British regulars were part of Montreal's social, religious, and economic life for more than a century after the first redcoat marched through the Recollet Gate in 1760. In this blend of military and social history, Elinor Kyte Senior examines the garrison's impact on the city in the troubled years 1832–1854. It was during a turbulent election in 1832 that the first fatal encounter occurred between troops and townsmen; by 1854, when most of the regulars departed for the Crimea, the garrison had suffered its most serious decline in public esteem over the Gavazzi riot of 1853.

By drawing upon local newspaper accounts, military and civilian memoirs, and military records in Ottawa and Montreal, Dr. Senior has reconstructed many aspects of the life of the garrison and fully explored its peacetime role. The rapid growth of the city, without a concomitant expansion in the local police force, threw the burden of internal security on the imperial garrison at a time when civil order was often precarious. Political turmoil bubbled over into rebellion in 1837 and 1838, and the aftermath left a residue of tension that darkened the decade of the 1840s.

If the garrison proved unpopular in times of civil tension, its contributions to the life of the city were not unwelcome. Montrealers enjoyed the largess of the military chest, which rivalled the Bank of Montreal in reserves and at times surpassed it in resources, and also the garrison's musical and dramatic performances. For their part, the military joined the local population at church, at sporting events, and at meetings of cultural societies. These close associations helped to maintain the imperial connection between the old world and the new when other such links were broken.

Elinor Kyte Senior is a historian-writer currently living in Montreal. She has contributed several entries to the *Dictionary of Canadian Biography* and has written for the *Journal of the Society for Army Historical Research*, *Military Affairs*, and the *Canadian Historical Review*.

British Regulars in Montreal

An Imperial Garrison, 1832–1854

Elinor Kyte Senior

McGill-Queen's University Press
MONTREAL

© McGill-Queen's University Press 1981
ISBN 0-7735-0372-2
Legal deposit 2nd quarter 1981
Bibliothèque nationale du Québec

Design by Naoto Kondo
Printed in Canada

This book has been published with the help of a grant from the Social
Science Federation of Canada, using funds provided by the Social Sci-
ences and Humanities Research Council of Canada.

To Hereward Senior
whose interest and encouragement
made the research and writing possible

Contents

Contents

Illustrations

Illustrations

reface

In the early nineteenth century Canada was an imperial frontier defended by a force roughly equal to the standing army of the United States. With a population smaller than its southern neighbour, Canada was, consequently, more aware of the presence of and need for its imperial garrison. This was particularly true of the metropolis Montreal, with a garrison which was seldom less than 1,500 in a city whose population was under 50,000 from 1832 to 1854. These years form a convenient unit of study, as in 1832 the garrison was involved in the first fatal encounter between troops and townsmen during a turbulent election and in 1854 the outbreak of the Crimean War resulted in the departure of most of the regulars from the city.

In analysing the nonmilitary impact of such an imperial institution on a colonial city, this work confines itself to four broad areas—the garrison's role as an aid to civil power, its influence on the development of the Montreal police force, the cultural dimension of the garrison, and its financial aspects. The presence of professional soldiers, commanded by officers drawn from the social elite of British society, was an experience that Montreal shared with most larger cities of British North America and Commonwealth countries. Today Canada provides its own forces, and in their turn Canadian soldiers on overseas service relive some aspects of the experience of the British garrisons of the last century.

I wish to acknowledge my debt to Professor Peter Marshall of Manchester University and to Professor John Cooper, both formerly of McGill University. To a number of senior military historians I am deeply grateful for the encouragement and advice they gave to me, especially Col. C. P. Stacey, Professor Reginald Roy, Professor of Military History and Strategic Studies at the University of Victoria, Dr. Alec Douglas, Director, Directorate of History, Department of National Defence, Ottawa, and Professor Richard Glover. I owe and acknowledge a particular debt to Professor Richard Preston, Professor Emeritus, Duke University, who on several occasions made available to me items from his own research. The Earl of Cathcart kindly provided me with material from his family papers relating to Sir George Cathcart.

From the staff of the Public Archives, Ottawa, I have received substantial and courteous help, particularly from Miss Barbara Wilson and Mrs. Mary Coughlin. I wish to convey my thanks also to Canon A. E. Hawes and Miss Florence Holmes of the Anglican Archives, Miss Audrey MacDermot of Christ Church Cathedral Archives, Mrs. Pamela Miller and Conrad Graham of the McCord Museum, Mrs. Mabel Good of Molson Archives, Sergent R. DuFault of the Recherche-Planification, Montreal Police Department, Mrs. Emmanuel Miller of the Jewish Public Library, Laurent Godin of the Old Court House Archives, Gilbert Chapados of the Bar Library Archives, and Pierre Brouillard of the Château Ramezay Archives. I am grateful to staff members of the McLennan Library of McGill University, particularly those in the rare book room, the interlibrary loan department, the microfilm room, and reference department. Mrs. Nellie Reiss and Mrs. Janet Sader of the Lawrence Lande Room met all my requests with courtesy and efficiency. To Mrs. Elizabeth Hale and Bruce Bolton of the Montreal Military and Maritime Museum, I express my deepest gratitude for help far beyond the call of duty.

I wish to express my sincerest thanks to the Canada Council for a fellowship awarded in 1970 and again in 1971. To Col. David Macdonald Stewart, Col. Ralph Harper, and other members of the Montreal Military and Maritime Museum, St. Helen's Island, I am most indebted for a summer research grant to complete work on the manuscript in Ottawa. My sister, Miss Jean Kyte, not only assisted in proofreading but provided valuable literary criticism.

To Mrs. Margaret Blevins who typed the manuscript with such care, I am deeply grateful. Finally, to Miss Audrey Hlady and McGill-Queen's University Press I am most indebted for editorial assistance and advice.

Part

The Garrison and the City

To stand at a street corner for a moment is to see
pass by the Indian woman in her heavy blanket,
the French habitant, Scotch, Irish and English
residents, and emigrants of all social conditions,
the American from the United States, officers of
the British Army, Priests in their robes, the Sisters of Charity, groups of neat-looking soldiers,
and the burly policeman, clad in his dark blue
military uniform.
A traveller in Montreal, cited in Alfred Sandham's *Ville-Marie*

1. The Garrison in Montreal

When the first British redcoat marched through the Recollet Gate into Montreal in September of 1760, it was the beginning of a British military presence in the city that was to last over a century. For Montrealers, a military establishment was no novelty. The city had been founded by a soldier on the frontier of New France and in the face of an Iroquois offensive against the colony. From its earliest days its inhabitants had shouldered a musket as well as ploughed a field. By 1760, with the fall of Quebec City, Montreal was military headquarters of the French army in Canada and some 1,000 of its 5,000 inhabitants were under arms.[1] Surrounding the city were towns whose names bore witness to the military heritage of New France—Sorel, Tracy, Berthier, Varennes, Saint-Ours, La Valtrie, Île Bizard, Verchères, Chambly— all were named for officers of the Carignan-Salières Regiment.

From 1760 until 1870 the main job of the British garrison was to defend the province and to maintain internal security. These were tasks that had to be undertaken by the regulars only five times during the 110 years that they formed the country's defence force. Their first effort at Montreal's defence was a failure. For a brief interlude in 1775–76, the British garrison suffered an eclipse as invaders from the south turned Montreal into a garrison town of the Continental army. During the War of 1812–14

3

Montrealers of both French and British origin once more joined as comrades-in-arms to repel another American invasion. From the time of the first American occupation of 1775–76 and especially since the War of 1812–14, the British garrison was regarded by all Montrealers as a purely defensive force. In the more bitter moments of the rebellion years of 1837–38 when the garrison shared in the onerous and unpopular task of suppressing internal revolt, members of the physical force wing of the Patriote party referred to the garrison as an "army of occupation," but this hostility was confined both in time and in extent. As soon as the rebellions were suppressed and imperial policy moved in the direction of reduction or removal of the overseas garrisons, such moves met with loud and long protest. None was more strident than that of the erstwhile rebel of 1837, George-Etienne Cartier, when, as minister of militia and defence of the new Dominion of Canada, he received word that all British troops were to be withdrawn from Canada in 1870.[2]

During the years that British troops formed the garrison of the city, Montreal rivalled Quebec City as the major British military station in the Canadas, though it could not compare with Halifax's status as military headquarters of the maritime command and senior station of the Royal Navy. Yet Montreal's military importance became apparent whenever internal or external tensions arose. Situated on three great waterways—the St. Lawrence, the Richelieu–Lake Champlain–Hudson route, and the Ottawa River—Montreal, though a natural base for offensive operations, lay open to attack. With the rapid growth of Upper Canada by the early nineteenth century, Montreal acquired a new dimension. Not only was it the commercial centre of the country and the largest city in British North America, it was also the "main central point for . . . the defence" of the two provinces.[3] Thus in 1814 military headquarters was moved to Montreal from Quebec City. Again, in 1836, as civil tension increased under the impact of Patriote party agitation, Maj.-Gen. Sir John Colborne, the commander of the forces,* reluctantly fixed his headquarters in the city.[4]

The presence of the highest ranking officers of the military establishment, together with their aides-de-camp, deputies, clerks, and servants, gave Montreal a military preeminence over the other garrison towns of Quebec, Kingston, Toronto, and London.

*The rank ascribed to an officer is that which he held at the time referred to.

4

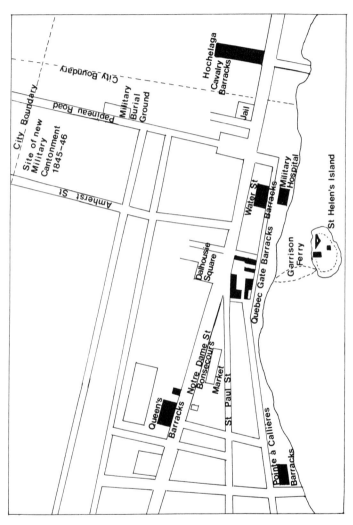

The major military establishments in Montreal. This map shows the location of the Quebec Gate Barracks; Queen's Barracks in the Old Gaol, 1838–46; New Barracks on Water Street, 1846–50; and Hochelaga Cavalry Barracks, which was converted to a military prison in 1849.

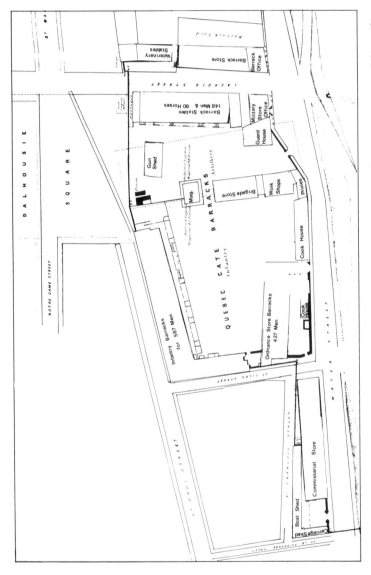

Quebec Gate Barracks, 1849. This property was obtained by right of Conquest and was appropriated for military purposes in 1760.

And, for much of the decade of the forties, when the city was the political capital of the united Province of Canada, Montreal resembled a European metropolis, since the seat of government and military headquarters were both located in the most important commercial centre of the country.

To the traveller coming up the St. Lawrence River in the early 1830s, the military presence in Montreal was all too evident. The first glimpse of Montreal would take in the imposing Quebec Gate Barracks of the British garrison, which fronted the north bank of the river. Here some 500 men of the 15th East Yorkshires and 75 Royal Artillerymen were quartered, surrounded by all the appurtenances necessary to garrison life—the commissariat store, bakery, brew house, stables, fuel yard, and even a small garrison theatre. East of the main cantonment was the garrison hospital, and, directly below, a jolly boat awaited those officers and men on their way to quarters on St. Helen's Island—the second major military establishment in the city and the main ordnance depot for the Montreal station. If the traveller was an officer's wife, she would find the "white tents of the soldiers on St. Helen's a pleasing sight as they glittered in the beams of the sun, and the bugle-call wafted over the waters so cheery and inspiring."[5]

The Quebec Gate Barracks and the Champ de Mars parade ground were reminders to French Montreal of the Conquest, for these were the two most important direct confiscations of property immediately following the occupation of Montreal by British troops.[6] Originally a nunnery, the Quebec Gate Barracks took its name from the old gate of the city that stood just northeast of the cantonment. Located as it was in the most populous part of the city, the garrison could not be ignored. As its soldiers and officers marched in and out of the main entrance that faced Dalhousie Square, they rubbed shoulders on every side with the 27,297 French- and English-speaking inhabitants of the city.[7]

With the garrison increasing in size by leaps and bounds in the 1830s, overflow troops from the main cantonment went into the old jail on Notre Dame Street near the Nelson monument. Efforts by army engineers to disguise or efface its origins met with indifferent success, but by gracing the old jail with a new name, the Queen's Barracks, a gesture was made to obliterate the past. Cavalry troops were stationed at Hochelaga just beyond the city's eastern boundary where stables and barracks were erected during the rebellion. Artillery reinforcements poured into the jolly

7

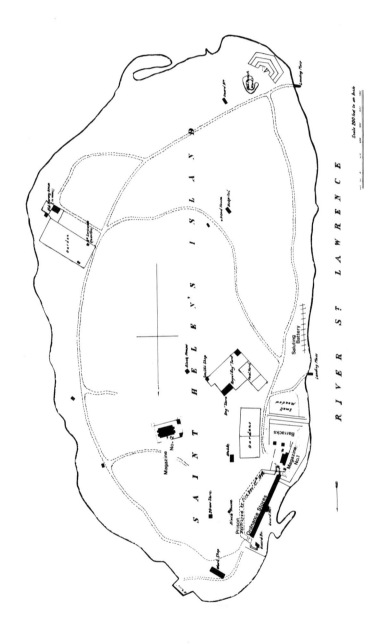

St. Helen's Island, 1849. This war property was acquired by deed of exchange on 8 April 1818 from the Hon. C. W. Grant and his wife.

boat at the King's Wharf and made their way to St. Helen's Island where temporary wooden barracks supplemented the permanent barrack accommodations for 100 men. Other troops were scattered about in temporary quarters as close to Dalhousie Square as possible to be within the orbit of the main military cantonment of Quebec Gate Barracks. For the officers, from the commander of the forces down, they found what accommodations they could in private dwellings and hotels, for the Montreal station never managed to provide permanent officers' quarters.

The Montreal garrison was a mixture of Irish, Scots, Welsh, and English, divided along religious lines between Roman Catholics and Protestants of various affiliations, resembling the religious divisions of the city itself. Its social hierarchy was even more formidable than the somewhat loosely structured colonial society it dwelt among. Moreover, the men of the garrison, even if they came from the same general background as the more recent British immigrants, were distinct in their roles and prospects for, unlike the immigrant, the regulars were transients.

Since the garrison's main job of defending the province or suppressing internal revolt took up only about 6 of the 110 years it spent in Montreal, it meant that this fairly large aggregate of bachelor men—for most rankers could not afford to bring out their wives and families if they had such—found themselves in the heart of Canada's metropolis with little to do of a practical nature, consuming a good deal, and officered by men of education, leisure, and, frequently, of wealth. Montrealers enjoyed not only the garrison's outlay for food, transport, medical supplies, wood, and rents, but also its band concerts and troop reviews on the Champ de Mars in summer and its amateur theatricals in winter. Up to 1832 officers found it a small, easy, if somewhat dull station, agreeable enough for a three-year stint of duty in the Canadas, though they much preferred Quebec City if given a choice.[8] For the ordinary soldier, peace and idleness were put up with as necessities. Their alternative was the border and many chose it. No less than 5,000 went over the line in the period from 1814 to 1836, causing regimental commanders to weep and others to exclaim, "What an army of deserters!"[9]

Breaking the pleasant monotony of this garrison life came the 1830s with increasing civil turmoil that erupted into open rebellion in 1837 and 1838. Reluctantly the garrison was drawn into these colonial quarrels that partly reflected immigrant pressure on the local balance of population. With the great waves of

9

British and Irish immigration in the early 1830s, Montreal's population projection indicated an increase in the English-language sector. By the 1840s this had become reality. By then Montreal was a city of some 17,109 French-speaking and 23,184 English-speaking inhabitants, including just under 9,000 Irish.[10] When to these was added the greatly expanded garrison that grew out of the rebellion period—some 1,500 soldiers instead of 500—Montreal's population was heavily weighted on the side of the English speaking and continued so until the 1860s.

It is not surprising, then, that it was the immigrant presence in local politics that involved the garrison in the first fatal encounter between troops and townsmen during an election. The incident, which was to be repeated several times during the next twenty-one years, involved the use of troops as an aid to civil power during turbulent Montreal elections or demonstrations. In England since the days of the Wilkes affair in the 1760s, troops were almost never used during elections, but in Ireland and the colonies they were used freely during elections and other disturbances.[11]

In Montreal in 1832 it was the Patriote party of Louis-Joseph Papineau, combining as it did political radicalism with social and economic conservatism, that began to court the Irish immigrant vote. From then until 1854, when the outbreak of the Crimean War resulted in the departure of most of the regulars from the city, there was no group in the city more anxious than the British military command to see the establishment of an efficient police, ready and able to maintain internal order and thus relieve the garrison of this unpopular duty. Yet, much as both civil and military authorities agreed on the need for such a force, the steadily deteriorating civil situation of the late 1830s and the continued unsettled state of Montreal after the Rebellions of 1837 and 1838 put the burden for the maintenance of public order largely on the garrison for much of this period. These years, then, form a convenient unit to study the impact of an imperial military institution on the cultural and commercial life of a colonial city as it grappled with the development of its own police establishment.

The Garrison and the Riot of 1832

On 20 May 1832 the commandant of the Montreal garrison, Lt.-Col. Alexander F. Macintosh, pushed his chair back from the dinner table and rose to greet his unwelcome guests. One was the self-assured and undisputed leader of the Constitutional party in Lower Canada, George Moffatt. His companion, an old army surgeon and now Montreal's leading medical man, was Dr. William Robertson. They had come directly to Quebec Gate Barracks from a special meeting of Montreal magistrates where voices were loud in their demands for help from the garrison. The election riots had gone beyond the control of either magistrates or special constables.

For almost three weeks the city had been in turmoil over the election in the West Ward, the ward represented in the Assembly since 1814 by Louis-Joseph Papineau, undisputed leader of the reform Patriote party.[1] But the second seat in the ward, traditionally held by an English Montrealer, was being fiercely contested by Daniel Tracey, editor of the Patriote party's English-language newspaper, the *Vindicator*, which was trying to lure Irish hearts and votes to the reform ranks. Not only was the editor recently arrived from turbulent Ireland, he was even more recently released from jail in Quebec City. Along with Ludger Duvernay, editor of Papineau's French-language newspaper, *La Minerve*,

11

Tracey had been imprisoned for libelling members of the Legislative Council. Tracey was now put forward by the Patriotes to cross swords with the American-born Montreal businessman of long residence, Stanley Bagg, who was favoured by the Constitutional party—often labelled the British party—which represented those supporting the established political system.

At this time a hard-fought election could be lost or won by the simple device of blocking the polls to prevent rival voters getting to the returning officer and proclaiming in a loud, clear voice the name of their candidate. If one candidate was leading, his victory was assured if he could keep rival voters away for at least a half hour, for the polls could remain open only as long as a vote was polled every thirty minutes.[2] Under this open voting system, clashes occurred day after day from 25 April until 20 May 1832, and they became more violent and more frequent, with both sides indulging in questionable methods. City magistrates tried to control the disorders by swearing in more and more special constables, the device usually resorted to when riots got beyond the few local police. Yet there could be no doubt about the partisan nature of some of the special constables. One was Orangeman George Perkins Bull, editor of the short-lived Montreal newspaper, the *London and Canada Record*. Bull, like his journalist contemporary Daniel Tracey, had recently arrived from Ireland where he, too, had spent some time in jail, charged with libelling a priest.[3] Bull was in close communication with Orangemen among the rank and file of the 24th Regiment,[4] then stationed at Quebec City, and likely in touch with Orangemen in the ranks of the 15th, the sole regiment in Montreal.[5] A sergeant of the 15th, Matthew Hayes, who had reform leanings, complained that "Bull's newspaper had a large circulation in the regiment particularly among the Orange faction who were numerous."[6]

The disorders at the polls finally mounted beyond the control of civil authorities. Returning officer Hippolyte St. George Dupré minced no words. "Yesterday evening, not wishing to submit my interpretation of the law to the will of Mr. Tracey and his partisans, I was surrounded with tumult and came very close to being assaulted. Mr. Tracey himself insulted me as a public officer and threatened to force me to do his will. I believe it is impossible to continue the election without having inside the poll a sufficient force of constables with their batons."[7]

On Sunday evening, 20 May, the magistrates admitted defeat

Left: Dr. William Robertson, a former surgeon of the 49th Regiment, was one of the magistrates involved in the 1832 election riot. *Right:* Benjamin Holmes; the Dublin-born cashier of the Bank of Montreal, was one of the Montreal magistrates trying to maintain order at the polls in May 1832.

and sent Moffatt and Robertson off to the Quebec Gate Barracks to secure troops.[8]

The commandant was well aware of the growing tension within Montreal society as Patriotes and Constitutionals vied for political power and patronage. He was also well aware that the increasing influx of immigrant Irish was adding variety and some spice to the colonial bickering. He greeted his guests warily and pointed out that he was particularly anxious that the military not be called "until matters had come to an extremity." Against a large and unruly mob that could move faster than troops, infantry was useless unless the troops fired. Macintosh looked at his guests. "That must, of course, be attended with almost certain destruction of life."[9] Robertson and Moffatt nodded in agreement. But without troops, there would also be destruction of life. Civil authorities had information of the "most positive kind that there was a plan for firing the Town and Suburbs in various places so as to draw the Military away in different and opposite directions and in small bodies, that they may be more easily overpowered."[10]

Reluctantly Macintosh agreed to reinforce the main guard near Nelson's monument on Jacques Cartier Square. He also took the precaution to order two six-pounders from St. Helen's Island. These were mounted at the head of St. James Street where Royal Artillerymen and soldiers of the 15th Regiment stood guard overnight. Patrolling the streets were the town major, Capt. B. Rooth, and a party of the volunteer Royal Montreal Cavalry under Maj. George Gregory.[11]

Next morning, 21 May, Capt. Henry Temple of the 15th took up his position at the main guard with a subaltern, sergeant, bugler, and forty-two rank and file. Serious disorders broke out at the nearby polling booth on Place d'Armes about three o'clock in the afternoon when three of Bagg's supporters were chased across the square by Irishmen and sought safety in Robert Henderson's store at the corner of St. James Street and Place d'Armes. While this trio was racing towards Henderson's, another ruckus broke out. One of the city police constables, Louis Malo, began berating one of Tracey's supporters, Alex Noon. Noon protested that Malo "struck him needlessly." Two members of the Patriote party urged Magistrate Benjamin Holmes, the Irish-born cashier of the Bank of Montreal, to dismiss Malo whom they said "was very obnoxious and if not removed would be the cause of further disturbance." Holmes ordered Malo away from the polling booth, and when

Malo hesitated to leave, Holmes "threatened him if he did not instantly depart."[12]

Shouts of "Have at their hearts' blood" rent the air as the crowd neared Henderson's store in search of the men who had sought safety there. Magistrate John Fisher ran to Lt. Jeremiah Dewson, the quartermaster of the 15th Regiment, crying, "What's to be done?" It had been Fisher's resignation as member of the Assembly for the West Ward that had precipitated the by-election that had turned into such a riotous affair. Dewson coolly replied, "If you go to the main guard with the order of the magistrates, Captain Temple will advance with a party of men." Without further ado Fisher raced off to Jacques Cartier Square and hurriedly informed Temple that he should immediately advance with a picquet to Place d'Armes. Temple asked for a written requisition from the magistrates, but he was told that "they were in such haste they had not sent it, but that as soon as I reached the ground, it would be delivered to me."[13]

Temple sent word to Lieutenant-Colonel Macintosh that his picquet had been ordered to Place d'Armes, and off he marched with twenty-four men. On arrival he found an "ill-disposed crowd using stones and bludgeons against the constables" who "ran towards the troops for protection." Temple immediately asked the magistrates for a written requisition for troop aid. Dr. Robertson had just relieved Magistrate Holmes as the troops arrived. Robertson and Pierre Lukin, the other magistrate on duty, agreed that "although we did not personally send for the troops, as it was now impossible for us to maintain the peace with the force of constables under our orders, we would instantly sign the requisition."[14] Amid flying stones and unnerving yells, Holmes obligingly stretched out his arm for them to lean the requisition against in order to sign it.

Holmes and Lukin then forced their way through the dense crowd to the returning officer to urge him to close the poll. As they did so, the young reformer, Louis-Hippolyte La Fontaine, cried out, "Go on, go on, there is no disturbance," although at the time, Holmes claimed, "there was a great deal of strong language around us and cause for the interference of the Peace Officer."[15] The appearance of the small picquet of troops brought no lessening of the tumult until their colonel ordered up a detachment of light infantry and urged Dr. Robertson to read the Riot Act, measures which brought a temporary lull in the tumult.[16]

One of the special constables, John Jones, a printer and Constitutionalist, had not been able to get near the poll. "Whenever I approached I was grossly insulted by Mr. Tracey's party and curses heaped upon me in profusion. At about 2.30 a mob, partizans of Mr. Tracey, quit the poll and attacked a party of Mr. Bagg's friends and the constables. . . . The Troops came down on this occasion from the Guard House, remained in the Square about twenty minutes, and then retired in front of the Church. I entered the poll and remained there until it closed."[17]

Jean Mondelet, a young student, became so alarmed at the tumult that he tried to persuade Tracey's supporters "to abandon the fight." Another of Tracey's supporters, the radical lawyer and man-about-town, Edouard Rodier, was of a different opinion. He moved among Tracey's supporters, assuring them that if the troops fired, it would be into the air. Scrutineer Alex McMillan observed that the movements of the crowd were not haphazard. To him it seemed that "the mob seemed under the guidance of certain people above the common class."[18] A sudden downpour of rain dampened mischievous spirits for a while. With the troops drawn off the square and placed under the portico of Notre Dame Church, polling went on sporadically until five o'clock. By that time Bagg, running three votes behind in the fiercely fought contest, decided "it was useless to fight against the violence in which we were menaced,"[19] and he withdrew under protest.

Jubilantly Tracey and his supporters paraded out of Place d'Armes, passed the Bank of Montreal, and headed down St. James Street. From his living quarters above the Bank of Montreal, Holmes had a ringside view of the proceedings on Place d'Armes. He watched Tracey's party move off while Bagg and his supporters left by way of Notre Dame Street. Just as both candidates quit the field, a serious fight once more broke out on Place d'Armes. Two men ran towards Tracey's party, beckoning them back. The fray became so alarming that Holmes prudently ordered his family to retire from the windows. He shut the blinds and ran to secure the door.[20]

Magistrate John Shuter was near Henderson's store when the affray burst out. There was a great crash of shattered glass as stones, weighing as much as two to three pounds, were hurled through the windows by the rioters. Unnerved, Shuter ran across the square to the church court shouting, "For God's sake, bring out the troops. The mob are murdering the people." Another man standing near the store was convinced that "every individual in

16

the shop would have been destroyed had the military not advanced and driven back the rioters."[21]

Lieutenant-Colonel Macintosh had been anxiously walking back and forth to Place d'Armes from the church court "to judge the strength of the mob and their disposition." When the fight broke out, Robertson, Moffatt, and several other magistrates, along with all the special constables, rushed out to the square while the regulars remained in the court to be ready, as Macintosh recalled, for there was "much noise and tumult in the Square . . . and I distinctly saw that the Mob was furiously engaged with the Constables."[22]

Suddenly the magistrates and constables all rushed back into the church court "followed by other persons, the last of whom were furiously assaulting the constables and others with bludgeons and stones."[23] Macintosh was hit. So, too, was Lieutenant Dewson. Shuter's back was covered with stones. Macintosh quickly dispatched Ensign Hay with instructions to bring up the rest of the regiment "if firing was heard," for Macintosh realized that the "troops could not, because of the volleys of stones discharged at them, either stand where they were or advance to disperse the voters, or far less, retreat without danger of destruction, unless they fired."[24] Fearing that the troops would be rushed upon and overpowered, Macintosh gave orders, "With ball cartridge, prime, and load." As he did so, he heard magistrates calling to him to bring out the troops. The crowd, seeing the soldiers prime and load their muskets, moved back into Place d'Armes where one man was lying as though dead near Henderson's store.[25]

Cautiously Macintosh ordered the soldiers to move from the church court to the north side of the square. He hoped that the appearance of the troops would disperse the crowd. Instead, the crowd became larger as the troops moved forward through Place d'Armes towards St. James Street. On the troops and police came showers of stones which the rioters grabbed up from a nearby construction site. Magistrate Moffatt was sometimes in front of the troops, sometimes at their side, waving his umbrella and entreating the mob to disperse.[26]

Near the Bank of Montreal Macintosh halted the troops, "with a view to give an opportunity to the mob to disperse without firing." When he called out loudly that the troops intended to fire, it seemed for a moment that the crowd was going to disperse, but then the showers of stones increased. What seemed strange to him was that the crowd moved with such regularity. "Whenever it retired or advanced, it managed to maintain about the same distance, and kept in a Body acting with great system in keeping up the Shower of Stones. Those in front kept near enough the Troops to do them injury, and when they retired or advanced ran through each other like light troops skirmishing."[27] This was high praise for the Patriote forces which had yet to begin any regular military exercises.

Macintosh ordered the troops to advance again, convinced that it "was better to make a last attempt to disperse them under a shower of stones than to make a sacrifice of human life," but the crowd, "apparently emboldened by the forbearance of the Troops, renewed the attack of stones." By this time Macintosh was sure that "firing was inevitable, and being again called upon by a magistrate on the spot to do so, I again advanced in front of the Troops and waving a stick, called out in the loudest tone of voice that the Troops were going to fire."[28]

A somewhat different account appears in the testimony of members of the Patriote party who were involved. According to Edouard Rodier, "The Troops advanced on St. James Street and put to flight all those they found in front of them. The troops were accompanied by a great crowd of people who threw stones at those who were fleeing and those who were fleeing threw stones at them." Rodier saw "an officer make a sign with his naked sword and immediately I heard the discharge of muskets." François Tavernier swore that not one of Tracey's men was throwing stones at the moment the troops fired. It seemed to him that "the constables who were behind the troops were throwing stones at the friends of Mr Tracey."[29] If Tracey's own supporters could give such contradictory testimony of what happened, it is not surprising that the testimony of rival witnesses should differ, either wilfully so or because of the confusion existing during the riotous proceedings. Yet no one denied that stones were being thrown or that the troops, officers, magistrates, and constables were targets.

As far as Macintosh was concerned, "stones were still being showered upon us to an extent that must, in a few minutes, have levelled at least half of the party to the ground. I ordered the Troops to begin firing man by man, that I might stop them the moment that I could see it had the effect of causing the mob to disperse." He was surprised that the crowd did not instantly run, which "seemed to me so extraordinary that I attributed it to some cause with which I was unacquainted. They, however, very soon after moved in the most sudden and precipitate manner. I in-

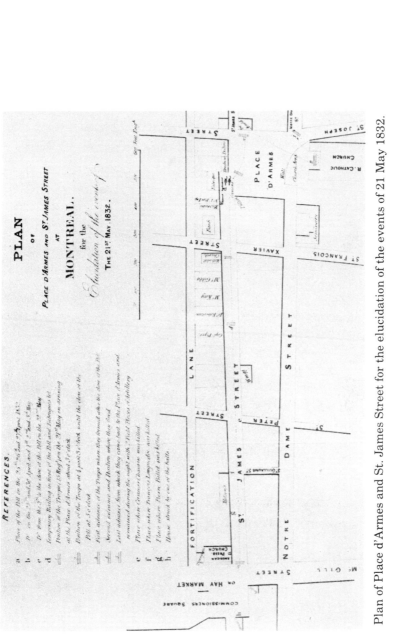

Plan of Place d'Armes and St. James Street for the elucidation of the events of 21 May 1832.

stantly ordered the men to cease firing which was immediately done." The crowd hesitated because they were convinced that the soldiers fired only blank cartridges. One member of Tracey's committee, on hearing someone behind him shriek and fall, thought it was from fear. He turned round and shouted, "Get up, you damned coward, what are you afraid of?"[30]

The action of the troops followed precise military procedure for the use of troops at riots. They were commanded by commissioned officers, in this case, their colonel and Captain Temple, and they were in the charge of a magistrate. They fired only after the Riot Act had been read and the magistrate had ordered the officer to quell the riot. The firing was accomplished with perfect discipline: the soldiers fired man by man and they ceased to fire instantly upon order. Three Montrealers lay dead—Casimir Chauvin, a printer from *La Minerve*, François Languedoc, and Pierre Billet, all French Canadians, an "accidental circumstance,"[31] as Lord Aylmer, the governor, put it, but one that gave French overtones to what had been a tory-radical election confrontation between a recent Irish immigrant and a not-so-recent American immigrant. As far as Patriote propagandists were concerned, St. James Street, where the shootings occurred, became the "Street of Blood."[32]

Immediately after the shooting two Patriote doctors, Robert Nelson and Guillaume Vallée, rushed to the side of the slain men. Other leading Patriotes, such as the lawyer John MacDonell and Côme-Séraphim Cherrier, moved quickly to the scene while younger supporters of Papineau's party scurried off.[33] Others, like Papineau's thirteen-year-old son Amédée, turned "Patriote on the spot."[34] For the Patriotes the events of 21 May 1832 became their "Boston Massacre."[35]

Papineau moved into action the next day at the inquest. Accompanied by several of his close associates, La Fontaine, Cherrier, and Clément Sabrevois de Bleury, he tried to persuade Macintosh to identify the magistrate who had given him the order to fire.[36] At this point Papineau seemed intent on keeping the fight local and was not particularly anxious to involve the garrison. Yet, when he failed to get Macintosh to identify the magistrate, he and his supporters then pressed the coroner, Jean-Marie Mondelet, into arresting Macintosh and Temple, along with the English-speaking magistrate, William Robertson, and the French-speaking magistrate, Pierre Lukin.[37] Macintosh and Temple were lodged in the city jail on 26 May by the high constable, Benjamin

DeLisle, in spite of the fact that the jury at the inquest had failed to reach a verdict. Normally a warrant for arrest in such cases could be issued only on the verdict of a jury, but the coroner proceeded on the strength of the evidence given at the inquest,[38] a somewhat irregular procedure.

Papineau tried a second time to persuade Macintosh to name the magistrate who had ordered him to fire, promising that if he did so, the proceedings against him and Temple would be stopped. The proposal was brought privately to Macintosh, who was still in jail, by a mutual friend, C. J. Forbes of Carillon, who told Macintosh he had received the message from Papineau by way of Jacques Viger.[39] If the charges against the military officers could be continued or halted by Papineau's personal intervention, there could be little doubt that their origin partook more of politics than of justice. The proposal also showed that Papineau and his chief advisers were still more anxious to involve the "British party" magistrates than they were to exchange blows with the garrison. Still Macintosh refused to identify the magistrate. Henceforth, Patriote policy was to whip up public resentment against the military over the incident. The imprisonment of Macintosh and Temple had a touch of an "eye for an eye" rough justice about it, since two members of the Patriote party, Tracey and Duvernay, had been kept in jail for over two weeks on the order of the Legislative Council. The two British officers were not admitted to bail until a week after the shooting when their release was secured by Charles Richard Ogden,[40] the solicitor-general, upon whom radical hostility became focused.

Ordered to stand trial on a charge of murder, Macintosh sought the protection of the governor, Lord Aylmer, in his role as commander of the forces. Macintosh quite rightly feared that "the good of the service must be materially affected by what may now occur, should the troops ever be called upon to act in a similar manner."[41] The charges against the two officers were eventually thrown out by an all English-speaking grand jury, despite a vitriolic campaign in *La Minerve*, the *Vindicator*, and *Le Canadien*, which attempted to arouse popular indignation against civil and military authorities. On 17 September 1832 *Le Canadien*, edited in Quebec by Etienne Parent, who had not yet broken with Papineau, spoke of Lord Aylmer as "complimenting the murderers" when Aylmer expressed approval at the dismissal of charges against the officers. Aylmer growled that the opposition newspapers were "becoming daily more outrageous and yet . . .

such is the state of public feeling in Montreal among the class who would be jurors that I should despair of obtaining a verdict of guilty in the case of the most atrocious libel penned against the government, the magistrates, or the military."[42]

The Patriote executive, whose headquarters was at Edouard-Raymond Fabre's bookstore on St. Vincent Street, kept up the harassment of Macintosh and Temple. In September two Patriote magistrates, Joseph Roy and André Jobin, issued new warrants for their arrest. Then, much to the chagrin of the Patriotes, Aylmer granted Macintosh leave to return to England. "Hitherto I withheld my assent to his leaving, being anxious to demonstrate to the Province at large that the military engaged on that occasion were anxious to court, rather than shun, an enquiry." But by October Aylmer was eager to comply with Macintosh's request for leave "as I have reason to believe . . . that some pretext might have been discovered for committing him to prison until the end of the [parliamentary] Session."[43]

Soldiers of the 15th Regiment were warned to walk in groups of six or eight when on the streets of Montreal,[44] and Lord Aylmer took the precaution of reinforcing the garrison by two flank companies of the 24th Regiment. In October, after a two-day visit to the city, the governor was "sorry to observe that the public mind still continues much agitated. A great deal of alarm was expressed to me by what may be termed the English party respecting the designs of the opposite or Papineau party." Although he thought the fears greatly exaggerated, Aylmer agreed that the "Papineau party may be urged on to some act of outrage during the ensuing winter, when the difficulty and delay of moving troops will be very considerable." He ordered two companies of the 79th Regiment from Upper Canada to reinforce the Montreal garrison for the winter. Orangeman Bull and other supporters of the government found comfort in the arrival of fresh troops and the fact that "a corps of Protestant Volunteers (Artillery) are now raising to counteract such seditious proceedings and the strong feelings of disaffection in this province."[45]

With the approach of winter and the firmness of the authorities in reinforcing the garrison, tensions aroused during the election subsided. By July of 1836 officers and troops mingled with Papineau and other members of the Assembly, as well as with members of the Legislative and Executive Councils and Montreal merchants to celebrate the opening of the first railway in British North America. Built to speed up travel between Montreal and the United States, the fifteen-mile long stretch of railway extended from Laprairie to St. Johns on the Richelieu River from where passengers could pick up the steamer heading for the American border. Scarcely within a year this line would carry troops and prisoners to and from military operations south of the St. Lawrence, possibly the first time that rail transport was used in military action.

Yet the encounter between troops and Montrealers in 1832 left its mark—not so much because French Montrealers were the ones killed. Indeed, François-Xavier Garneau, in his history of the period, does not even mention that those killed were French.[46] But the encounter was a prelude to the far more serious alienation between Montrealers in 1837–38, a prelude in which many of those destined to play important roles in Montreal and in Canadian history over the next decades appear together.

For the military authorities, it meant a reappraisal of their procedures in helping to quell civil disturbances if such aid could so easily involve their officers and soldiers in serious criminal charges, including arrest, imprisonment, harassment, and heavy financial outlay for legal counsel. For the civil authorities, the encounter was a portent of their inability to cope with increasing civil disorders. They had made extensive preparations to ensure order at the polls in 1832, enrolling 100 special constables on 26 April and adding another 175 on the last day of polling. Even though they had ordered out the Royal Montreal Cavalry and had the main military guard at Nelson's monument reinforced as a precaution against disturbances, it had been to no avail. Thereafter, Montreal magistrates tended to press for military aid as soon as there was any indication of serious trouble, but military authorities regarded such requests with increasing reluctance and insisted that during elections not only magistrates but the returning officer as well sign the requisition for military aid.

23

3. The Military and Police Establishments

Within the five years from 1832 to 1837 Montreal experienced a disintegration of civil order that included the suspension of both municipal and provincial government. Its first attempt at municipal government, under a charter from the House of Assembly in 1832, faltered in 1836 when the Assembly refused to renew the charter. By April of 1837 the twenty-nine man police force ceased to exist when funds ran out,[1] leaving the city protected only by local magistrates, the sheriff, and high constable who could call on special constables or the volunteer militia units in emergencies. Thus, as tension erupted into open rebellion in the late fall of 1837, the city of just under 40,000 was devoid of any police establishment whatever.

It is not surprising, then, that the military command, apprehensive at this breakdown of police arrangements and the increase in local disturbances, should issue new general orders on 26 May 1837 about the use of troops as an aid to civil power. The orders specified that no application for military aid was to be complied with unless accompanied by a written requisition from a magistrate, who was to state distinctly the service on which the troops were to be employed and that the ordinary civil force was insufficient to maintain peace. Troops were to be commanded by a commissioned officer, and as soon as the service was completed, the officer was to send a detailed report of the service to the military secretary.[2]

How vigorously the military command adhered to the new strictures can be seen in an exchange of letters between the Montreal commandant, Lt.-Col. George Augustus Wetherall, and the deputy adjutant general in July. When serious outrages were reported at Saint-Eustache, a small town northwest of Montreal, the commandant, at the request of the attorney general, kept 200 soldiers ready to move, but Wetherall assured the deputy adjutant general, "Sir John [Colborne] shall have no fault to find with me for too ready a compliance" with requests for military aid.[3]

By the autumn of 1837, as both rural and urban tension increased, the commander of the forces, Sir John Colborne, urged the governor, Lord Gosford, to lose no time "in establishing an armed police. . . . Montreal is the grand point to attend to till the Civil Authorities have tried their power. . . . The leaders of the disturbances, if arrested, can only be taken by an armed mounted Police."[4] As a result of pressure from the military command, Lord Gosford decided to send Attorney General Charles Richard Ogden to Montreal in early November with secret instructions to "enquire into the present state of the police force with a view to place it on an efficient footing."[5] Ogden's immediate solution to the lack of municipal police was to use the local volunteer unit, the Royal Montreal Cavalry, as mounted police and to organize a secret service to gather intelligence on the plans and activities of disaffected elements.[6] Funds for the secret service and for the makeshift mounted police were provided from the military chest.[7]

The man to whom the secret service was entrusted in the fall of 1837 was Pierre-Edouard Leclère who had, in 1832, founded and edited the French-language loyalist newspaper, *L'Ami du Peuple*, to counter the Patriote monopoly on the French-language media. To help in intelligence work, Leclère and Ogden drew upon the services of the Doric Club, a physical force group made up of younger Montreal loyalists whose president, John Shay, boasted of the work of the Dorics in "putting down the malcontents in the city before the outbreak of rebellion, and rendered services of a secret nature to the Government . . . in the apprehension of the seditious and suspected, in obtaining information of their proceedings for Sir John Colborne, conveyed through the Attorney-General."[8]

The ease with which these police arrangements were made indicated the immediate rapport which Ogden had established with

25

Colborne, a harmonious relationship that continued throughout the rebellion period when provincial government gave way to martial law. Out of this close cooperation between well-affected civilians and the military during the rebellions came a bond of sympathy and common interest that was to last throughout the forties, giving the military command in Montreal a chance to exert influence in areas such as the police system that normally would have been beyond the reach of an imperial military institution.

As soon as the first rebellion was suppressed in December 1837, the military command was anxious to relieve the regular troops of duties of a purely police nature. It was doubly anxious to ease the troops out of the role of auxiliaries to the civil power in suppressing internal disturbances. With Ogden's concurrence, Colborne, as administrator of the government, proposed a police ordinance to the Special Council in April 1838. Military authorities suggested that "in towns with large military establishments, a small force of police would be sufficient for the summer months. . . . It could be increased without much additional expense in the winter when the price of labour is low and crime is on the increase." It was assumed that the mere presence of a large garrison in Montreal would be a deterrent to serious disturbances. The Special Council, however, refused to pass the ordinance, most members considering it "too arbitrary for this free country."[9]

Colborne then awaited the arrival of the new governor, Lord Durham, before pressing another ordinance on the Special Council. Durham agreed wholeheartedly with Colborne and Ogden on the need to provide "an efficient system of Police in the Cities of Montreal and Quebec."[10] He was scarcely in the city a month when he implemented in June 1838 a police ordinance, largely the work of Colborne and Ogden.[11] Leclère was made superintendent of the new force at a salary of £500 a year. He was sent immediately to Quebec to confer with Thomas Ainslie Young, the inspector of police there, with a view to setting up a police system in Montreal similar to that in operation at Quebec. In introducing Leclère to Young, R. L. Morrogh of the civil secretary's department, described Leclère as "a magistrate of this City and for a long time a confidential employé in our office."[12]

Upon his return to Montreal, Leclère organized a force of 102 privates and 4 mounted patrols, commanded by 4 officers, 6 sergeants, and 6 corporals—an imposing establishment for a city which before the rebellion had but a small police force which had grown out of the lamplighter tradition.[13] Leclère drew on the old police service for some of his officers. Alexander Comeau, who had been so efficient at ferreting out hidden or fugitive Patriotes during the rebellion that he was described as "le horrible policier,"[14] was made captain, as was William Brown, former sergeant-major of the 32nd Regiment, who had been adjutant of the recently disbanded 1st Battalion of Montreal Volunteer Militia. The expense of the force, amounting to some £8,640. 17s. was borne by the provincial government.[15]

The coalition of loyalists which was so prominent in the suppression of the rebellion did not survive. The appointment of a French Canadian, albeit of impeccable loyalty, to the lucrative post of police superintendent was criticized by the *Herald*, which caustically commented that "his national origin was not the least of his merits" and wondered "if his origin had been English, would he have received the same marks of approbation from the Executive."[16] *L'Ami du Peuple*, which may still have been at this time partially financed by Leclère,[17] defended the appointment on 4 July 1838, claiming rightly that Leclère "had been secretly head of police since last November" and pointing out that it was only the "Constitutionals in the province [who] fear such appointments."

Supplementing the city police was a new rural police establishment under Lt.-Col. Augustus Gugy,[18] the bilingual loyalist militia officer who had served as intelligence officer with the regulars during the attack on the rebel stronghold at Saint-Charles. Gugy worked with fourteen stipendiary magistrates,[19] all drawn from loyalist ranks, both French and English, and including regular army officers such as Lt.-Col. W. C. Hanson of the 71st Highland Light Infantry, Capt. R. B. Cumming and Paymaster Thomas Coleman, both of the 15th Regiment, and Lt. Thomas Rainsford of the 66th. In towns which had been centres of disaffection, such as Saint-Denis, Saint-Remi, Sainte-Martine, and Napierville, the rural magistrates were aided by a number of paid and armed constables who were lodged in police barracks, much on the style of the Royal Irish Constabulary.[20] The main job of the rural police was to make reports on the state of the country, to keep an eye on strangers, and to observe any fresh grievances in the area or suspicious behaviour of disaffected elements.[21]

One of the surreptitious purposes of the new rural police was to build up a "government" party in the country. Fully aware that Patriote forces had been only too successful in winning over rural inhabitants by appeals to their economic interests, government supporters argued that even if the new police "fail to create a Government party," they would ensure that "no publican, except of Loyal feeling gets a tavern Licence, no Ferryman, a ferry licence, in fact, that no person openly avowing doctrines hostile to the British connection should receive any favour at the hands of Government."[22] It is not surprising that the exiled editor of the Montreal *Vindicator*, the Irish immigrant doctor, Edmund B. O'Callaghan, should speak uneasily of Durham sending spies through the "agricultural districts," or that the new rural police should be regarded with suspicion by erstwhile Patriotes.[23]

The paid rural magistrates were Colborne's answer to the situation he had found in 1837 when he complained that the local government was ignorant of the character of the rural population and of the extensive preparations that had been made for revolt.[24] In forming the new police, Colborne and Durham drew on the experience of Lt.-Col. George Cathcart, one of the more perceptive officers who was stationed at Saint-Hyacinthe in the spring of 1838. Cathcart's recommendations for a rural police force were drawn partly from his acquaintance with a system set up in Jamaica after the slave revolt there,[25] an example of how developing institutions in one colony can be influenced by those of another colony by way of ubiquitous British regular officers.

Colborne did not rely entirely upon the new rural police. He continued to receive his intelligence directly from the regular officers who were detached from their regiments and sent into the countryside on what was called "particular service." In this case, their particular service was to keep an eye on disaffected elements and to observe and report on the new police. Above all, they were to maintain a steady communication with commanding officers of the volunteer units that had begun to operate as border guards. Military men of great tact were needed for this service. Cathcart understood this well. In advising a fellow regular officer how to establish an effective rapport with the local corps, he hit upon the essentials. "An intelligent officer with good humour and a certain degree of tact would have no difficulty in understanding the line of conduct most likely to gain a *moral influence* over the officers of the Volunteer Corps without exciting jealousy." Cathcart urged that instructions be issued confidentially to the officers engaged on particular duty and warned them not to "assume any military command or interfere in the interior economy and drill of the corps" and especially to "cultivate a friendly intercourse

Above: Sir John Colborne, commander of the forces, 1835–39, urged the establishment of an armed police force in Montreal in 1837. *Below, left:* Lt.-Col. Augustus Gugy headed the first rural police establishment in the Montreal district. *Below, right:* Lt.-Col. George Cathcart, one of the British officers on particular duty in Lower Canada, was influential in establishing Montreal's postrebellion police force.

with the commanders and principal officers of the Volunteer Corps in their districts."[26]

Cathcart realized the importance of officers on particular service avoiding jealousy or resentment on the part of local volunteer officers and troops, especially as local troops would be the chief source of intelligence until the rural police began to function effectively. Even in the case of engagement with an enemy, Cathcart cautioned that regular field officers should "guide irregular and volunteer troops in the character of *adviser* to the Volunteer Commanders rather than attempt formally to assume the command."[27] In other words, regular officers would be in command without being ostensibly so, a most delicate relationship but one which proved workable and effective on several occasions.

This elaborate city and rural police establishment, organized largely at the instigation of the military and partially manned by British officers, had scarcely begun to operate when the second insurrection burst out in early November 1838. This well-organized conspiracy faced a well-prepared government and a greatly enlarged British garrison which promptly and, with some severity, suppressed the uprising. After the suppression the police began to move into more routine tasks, though the secret police continued to function under Superintendent Leclère. Until February 1840 he was still receiving confidential reports on the activities of Patriotes who had gone over the border during the insurrections. In reporting to Charles Montizambert, the assistant civil secretary at Montreal, Leclère included an affidavit of Félix Poutré of St. Johns, "a respectable individual attached to the police force for secret purposes, who was despatched by me to the American side of the lines to ascertain the state and feelings of the political refugees, by which it would appear that nothing of a serious nature is to be apprehended from that quarter."[28]

With the lessening of border tension and the return of disaffected elements to conventional politics by 1840, the new governor general, Charles Poulett Thomson, took a close look at the police establishment and expressed his displeasure at both its size and its cost. A three-man commission, composed of two British officers, Lt.-Col. George Cathcart and Capt. Thomas Edmund Campbell of the 7th Hussars, and the provincial secretary, Dominick Daly, was appointed by Thomson to inquire into the police to see "if the force was too large, the rate of pay more than sufficient for the duty performed and [whether] a great reduction may not be effected."[29]

30

Left: Lt.-Col. William Ermatinger, the son of an Ojibway Indian princess and a Montreal fur-trader, became the most important man in Montreal's police establishment in the 1840s. *Right:* Thomas Wily, the bilingual colour-sergeant of the 83rd Regiment, became Montreal's chief of police from 1844 to 1849 and subsequently lieutenant-colonel of the 1st, or Prince of Wales Rifle Regiment.

The result was a new police ordinance in June 1840 that reduced both city and rural police and eased military officers out of their role as rural magistrates.[30] The city police was reduced from 120 to half that number and the budget cut from £10,046 to £3,504.[31] In the reshuffle of top personnel, one of the first to be ousted from office was Police Superintendent Leclère.[32] Not only was his appointment regarded with jealousy by the still-militant Constitutionals, but undoubtedly his work as head of the secret service had marked him as one of the more obnoxious of the civil servants in the eyes of former Patriotes. Leclère's removal from office demonstrated the plight of loyalists whose services during the insurrections were of such importance but whose subsequent employment was hampered by their increasingly isolated position. Leclère was given a post as magistrate at Saint-Hyacinthe at a reduced salary.[33]

The rural police for the Montreal district was reduced, and its budget was cut from £24,867 to £14,452.[34] The reduction of the rural police brought a protest on 18 June from the editor of the *Transcript*, who warned that the "use and activity of the Rural Police will force itself upon public notice, despite the numerous enemies of the institution." Thomson's policy of retrenchment also wiped out the post of inspecting stipendiary magistrate of rural police held by another prominent loyalist, Lt.-Col. Augustus Gugy. He was given Leclère's job at a salary of £450.[35] Some indication of the usefulness of military officers serving as rural magistrates and the rapport they had established in what had been centres of disaffection is shown in the memorials that were presented to them upon their removal. When Lt. Thomas Rainsford stepped down as stipendiary magistrate at Saint-Denis and Saint-Hyacinthe, it was a former insurgent officer who,[36] when expressing the good wishes of the people of Saint-Hyacinthe towards Rainsford, observed, "You will soon see that the greatest and most inveterate enemies are not those who have met on the battlefield."[37]

One of the rural magistrates to survive the reduction was Capt. Charles Wetherall,[38] the half-pay Dragoon officer and brother of Lt.-Col. George Wetherall. Captain Wetherall was to become one of the key men in the Montreal police establishment, serving as police magistrate in the city and in 1843 taking on the difficult post of magistrate at Beauharnois after canal labour riots there. Perfectly at ease in French and English, Wetherall organized a police force for service on public works,[39] and it was because of his success in raising this force that Lord Elgin turned to him in 1849 to raise a mounted constabulary.

Serving with Wetherall as stipendiary rural magistrates in 1840 were William King McCord, brother of Lt.-Col. John Samuel McCord who had commanded the Montreal volunteers during the rebellions, David Kinnear, later to become editor of the Montreal *Herald*, Elzéar Juchereau-Duchesnay, whose job as assistant adjutant general of military had been abolished, and Thomas Coleman, former paymaster of the 15th Regiment.[40] Undoubtedly, the hierarchy of the new police establishment, thinned as it was, was still solidly loyalist and exclusively of the British party.

When Gugy became adjutant general of militia in 1841,[41] the superintendency of the city police shifted temporarily to a former British officer, Henry Driscoll, who had served as major in the Montreal Volunteer Militia in 1837 and had been made Queen's counsel by Colborne.[42] In February of 1842 the man who was to be the most important man in the Montreal police establishment for the next twelve years took office as commissioner. Lt.-Col. William Ermatinger, the son of a Montreal fur-trader and an Ojibway Indian princess, began his military career in the Royal Montreal Cavalry in the early 1830s.[43] After studying law in the office of Judge Samuel Gale, he served with the British Legion in Spain during the Carlist Wars.[44] He left the Spanish service with the rank of lieutenant-colonel and was decorated by Queen Isabella. More than any other man, Ermatinger forged a police force capable of handling all but the most serious civil disturbances. His jurisdiction extended not only to the city and its suburbs, but also to the island of Montreal and neighbouring parishes such as Laprairie, Longueuil, Boucherville, and Île Perrot. Under the general control of a police committee of the city corporation, Ermatinger's force in 1843 consisted of Alexander Comeau as inspector; three chief constables, one English, one French, and one Irish; five mounted constables, two of whom were French; and fifty-two subconstables, for a total force of sixty-two. Their wages of three shillings a day, paid now by the city corporation, were a little higher than that of a common labourer, whose pay in 1843 ranged from one shilling and threepence to two shillings a day.[45] As the force did both day and night duty, it meant that the city of 40,000 was guarded by about thirty policemen, armed with batons only.

During the decade of the forties when riots on the Lachine and Beauharnois canals and civil disturbances in Montreal were to tax the police beyond endurance, Ermatinger provided stability to the force. With him and Wetherall for most of the forties was another British regular soldier, Thomas Wily, the former colour-sergeant of the 83rd Regiment. The son of an indigent half-pay captain who could not afford to buy commissions for his sons, Wily entered the army as a private and worked his way through the ranks. When he arrived in Quebec with his regiment in 1837, his fluency in French made him particularly useful, and he was named drillmaster of the Royal Quebec Volunteers. Disappointed in not receiving a promised commission in the regulars, in 1838 he purchased out and immediately secured a commission as adjutant of the 1st Provincial Regiment stationed on the border, remaining with this corps until it was disbanded in 1842.[46] The genial and competent Wily was made Montreal's chief of police in 1844 and remained chief until the Rebellion Losses Bill agitation in 1849.[47]

Throughout the forties, then, as Montreal's postrebellion police force took shape under the direction of three former British military men, the garrison of the city resumed its peacetime functions. The most onerous and the most important of these during the next thirteen years was that of aiding the civil authorities in times of disturbance, for, as militant Patriotes gave up radicalism and returned to conventional politics, elements within the English-language sector of the city, often the recently arrived Irish, stepped in to keep the city on the brink of turbulence for most of the decade. Elections, whether to the provincial Assembly or to the reestablished municipal council, could generally be counted on for "broken heads" or worse and for military intervention.[48]

In judging the temper of a crowd and anticipating its intention, men who knew local conditions and residents were of prime importance. During the forties and early fifties, the garrison numbered among its 1,500 men senior staff officers whose service in the city dated back to the rebellion era. These were officers who knew the city, its temper, and its people intimately, none more so than the deputy quartermaster-general, Col. Sir Charles Gore,[49] who had commanded the unsuccessful attack on Saint-Denis in November 1837. Gore became commandant of Canada East in 1846 and, as such, was the man to whom the city magistrates had to apply for military aid. The other major link between the civilian and military hierarchies in times of trouble was the town major, Ensign Colin Macdonald, a Peninsular veteran of the 79th Cameron Highlanders.[50] Macdonald's job was to keep things running as smoothly as possible between soldiers and townsmen, an unenviable task when troops confronted rioters. Other senior officers of this period included the deputy adjutant general, Lt.-Col. John Eden; Commissary General Sir Randolph Routh; and Lt.-Col. George Wetherall, the victor of the battle of Saint-Charles, who, after a brief tour of duty with the 1st Royal Scots at London, Canada West, returned to Montreal as deputy adjutant general.

Military authorities felt no need to hasten from Montreal those troops that had been involved in the suppression of the rebellions. The 24th Regiment and the Royal Scots did not leave until the late spring of 1840. The Grenadier Guards returned to Quebec in May 1840, and the 7th Hussars remained in the Montreal area until 1842. The 1st King's Dragoon Guards remained until 1843, serving at Chambly, Laprairie, and Montreal.[51] The 73rd Highland Regiment and the 85th Buckinghamshire Light Infantry were both posted back to Montreal in 1841, and the 93rd Sutherland Highlanders returned to Montreal in 1844.[52] The regiment that remained at the Montreal station from the rebellion era throughout the entire forties was the 71st Highland Light Infantry, its officers and men becoming as familiar with Montreal and its residents as were the men and officers of the Provincial Cavalry with whom they so often acted in the suppression of civil disturbances.

How many of these and other British soldiers of the rebellion period remained on the Montreal station after their regiments had left the country is difficult to ascertain, but there were many. A new military policy, designed to combat the waves of desertion that occurred whenever a regiment received its posting from Canada, permitted soldiers to transfer to regiments remaining in Canada. Thus from 1840 on vacancies in regiments were quickly filled by men anxious to finish their service in Canada.[53] In 1843 alone there were 1,015 such transfers.[54] These were soldiers, then, whose long residence in Montreal made them as knowledgeable as the soldiers of the 71st Highlanders who spent fourteen years on the Montreal station before their return to England in 1852.

A new regiment, the Royal Canadian Rifles, which was raised for frontier service, constituted another group of men from the rank and file who chose to remain in Canada.[55] The Royal Canadian Rifle Regiment was organized and recruited in Montreal in the fall of 1841. It was designed to place on the border only older mature soldiers, preferably married, whose conduct had been exemplary and whose fifteen or more years of service would guarantee their pensions, presumably a deterrent to desertion.

Recruits for the new regiment could be enlisted from line regiments serving in Canada or from those posted back to England;[56] at the same time discharged soldiers with fifteen years' service were permitted to reenlist.[57] This was a departure from military policy that had prevailed since the end of the 1812–14 War, a policy that strictly prohibited the reenlisting of discharged soldiers or of colonials for fear it would drain settlers from the colonies at a time when imperial policy was to encourage the settlement of the Canadas "by a British-born population."[58] The policy of forbidding colonials from enlisting in the British army was not changed for the new regiment; only those colonials who could secure a commission by purchase or examination were acceptable.[59] Ten companies were filled quickly, for the regulations of the new regiment had several attractions. Twelve wives per hundred soldiers, rather than the usual six, were permitted to receive army rations and barrack accommodations.[60] Men of the new regiment were allowed to engage in part-time farming or other activity outside their military duties.[61] The Rifles remained at the Montreal station until 1843 when seven companies were posted to frontier duty in the upper province.[62]

The Montreal garrison in the early forties, then, not only had senior staff and regimental officers who were aware of the past tensions of the community, but also had one regiment that remained on the station throughout the decade and a number of soldiers transferring into regiments that stayed in the country. Their role in preventing or suppressing civil disorders and riots was paramount in the decade of the forties when local police arrangements were developing from an embryo prerebellion force of watchmen into a more sophisticated establishment of officers and constables, paid and controlled by the city council.

4. The Garrison and Its Social Milieu

In the early 1840s Montreal society was still recovering from the wounds of the Rebellions of 1837 and 1838. The city had been the breeding ground of both revolts, and each revolt had been suppressed by a combined military force that included not only the Montreal garrison, but also regulars and volunteers from the upper province and the maritime command. Though Montreal escaped all but a slight street skirmish as far as field action and repressive measures were concerned, its people had been deeply seared by the events of the rebellions. Rebel and loyalist emerged from the same family tree. Other townsmen, torn by divided loyalties, aided neither rebels nor Crown forces but watched the fratricidal struggle in a state of paralyzed neutrality.

In the aftermath of rebellion, bitterness replaced aggressiveness, a bitterness that reflected the hostility of the loyalists against those whom they considered responsible for the rebellions, especially those rebel leaders who resumed conventional politics and began to assume government jobs. For their part, those Montrealers who had taken up arms or those who had simply been political supporters of the Patriote party were embittered by the severity of the suppression of the rebellions and by what seemed a boycott directed against them as far as government jobs and militia appointments were concerned.

37

Added to this troubled social setting of Montreal in the early 1840s was a new factor. Montreal's population had become predominantly English speaking largely because of the influx of Irish immigrants in the 1830s. Along with this change in population came an increase in the city's Roman Catholic character, for the incoming Irish straddled both dominant communities, adhering to the English community linguistically and to the French community in their faith. This was just as true of the Irish soldier quartered in the Quebec Gate Barracks. If the soldier sought out the Irish taverns in Griffintown on his off-hours, on Sundays his church parade moved off in the direction of Notre Dame, the Roman Catholic parish church of the French community, for St. Patrick's Church was not built until the end of the 1840s. Here the Irish soldier would find common ground with the French and Irish Roman Catholics of the city. It was this increase of Irish within the city that gave the disorders of the 1840s a new direction. Though the more recent Irish may not have been able to vote, they were capable of being organized into a physical force wing for election or other purposes. Revolt had failed but there were still elements within the city prepared to use limited physical force to gain political or religious objectives. Within this precarious and complex racial and religious setting, the British garrison, with its highly sophisticated officer corps, carried out its postrebellion duties.

For a stranger, including the newly arrived British officer, entry into what was then Montreal's "first society" was almost impossible without a formal introduction, as a British traveller discovered, but "let a stranger be but once well introduced, and in no place will he meet with more liberal and kind attention."[1] A visiting clergyman in the 1840s found the city as "an agreeable a residence as any person possessed of some means could wish . . . though a clergyman, if young, would find a great watchfulness to guard against the fascinations of its gay society."[2] Not so impressed with the city was a young American actress who arrived to perform at the Theatre Royal on Notre Dame Street. She found "the heat while we were in Montreal intolerable, the filth intolerable, the bugs intolerable, the people intolerable, the jargon they speak intolerable," and she lifted her hands in thankfulness when she again set foot in the United States.[3]

For the military hierarchy, guidelines on colonial society had been formally drawn up by the Queen's herald in an attempt to avoid conflicts over social precedence and rank. Distinctions of

38

rank tended to become blurred in the colonies where one officer's wife observed "the saucy familiarity of servants, [who] . . . republican in spirit, think themselves as good as their employers."[4] The military hierarchy was the only group with a clear guide to social distinction, and it is not surprising, then, that it was from military personnel that advice was sought as to where to place local officials at the governor's dinner table or what precedence should be given to the mayor of Montreal who might, apart from his office, hold an inferior social rank to another member of an official procession.[5]

The order of precedency in the colonies ranked the commander of the forces above the governor general.[6] Ranking below them were general staff officers, visiting governors from other provinces or colonies, colonels, lieutenant-governors, presidents of councils, and field officers below the rank of colonel. To avoid problems of rank at official functions such as the opening and closing of the House of Assembly, government dinners and levées, it was carefully stipulated that a governor as well as members of the Assembly and Crown officers of another province "have not in that Province where they visit any Precedency above their rank in Private Life."[7] The rules governing precedency in the colonies were supplemented, when necessary, by a reference to the rules governing precedency in England itself.[8] But even here there was room for confusion, for the order of precedency in England was in several large categories, that is, royalty, clergy, nobility, aristocracy, royal household officials, military, gentry, professional classes, and, at the bottom of the social hierarchy, tradesmen, artificers, and labourers, in that order.

As well as fitting French social ranks such as seigneurs, bourgeois, and habitant into a formalized English social order, there was the additional difficulty of fitting imperial ranks into a colonial milieu. Where to place at the governor's table a man like Sir William Logan posed problems for the governor's secretary. Logan was a native Montrealer, the son of an immigrant baker,[9] but as an eminent geologist and the first Canadian to be knighted for service to his country, he could not be put "below the salt." Maj. Thomas Edmund Campbell of the 7th Hussars, who had, in turn, acted as private secretary to both Lords Sydenham and Elgin, and to whom the problem was referred, could not help. He replied simply, "His rank is imperial; it is for you to decide what place you will give it at your house."[10]

The difficulty of adhering to the official colonial ranking was indicated by the manner in which Montreal society was presented at the first levée of Governor General Charles Poulett Thomson in 1839.[11] The commander of the British forces, Sir Richard Downes Jackson, was presented first, followed by Maj.-Gen. Sir George Arthur, as lieutenant-governor of Upper Canada. Then Maj.-Gen. John Clitherow, commanding the Montreal station, and Commissary General Sir Randolph Routh were presented, followed by colonels, lieutenant-colonels, majors, captains, and surgeons of the regular garrison in Montreal. The presentation of the regular military hierarchy was straightforward.

What to do with the 271 Montrealers, including colonial military officers, 72 French Canadians, and 4 Jews was resolved by presenting everyone in alphabetical order. This lack of any attempt at colonial precedency may be explained by the confused state of society following the rebellion and the forfeiture of local colonial government. The formal rules of precedency called for the presentation of the presidents of the Executive and Legislative Councils, followed by members of the Councils, the speaker of the House of Assembly, the chief justice, treasurer, associate judges, baronets, attorney general, judge of the admiralty, secretary of the province, and members of the House of Assembly. Then would come the mayor, aldermen, and members of the city corporation, together with their wives.

Had Montreal society and government institutions been functioning normally, undoubtedly Peter McGill would have headed those being presented, for not only was he a member of the Special Council and the Legislative Council, but he was also president of the powerful St. Andrew's Society, of the Constitutional Association of Montreal, of the Ward Association, and head of the Bank of Montreal. His presentation would have been followed by George Moffatt, who, like McGill, was a member of both the Special Council and the Legislative Council. In addition Moffatt was president of the St. George's Society and an officer of the Constitutional Association.

After McGill and Moffatt would have come other members of the Legislative Council such as Joseph Masson,[12] reputedly the wealthiest man in the two Canadas, Toussaint Pothier, Andrew Stuart, Pierre de Rocheblave, Hughes Heney, Dominick Daly, Pierre Debartzch, Judges Samuel Gale, Jean-Roche Rolland, and George Pyke, the Roman Catholic bishop of Montreal, Monseigneur J. J. Lartigue, and other dignitaries of the church including Joseph Vincent Quiblier, superior of the Sulpicians. But neither the House of Assembly nor the city corporation were functioning, and many of the militia officers were still in a somewhat anomalous position.[13] Yet, despite this somewhat confused state of society, some gesture at precedency was made. Certain townsmen, including members of the Special Council, the chief justices, and Crown officers, and a small number of the church hierarchy, were "in attendance" upon the new governor general. This meant that they would be with the governor before the formal presentation of the others.

The egalitarian method of presentation of prominent Montrealers to the new governor general could suffice for official occasions, but a more precise ranking could not be avoided for less official functions such as dinners. Official position, although it permitted entrance into first society, did not necessarily mean acceptance into first society, nor did it necessarily smooth social relations. Eleazar David David, son of the socially prominent and wealthy Jewish family of Montreal, and himself possessing an established place in society because of his military rank as major, could be snubbed socially by the colonial son of a prominent English military family, Edward Hale of Sherbrooke. When Major David, tall and handsome in his cavalry uniform, and fresh from his military glories at Saint-Charles where his horse was shot under him and his bravery mentioned in dispatches by Sir John Colborne, leaned upon the wagon of Edward Hale to speak to his daughter Bella, Hale ran the wheels of the wagon "over [his] toes to pay him for his pains."[14]

Whether Hale's dislike for David sprang from a personal antipathy, an antipathy shared by Sydney Bellingham,[15] David's fellow captain in the Royal Montreal Cavalry, or whether it sprang from the aversion to which David's brother referred when he moved from Montreal to Three Rivers because "the people in Three Rivers . . . have not the same aversion to our religion as in Montreal" is uncertain. The fact that Jews of the professional class could and did become militia officers, justices of the peace, and members of the Assembly tends to strengthen Benjamin Sack's contention that "Jews were neither disliked nor discriminated against generally in Montreal" in the first half of the nineteenth century.[16]

The hostility against the Davids just after the rebellion may have owed much to Maj. Eleazar David's indiscretion in eloping with the wife of a British army officer, herself the mother of three young children, the youngest of whom, a babe in arms, she took with her and whom David later acknowledged as his child.[17] David's subsequent return to Montreal with his family a decade later and his acceptance into society and military circles, as well as the marriage of three of his daughters into prominent English families, all indicate how completely he was accepted into high society.[18]

Towards the sons of an Ojibway Indian princess there was never a hint of social ostracism by Montrealers or of aloofness on the part of British officers.[19] No two men in Montreal received or deserved more genuine deference and affection than William and Charles Ermatinger. William Ermatinger, subsequent to his appointment as police superintendent in Montreal, became field inspector of the militia. His elder brother, Charles Oakes Ermatinger, served in the Royal Montreal Cavalry from 1837 to 1850 and became chief of police in Montreal in 1853.

Social relations between the British and French in Montreal presented some ambiguities. Stewart Derbishire, an English lawyer employed by Lord Durham in 1838 as a confidential agent, concluded that "the habitants . . . consider themselves superior to all the other peoples, and too good to mix with any other race."[20] A member of an old Anglo-Irish family, Sydney Bellingham, who came to Canada to better himself financially, believed that relations between the English and French communities, through intermarriage, had been cordial until the advent of Papineau.[21] By 1833 British traveller John McGregor observed that "the English and Canadians [do not] mix cordially with each other." He believed that this arose "from the English having formerly assumed an arrogant superiority over the French, at a time . . . when the latter were far above the former in the scale of manners and acquirements which shed lustre over, and give a tone of well-bred gentility to society." This observer remarked, "The Canadian gentry all over the province, consisting chiefly of descendants of the old noblesse and gentry, retain the courteous urbanity of the French school of the last century . . . [and] although their disposition is kind and their manners agreeable, their society is not sufficiently appreciated by the English."[22]

To a visitor such as John McGregor in 1833 and, indeed, to Lord Durham during his brief residence in Canada in 1838 when hostility within the two communities was at its height, this may have seemed the case. But the reverse was true. So interrelated were leading French and English families by 1837 that there were few which did not share cousins, and this included the Papineaus. It may even have been members of mixed families who experienced the most intense feelings during the rebellion and postrebellion era. Robert Shore Milnes Bouchette, the Patriote son of Joseph Bouchette, the impeccably loyal surveyor general of the province, married an English girl. Another insurgent chief, Dr. Cyrille-Hector Côté, took as his bride the daughter of the barrack master at St. Johns, and as soon as tempers cooled after 1838, it was soldiers of the provincial forces at the border who rowed Madame Côté across Missisquoi Bay to a rendezvous with her husband still in exile at Highgate, Vermont.[23] The wife of Dr. Wolfred Nelson, the victor of the battle of Saint-Denis, was Josephe-Charlotte Noyëll de Fleurimont, a granddaughter of the Marquis de Fleurimont, one of the French officers wounded at Quebec in 1759 and who later, in the service of England, was wounded again at the repulse of Montgomery before Quebec in 1775.[24] Alexandre-Maurice Delisle, the influential businessman and later sheriff of Montreal, was the son of an English mother, Mary Robinson.[25] Col. John Jones, father of the legislative councillor Robert Jones, and of Capt. Walter Jones of the Queen's Light Dragoons, was married to Mary Magdalen Heney, a granddaughter of Charles René Lapailleur. It was owing to the influence of the Jones family that the insurgent François-Maurice Lapailleur was banished to Australia instead of being hanged in 1838.[26]

John MacDonell, the Montreal advocate at whose home the St. Jean Baptiste Society was founded in 1834 and who, by 1838, was one of the leaders of the Chasseur conspiracy in the city, was the son of a Scottish lieutenant of the Royal Artillery and his mother was a member of the prominent royalist French-Canadian family, the de Bélestres.[27] The wife of Théophile Dufort, the Montreal magistrate who acted as liaison between Papineau and Mackenzie in the fall of 1837, was Maria Louisa Pickel, daughter of reform lawyer John Pickel. These were men with ties in both communities whose families were scarred by the fratricidal strife of 1837–38. Others such as Jacques Viger, Montreal's first mayor, whose wife was a member of the Lennox family,[28] were among that large sector of the population which was paralyzed into neutrality by the bitterness of the rebellion era.

A prominent English military family with French connections was the Grants who married into the LeMoyne family of Longueuil, Seigneurs of Beloeil, as did Lt.-Col. John Whyte of the 7th Hussars. His fellow officer, Maj. Thomas Edmund Campbell, married Henriette-Julie Duchesnay, a daughter of the Seigneur of Fossambault.[29] Lt.-Col. William Ermatinger's wife was also of the Duchesnay family, and Philippe-Joseph Aubert de Gaspé, Seigneur of Saint-Jean-Port-Joli, married Susanne Allison, daughter of Capt. Thomas Allison of the 5th Regiment of Foot.[30] One of the most important military-French alliances was Commissary General Sir Randolph Routh's marriage to Marie-Louise Taschereau, sister of the future cardinal, Elzéar-Alexandre Taschereau of Quebec City.

Almost as important as the marriage relationships between British army personnel and prominent English and French families of Montreal were the linguistic abilities of both military men and Montrealers generally. Many of the regular officers of the rebellion period were bilingual. Sir John Colborne rose at four o'clock in the morning to master foreign languages. He spoke not only French but several other languages including Swedish.[31] Capt. Charles Wetherall spoke French fluently as did his brother, Lt.-Col. George Augustus Wetherall. Lt. Daniel Lysons of the Royal Scots was likely chosen for staff work upon his arrival in Montreal because of his fluency in French. Similarly, the colour-sergeant of the 83rd Regiment, Thomas Wily, who became police chief in 1844, spoke French perfectly. Lt.-Col. William Denny who commanded the 71st Highland Light Infantry, which was in the Montreal district for most of the 1840s, was perfectly at ease in French as were Capt. Brook Taylor, military secretary to Sir Richard Jackson, and Capt. Robert Lovelace of the 19th Regiment who immigrated to Canada in 1840 and eventually resumed a military career in both the Canadian militia and British army during the Crimean campaign. For those officers unable to speak French, their patronage was earnestly solicited by Georges Girard who promised that under his private tuition they would shortly speak French fluently.[32]

Montrealers of the professional and business world were just as adept and ready as British officers to master both major languages of the city. Papineau sent his eldest son, Amédée, at the age of four to an English school run by the daughter of Jocelyn Waller, Irish editor of the Montreal reform journal *Spectateur Canadien*, which was published in both French and English.[33] When this journal collapsed at the end of the 1820s, Papineau, anxious to convert English as well as French voters to reform measures, soon established the *Vindicator* to replace *Le Spectateur Canadien*. The editors of the *Vindicator*, Daniel Tracey and

Edmund B. O'Callaghan, were fluently bilingual. For newspaper-men of the English community, bilingualism was also essential. Both Brown Chamberlin and John Lowe of the *Gazette* were flu-ent in both languages as was Sydney Bellingham who worked for a while on the *Times*.[34]

Lawyers could not function unless they were bilingual. Sir Francis Johnson, the son of an army officer, who was to become a Queen's counsel and judge, was so fluent in both languages that it was said of him, "On ne peut avoir l'aire plus anglais et avoir l'ésprit plus français."[35] Lt.-Col. John Samuel McCord who raised the Montreal volunteers during the rebellion and later became a judge, was perfectly bilingual, having studied at the Sulpician Seminary. Judge Thomas Cushing Aylwin was interpreter at the criminal court at Quebec when only sixteen years old.[36]

Businessmen found it to their advantage to be bilingual in a city divided between English-speaking and French-speaking peo-ple. When William Molson ran against Irishman Lewis Thomas Drummond in the 1844 provincial general election, he spoke in both languages. Stanley Bagg, described as the wealthiest man in Montreal, gave his election address in 1832 in French. When young William Weir immigrated to Lower Canada in the early 1840s, he immediately went to Lachute "to acquire a knowledge of the French language, which was then necessary to secure a good situation."[37]

Most doctors of both communities were bilingual, and those of German background, such as the Arnoldi family, usually ac-quired fluency in English and French as well. Drs. Wolfred and Robert Nelson were at home in both languages. When Wolfred Nelson was confined to a Montreal jail in the spring of 1838 for his part in the rebellion, he was so concerned that his children would lose their fluency in English that he wrote to his eldest daughter and admonished her to practise English. "I am so very anxious, my dear Sophia," he wrote, "that you, Julia and your brothers should speak English with fluency that I beg Miss Hen-nessy [their tutoress] in a very *particular manner* to converse with you all entirely in English and if my children love me and wish me to bear with some resignation my captivity, they will not fail on all occasions to use among themselves the English. Tell Horace [his eldest son] how much he will oblige me by observing this request of mine."[38]

Nelson's family typified the dilemma of those children of mixed marriages who were absorbed into one or the other culture. In

Nelson's case, the eldest daughter remained within the French cultural and linguistic milieu, while the younger children came within the English-language orbit.[39] Horace, who helped to cast bullets for his father during the attack on Saint-Denis by Crown forces, eventually became dean of the medical school at Bishop's University in Lennoxville.

In seigneurial rural areas, a passing knowledge of French was often inadequate. Sir John Colborne advised his soldier son, James, that "a knowledge of the French language is not only necessary for every gentleman, but an officer cannot even be sent to an outpost [in Lower Canada] without it."[40] Indeed, in the Montreal of the 1830s and 1840s bilingualism was taken for granted as a prerequisite to office within the military, legal, medical, journalistic, and business hierarchies.

There had been a long-established entente cordiale between the upper ranks of French-Canadian society and the military hierarchy, dating from the post-Conquest period, but it was most evident during the service of the Duke of Kent in Lower Canada at the turn of the century. The Duke of Kent, who was fluently bilingual, was described as "one of the finest harmonizers . . . among the old and new subjects of the British Crown." When an election fight broke out at Charlesbourg in 1792, he calmed the rioters by addressing each in his own tongue. "Can there be a man among you that does not know the King to be the father of all his people? Let me hear no more about these hateful French and English questions; you are all His Majesty's well-loved Canadian subjects."[41]

Under the aegis of the Duke of Kent, several cadet members of prominent French-Canadian families entered the British army as officers, among them Lt.-Col. Charles de Salaberry and his three brothers,[42] as well as sons of the Desrivières and Duchesnay families. These young French-Canadian officers served with the British forces in the West Indies during the Napoleonic Wars, and because of their French names, they faced a duel almost every week with their fellow officers who taunted them with being French.[43] Yet these officers could forgive such treatment. Charles de Salaberry, who had seen service in Dominica and in the Walcheren campaign as aide-de-camp to General de Rottenburg, was asked by Gen. George Prevost to raise the Canadian Voltigeurs in 1812, and he did so willingly even though his relations with Prevost were anything but cordial.[44]

One of the young French Canadians who would leave his law

studies to raise a quota of sixteen men for the Canadian Voltigeurs being organized by de Salaberry in 1813 was the man upon whom Sir John Colborne would rely so heavily during the rebellions in Lower Canada twenty-four years later.[45] Louis Guy served as lieutenant under de Salaberry at the battle of Châteauguay, and at the actions at Four Corners and Lacolle Mills was "employed on the most hazardous and dangerous services . . . [when] his good conduct and bravery were equally conspicuous."[46] Instead of returning to his legal studies at the end of the war, Guy, like his admired senior officer, chose to enter the regular army and served as a lieutenant in the 81st Regiment.[47] It was to Louis Guy that Sir John Colborne turned when he wanted loyalist members of the Montreal militia enrolled for service in Montreal in November of 1837,[48] and Guy led the first Montreal volunteers out of the city for general service on 2 December 1837.[49]

Among French Canadians who served in the 1812–14 War, became rebels in 1837, and then returned to conventional political opposition in the forties were Louis-Joseph Papineau and Etienne-Paschal Taché. Papineau served as a militia captain in 1812–14, but in 1837 he was among those dismissed from the militia because of his ambivalent attitude. He could hardly forget a horsewhipping administered to his followers who came armed to the Longueuil horse ferry to escort him to Saint-Charles on 23 October 1837. With Papineau on the Longueuil horse ferry were a young British lieutenant and some brother officers on their way to hunt on the south shore with a pack of hounds. When they discovered that Papineau was being met by a mounted armed escort, the British officers promptly "mounted our hunts and charged, hunting-whips in hand, on which [the men] fled [while] Papineau stole off by another road."[50]

Yet Papineau could forgive such treatment. Thirty years later when he met the same lieutenant at a reception in Montreal given by Governor General Lord Monck, Papineau teased the officer and reminded him, "I hear you were the officer who came to call on me . . . in 1837 in St. Hyacinthe." The lieutenant, Sir Daniel Lysons, had been sent to the home of Papineau's sister, Madame Rosalie Dessaulles, where Papineau was reported to be hiding,[51] but Papineau had already made his way out of the province.

Like Papineau, Etienne-Paschal Taché was an officer in the 1812–14 War, who had served as a lieutenant in the Chasseurs Canadiens.[52] In 1837 Taché tried unsuccessfully to provoke

47

a minor uprising in Montmagny. By 1846 the erstwhile rebel stirred both French and English Canada by his powerful affirmation of French-Canadian loyalty during the crisis in American-Canadian relations in 1846 over the Oregon border dispute. Taché's stirring speech was to gain for him the post of deputy adjutant general, while the incumbent of the past six years, Augustus Gugy, who had played a vital role in putting down the rebellion, found himself, as he termed it, "legislated out of office."[53] As the new militia bill was being debated, Taché, amid tumultuous applause from French ranks as well as from those who understood French among the liberals of both Canada East and Canada West, and Draper tory ranks of Canada West, asserted,

> Notre loyauté à nous n'est pas une loyauté de spéculation, de louis, schellings et deniers, nous ne l'avons pas constamment sur les lèvres, nous n'en faisons pas un trafic. Nous sommes dans nos habitudes, par nos lois, par notre religion, comme l'a très bien remarqué mon honorable ami pour la cité de Québec, monarchistes et conservateurs. . . . Messieurs, traitez-nous comme les enfants d'une même mère . . . et je réponds que si jamais ce pays cesse un jour d'être britannique, le dernier coup de canon tiré pour le maintien de la puissance anglaise en Amérique le sera par un bras canadien.[54]

The applause from the benches and galleries where Montreal and Township tories were seated was a little less enthusiastic. Taché's bite did not go unnoticed. Their loyalty during the rebellions, they felt, had not been one of pounds, shillings, and pence either.

Sitting with Taché in the reform ranks of the House of Assembly was George-Etienne Cartier who, like Taché, had fought with the rebels, shouldering a musket beside Wolfred Nelson at Saint-Denis against British regulars and bringing additional ammunition to Nelson from Saint-Antoine.[55] Cartier fled over the border with a price on his head, but returned to Lower Canada when a general amnesty was declared. Thirty-three years later as minister of militia in the Dominion of Canada, Cartier, named in honour of one British monarch and knighted by another, received from the imperial government all the fortifications, armaments, stores, and ordnance lands of the imperial garrisons on the withdrawal of British troops from Canada.

Cartier's initial confrontation with British regulars paralleled that of another scion of a leading French-Canadian family—

Robert Shore Milnes Bouchette, the godchild of Sir Robert Shore Milnes, lieutenant-governor of Lower Canada at the turn of the century. Casting off traditional family loyalties, Bouchette, whose English wife died of cholera in 1834, took up arms against Crown forces in 1837 and was wounded at Moore's Corner.[56] In 1866 Bouchette, a commissioner of customs in Ottawa, served as captain in the Civil Service Rifle Regiment under the command of a former colour-sergeant of the 83rd Regiment, Thomas Wily. The colour-sergeant, now colonel of the Canadian militia, commented, "Surely there must be something just and magnanimous in the character of a people who in so short a time can convert bitter foes into loyal and devoted subjects."[57]

This chameleon quality of French-English relations in Montreal and in Lower Canada was evident in the attitude of the daughter of a French officer who had fought against British soldiers on the Plains of Abraham. When Paul-Henri de Belvèze, commandant of the first French warship to sail up the St. Lawrence since the Conquest, visited Mademoiselle de Lanaudière, he could not understand how anyone with such a "reminiscent French heart" could ever have become so loyal to the British Crown. Her reply was simply, "Nos coeurs sont à la France, mais nos bras à l'Angleterre."[58]

The development of this intellectual loyalty to the British Crown grew out of the tension and turbulence of the late 1830s and 1840s when French and English Canadians, Protestant and Catholic, native and immigrant, were jostling for position. The imperial garrison found itself acting in the role of referee and oftentimes a somewhat reluctant policeman as the divergent forces clashed in 1837–38, coalesced in 1841, and then clashed again in 1849.

Yet relations between the British military and French Canadians, even when they faced each other's bullets, were usually tinged with mutual respect. British regulars knew the mettle of the countryside French. When troops attacked Saint-Denis, they were turned back by an almost equal number of French habitants, commanded by an English Canadian, Wolfred Nelson, himself the son of a royal navy commissioner in America who came to Canada during the revolution.[59] Nelson later spoke of his distress at being forced into battle against the "soldiers of England . . . the land of his honored and venerated Father. Had he been placed side by side and acting in concert with the troops, in resisting a common foe," Nelson wrote, "his emotions would have partaken of exultation and delight. . . . as it was, he had a weight upon him that he could not dissipate . . . and the retreat of his assailants gave him but little satisfaction."[60] At Saint-Eustache it was a French-Canadian doctor, Jean-Olivier Chénier, who commanded and stood by the habitants who remained to fight the overwhelming numbers of British troops on 14 December 1837. It is not surprising that a British general would later say, "Given a Canadian gentleman and you generally have the making of a good officer, for, as a people, they have military aptitudes of no mean order."[61]

This mutual respect between the upper ranks of French-Canadian society and the military prevailed sufficiently for rebel leaders of the gentleman rank to expect and receive the courtesies of an *affaire d'honneur* from British officers, although some officers complained that it was only because "the British troops were left perfectly unsupported by their own authorities . . . that the officers felt obliged to accept the challenge."[62] One such incident occurred when Lt. A. H. Ormsby of the 1st Royal Scots was making his nightly rounds on 29 October 1837. The sentry at the commissariat office complained that two gentlemen had been trying to force him off his post and take away his musket. Ormsby told the sentry to use his bayonet in such circumstances, upon which one of the Canadians stepped forward and challenged the lieutenant. The Canadian, dressed in *étoffe du pays*, was the amiable and reckless Son of Liberty, Edouard Rodier. He sent, as his second, Thomas Storrow Brown, accompanied by Ludger Duvernay, the editor of *La Minerve*, to the officers' mess of the Royals the next morning to arrange the duel.[63]

The boldness of the challenge was heatedly discussed in the mess on St. Francis Street where officers likened it to the effrontery of the "rebels [who] drilled on our parade grounds, and complained if they were interfered with." The officers decided that the challenge had to be accepted, but it was ordered that Ormsby's second, Capt. John Mayne, was to remove Ormsby from the ground after the first shot. The duel took place at the racecourse in Côte St. Pierre. Neither shot took effect and Ormsby left the ground with his second. A brisk exchange of notes ensued, the Canadians demanding to know what Mayne intended to do and the officers replying that they had determined that no other officer was to accept a challenge. When Colborne was informed of the duel, although officially expressing his disapproval, he "allowed that there was much to be said on our [the officers'] side."[64] Undoubtedly, the affair enhanced Rodier's reputation and the Patriotes "furent enchantés de voir avec quel succès il avait tenu tête aux militaires, et ceux-ci furent les premiers à louer son courage et son sangfroid."[65]

While individual officers could praise the boldness of French Canadians, undoubtedly the rebellion called forth animosities and contempt that would not have otherwise been expressed. Lt. René Hertel de Rouville, who had fought with the Canadian Voltigeurs at Châteauguay in 1813 and who supplied food and quarters for Wetherall's troops when they stopped overnight en route to Saint-Charles, was only "a little mean-looking old man dressed like a labourer" to Lt.-Col. Charles Grey of the 71st Highland Light Infantry.[66] Similarly, the virulent outburst of an officer of the 43rd Regiment, a regiment that had been hastily ordered to trek through the New Brunswick forests in mid-winter to Lower Canada, showed how deeply the events of 1837 had seared the normally amicable relations between British officers and French Canadians. The officer described the regiment's arrival in Cornwall, "a town whose name, language and inhabitants reminded us that we were now in Upper Canada. The shrill 'sacrés' and 'marche donc' of the French Canadians no longer grated upon the ear, and instead of the puny, swarthy, stove-dried and monkey-like Jean Baptiste, we encountered a sturdy, florid and grave-demeanoured race evidently drawing their characteristics from Scotland."[67] Such comments, printed in one of the most widely read newspapers in British North America, did not go unnoticed by French Canadians.

Yet other forces were at work to lessen the bitterness of the rebellion. The editor of the Kingston *Loyalist*, Maj. John Richardson, a former British officer, urged that young French Canadians be encouraged to enter the British army, thus "identifying their honor, as well as their interests, with those of the Empire." Richardson praised the French, saying, "They are, like their ancestors, a sensitive and chivalrous people more easily won through a consideration of their honor, than their interests." In an unusual burst of homage, the *Loyalist* editor exclaimed, "Open the way to distinction, in the proudest service in the world, to a young French Canadian, and you secure, not only his unswerving fidelity, but the affections of the whole body of his countrymen. Warm in the generous enthusiasm which is common to their race, they will rally round the glorious standard the choicest of their children have already hastened to defend."[68]

Such a path was followed in the decade following rebellion by

Edmond Joly, son of the Swiss Protestant Seigneur of Lotbinière and brother of the future premier of Quebec, Henri-Gustave Joly. Edmond Joly became an officer of the 32nd Regiment that had seen service at both Saint-Denis and Saint-Eustache during the rebellion. Having served in the Crimea, Joly hastened to India to rejoin his regiment which was surrounded by mutinous forces at Lucknow. How devoted these young officers were is indicated in letters to relatives. On the eve of his departure from Calcutta to join the small force under Sir Henry Havelock that attempted the relief of Lucknow, Joly wrote, "I believe the most glorious day of my existence would be that in which I should throw myself amongst the first into Lucknow, to meet my brave 32nd or perish."[69] The son of the Seigneur de Lotbinière was among those slain at the siege.[70]

Joly's military career paralleled that of George Sheaffe Montizambert, a major in the 10th Regiment, who met his death at the age of thirty-five while leading his men in an attack on an outpost at the siege of Mooltan in India in 1848.[71] A member of the family of Charles de Salaberry, Alphonse de Salaberry chose to serve within the militia hierarchy, becoming adjutant general of militia for Canada East from 1848 to 1867, and a Duchesnay served as ensign with the provincial forces on the frontier in 1839.[72]

Thus French Canadians had had mixed relations with the British garrison. At one time they fought beside regulars against a common foe; at other times some took up arms against the Queen's soldiers and their fellow loyalist countrymen. Still others entered loyalist volunteer units and fought against their insurgent compatriots,[73] confounding Amury Girod's prediction that French Canadians would not fire upon one another in the event of civil war.[74] Yet the British military command tended to agree with Girod's prediction and hesitated to mobilize the Lower Canadian militia at the outbreak of the rebellion. The intimidation of militia officers of both the French and English communities by militant Patriotes,[75] and the dismissal of others because of their share in the disturbances in the summer and fall of 1837, convinced authorities that it was better not to risk calling out the militia when French Canadians might be forced to take sides against their own people. Recourse was had, instead, to volunteers, most of whom were English speaking. This was the beginning of a close association between the regulars and volunteers that was to continue until the agitation arising out of the Rebellion Losses Bill shattered existing alignments.

At the lower level of society there was little of social mixing between soldiers and members of the French community, partly because of language and religious differences. A French-speaking soldier was a rarity and the Irish Roman Catholic soldier tended to socialize within the Montreal Irish community. In rural areas the isolated soldier seeking to join in French social festivities found little encouragement. Even two years after the rebellion, when a young trooper of the 7th Hussars tried to join in the dancing and singing at the house of a habitant, he was ordered away by the host, a man named Longtin of Laprairie. Upon the refusal of the soldier to leave, the habitant picked up a stone and struck the trooper so forcefully that he died.[76] In the city the same exclusiveness existed among the lower classes of society. British officers found it expedient to have all English or all French servants "to make the establishment work well." Most officers opted for French servants not only to avoid bickering in the servants' quarters, but also because "an English servant can not get on well in marketing unless he can speak French."[77]

Montreal in the 1840s and 1850s was not the easiest of British garrison towns to serve in, but it assuredly was one of the most interesting. Its populace, divided as it was almost evenly between the French-speaking and English-speaking communities, had been torn apart by the troubled political squabbles of the 1830s that had led to rebellion. This was a society in which family relationships and feuds among both cultural groups, the changing political affiliations among individuals, and their memories of rebellion resentments and loyalties all shaped the political tendencies and tensions that erupted in the city with such bitterness in 1849 and ended with such tragedy in 1853. It was within this volatile and racially mixed society that the British garrison carried out its peacetime duties in the postrebellion era, duties that too often resulted from the conflicts within that society.

Part

The Garrison as an Aid to Civil Power

The times we write of were the halcyon times of
peace, when the Queen's troops were not exposed
to any serious professional perils. Parades were
observed and repeated with scrupulous regularity. Sentinels were posted at exact intervals.
Battles were heard of, none had been seen. War
and the army list were studied as duties. Peace
and idleness were put up with as necessities.
John Fennings Taylor, *Portraits of British
Americans*

5. Order and Disorder in Montreal, 1843–1848

Senior staff officers and regimental commanding officers in Montreal in the 1840s usually knew enough military law to be able to define riots and unlawful assemblages, but the precise point at which a lawful assembly, such as a gathering of citizens to vote, becomes so unruly as to cause alarm and thus become unlawful was never easy to judge, even for experienced law officers and military men. Military law defined a riot as a "tumultuous disturbance of the peace by three or more persons assembling together of their own authority with an intent mutually to assist one another against anyone who opposes them in the execution of some enterprise of a private nature, and afterwards actually executing the same in a violent and turbulent manner to the terror of the people," that is, some act of violence had to be committed for a riot to exist. An unlawful assemblage differed from a riot in that it was a meeting of "great numbers of people with such circumstance of terror as cannot but endanger the public peace."[1] Violence need not have broken out to render the meeting unlawful; it was enough if the assemblage produced alarm.

If a violent act occurred, a magistrate could, under common law, call upon not only the military but other citizens as well to help maintain order. It was not necessary for him to read the Riot Act before the military intervened. The reading of the act simply enabled the magistrate to make the assemblage illegal and to disperse it by force of arms if necessary. Anyone remaining at the assemblage after the Riot Act was read and beyond the time limited by the act was guilty of a felony, whether he committed a breach of the peace or not.[2] The military, however, faced a dilemma when called upon to assist the civil power in maintaining order. If a soldier refused an order to fire on civilians, he was liable to be tried by a court-martial for disobedience; if he obeyed the order and killed a rioter, he could be tried in the civil court on a charge of murder.[3] Great judgement, coolness, and experience, therefore, were required of officers in charge of detachments sent in aid of civil power, and military authorities in Montreal had worked out with care the procedures to be followed in such circumstances. To make sure that newly arrived regimental and staff officers were aware of the local general orders about the use of troops in aid of civil power, these orders were reissued several times throughout the decade of the forties in Montreal.

Serious rioting requiring military intervention began in the spring of 1843 when feuding Irish workers on the Lachine Canal began pulling down each other's shanties and resorted to firearms.[4] On the first day of rioting, a party of the 1st King's Dragoon Guards and the 71st Highland Light Infantry, stationed at Lachine, was called out. The troops did not interfere, as the magistrate did not ask them to although firing was kept up by the rioters. The next day one of the factions tried to seize the powder supply kept for blasting on the canal. The Dragoon Guards removed it to safety, but as the burning of shanties continued all morning, additional troops from the city were requested. Police Superintendent William Ermatinger, with a party of the 71st Regiment, hastened by sleigh to Lachine with orders to read the Riot Act. If the rioters did not disperse within an hour, he was to fire upon them with blank cartridge. Should this prove ineffective, then the military was to fire with ball.[5] Ermatinger's instructions were precise and moderate. As most of the rioters fled with their arms on the approach of the troop reinforcements, none of these steps was necessary.

On the surface, the fight seemed to be straight factional feuding between Corkonians and Connaughtmen, but it may well have sprung from a combination of religious animosities, discontent with contractors, and even political differences.[6] When the riots were investigated by a committee from the House of Assembly, which included the influential Irishman Benjamin

58

Holmes, the question of wages was raised and complaints were heard from canal men about being laid off.[7] The Corkonians were reputedly the aggressors and the stronger party, and if they were from the Bandon area as well, were likely Orangemen, though accounts of the riots make no mention of Orange overtones. Certainly Holmes, whose religious affiliation was with the very rational Unitarian Church, was anxious to keep internal disorders as free of racial and religious overtones as possible.

The need for troops in aid of the civil power at this initial canal riot prompted the executive government to take measures to organize canal police both at Lachine and along the Beauharnois Canal. Ermatinger was ordered to "lose no time in organizing a temporary force of ten men to serve as police on the line of the Beauharnois Canal, under the immediate command of Mr. Laviolette, the Stipendiary Magistrate at Saint-Timothée,"[8] on the same terms as the force he had raised for service on the Lachine Canal.

These police measures were none too soon. Within three months of the Lachine Canal riots, serious labour riots broke out along the Beauharnois Canal when Irish workers went on strike for better wages, a twelve-hour workday, free shanties, and the right to buy provisions at shops other than those of the contractor. The local magistrates, J. B. Laviolette and George Crawford, one of the contractors, had taken the precaution to apply for troops to augment the newly raised canal police force and by 10 June a detachment of fifty soldiers of the 74th Regiment had been sent to Saint-Timothée. As the depot of the 74th Regiment was at Kinsale in the south of Ireland, it is likely that many of the soldiers of the regiment were Irish.[9]

On 12 June thirty soldiers of the 74th were ordered out in aid of the civil power and soon found themselves completely surrounded and overpowered by the more numerous canallers, who then forced two contractors to agree to raise their wages to three shillings a day. Having gained their wage objective, the crowd dispersed in the direction of the premises of other contractors, while the magistrates and the detachment of soldiers moved off towards Grant's Hotel in Saint-Timothée. Here they were reinforced by thirty troopers of the Queen's Light Dragoons of the Provincial Cavalry, who had been ordered up from their post on the border.

The cavalry and infantry took up positions outside the hotel when they saw canallers, brandishing shillelaghs and bludgeons, approach. Magistrate Laviolette, along with Maj. A. Campbell, the regular officer in charge of the detachment of troops, took a stand on the hotel gallery from where he called upon the crowd to disperse. Instead, they began to surround the hotel, whereupon Laviolette lost no time in reading the Riot Act in "a loud and distinct voice, after which I again enjoined them two or three times to disperse,—this they refused to do, saying that they were about their business, and would go when they chose, and some of them, shouting and hissing, continued to advance towards the troops and round the house."[10] Fearing that the troops would again be overpowered, Laviolette ordered them to fire. Both the infantry and cavalry fired, after which Capt. Walter Jones ordered the cavalry to charge.

One canaller was killed instantly and five others died from wounds. The crowd fell back into the thick bush that lay between the hotel and the rapids that ran in front of the hotel. The Queen's Light Dragoons set off in pursuit and the canal police eventually arrested some twenty-seven, who were lodged in the nearby mill. All but three of the strike leaders were released by Laviolette within a few days, as he believed that "one-half of the poor men, who had shewn themselves in the mob, had been compelled to do so against their wishes."[11]

In this case there was less hostility towards the troops than towards Laviolette, whose life was threatened daily by the more violent of the canallers.[12] Yet, military authorities regarded the encounter with uneasiness and were somewhat relieved when an inquiry into the riots was set up under Capt. Charles Wetherall, together with R. L. Morrogh of the civil secretary's office and Lewis Thomas Drummond, the popular young Irish lawyer who had acted as legal counsel for the insurgents charged with high treason after the rebellions. The inquiry revealed the economic basis for the discontent among the canallers and tended to exonerate the troop action. For their part, military authorities commended the troops for the way they had suppressed the riot and especially praised the action of the Provincial Cavalry.[13]

These canal riots of 1843 were but a prelude to far more serious election riots in the city itself in 1844 when the garrison found itself once more reluctantly drawn into local political squabbles. The occasion for the first outbreak of rioting was a by-election in April. The election was precipitated by the resignation of the member of the Assembly for the West Ward, Benjamin Holmes, who had been one of the magistrates active during the 1832 election riots. Holmes, now also a city councillor for the West Ward in the newly established municipal government, had supported the shaky liberal administration of Louis-Hippolyte La Fontaine and Robert Baldwin. When it resigned in the fall of 1843, Holmes, who was on leave of absence from his post as cashier of the Bank of Montreal, decided to resume his banking career and resigned as member of the Assembly on 1 February 1844.[14]

When Holmes's seat became vacant, Sydney Bellingham, the genial Irishman of letters and former captain of the Royal Montreal Cavalry during the rebellion period, came forward in the liberal interests. William Molson of the great brewing-banking combine entered the electoral race as the conservative candidate. Bellingham soon found that elements in the Irish community from whom he had expected support had decided to back Lewis Thomas Drummond as the Irish candidate for the city. Bellingham "very handsomely resigned," as the *Gazette* editor put it, and he threw his weight behind the Molson campaign, thereby splitting the block Irish vote and opening the door to such a vigorous by-election campaign that military authorities prepared in advance for disturbances.[15] Soon three-cornered racial overtones overtook the campaign. At one of Molson's first meetings in Griffintown, in the heart of the Irish section of the city, his supporters heard "without surprise but not without indignation of the attempts of our opponents to defeat . . . our candidate by representing him as being prejudicial against our fellow subjects of French origin."[16] No holds were to be barred when it came to securing Irish or French votes or preventing such votes from going to a rival candidate.

Molson's meetings continued to be interrupted by yelling and hooting supporters of Drummond, even though Molson had the support of former Patriotes such as lawyer John MacDonell and man-about-town Clément Sabrevois de Bleury, as well as the fugleman of the Irish ward, John Tully.[17] Constitutionals crowded into John Orr's Hotel on Notre Dame Street to roar their approval of Molson, while their leader, George Moffatt, praised the governor general, Sir Charles Metcalfe, as the man who wished to bestow the patronage of the Crown only upon those "best fitted to do service while the late ministry . . . wished to use it to buy one part of the community."[18]

Drummond had a show of strength on 8 April 1844 when he called a meeting of "Repealers and Friends of Ireland," an indication that not only had the Irish arrived in force in the city, but that they had added Irish political issues to the cauldron of local

party politics. Drummond's invitation was taken up by the Lachine Canal workers who turned out in large numbers to hear
spirited addresses by Francis Hincks, Irish editor of the newly established reform journal, the *Pilot*, along with Drummond himself and City Councillor Peter Dunn.[19]

The presence of the canallers in the election campaign had
been anticipated. Early in March the chairman of the Board of
Works, H. H. Killaly, had warned that "labourers on the Lachine
Canal will be present in large numbers at the approaching elections for this city and that a quantity of bludgeons have been prepared."[20] Killaly wrote to the various contractors on the Lachine
Canal and told them to warn the labourers that if they quit their
work to come into the city during the election, they would be
dismissed.

The increasing rowdiness of the election campaign was only too
evident on 11 April when Molson and Drummond arrived with
their respective contingents of supporters at Place d'Armes to
make their nomination speeches. While Molson tried to shout out
his carefully prepared speech in which he denied that he had
"ever discriminated against giving employment either to Protestant, Catholic, Frenchman, Irishman or Englishman," a ruckus broke out. The very pro-Molson *Gazette* reported, "We think
the Drummondites began it, but we must admit the Molsonites
showed the most sticks."[21] The returning officer, A. M. Delisle,
jumped down from the hustings and drew his sword, followed by
Police Superintendent Ermatinger and the two candidates themselves, who walked arm in arm through the riotous crowd, Drummond waving a white muslin handkerchief "as a signal for the
suspension of hostilities" until order was restored."[22]

The rowdy meetings prompted the deputy adjutant general,
Col. George A. Wetherall, to reissue the general orders concerning military aid to the civil power, which stressed that an application for military assistance was to be complied with only if
accompanied by a written requisition from a magistrate specifying distinctly the service on which the troops were to be used.[23]
He also sent to the Montreal commandant a memorandum warning him to "keep all the troops within the limits of their Barracks
. . . ready to turn out at a moment's notice" and to have a "picquet
of one hundred rank and file from each Regiment at all times
ready in the Barrack Square of their respective Regiments."[24]
Officers were provided with a list of the returning officers and
their deputies, and were instructed to comply with their written

requisitions for aid. Arrangements were made to have a troop of the Provincial Cavalry come in from the frontier to assist the regulars, for their usefulness in quelling riots had already been demonstrated the previous spring when the Queen's Light Dragoons had effectively cooperated with regulars in suppressing the disturbances on the Beauharnois Canal. To complete military preparations, a six-pounder and howitzer were held in readiness.

The care with which these arrangements were worked out reflected the experience of the commander of the forces. Sir Richard Jackson, a distinguished Peninsular officer, had been in command of the northern military district in England during the Poor Law agitation and the opening phase of Chartism.[25] His military secretary, Sir Charles O'Donnell, had been brigade major of the northern district under both Jackson and his successor, Maj.-Gen. Sir Charles Napier.[26]

The deputy adjutant general was not being overly cautious. The very first day of the election, 16 April, affairs took an ugly turn when Irish labourers from the Lachine Canal, "persuaded that their religious interests were involved . . . in a contest with Orangemen," came into Montreal where they were met by agents who distributed them at various polls. They began to rip the clothes off merchants voting for Molson, a stratagem which City Councillor Tully claimed could be traced to an article in the *Pilot*. The article made an unfavourable comparison between the "coats worn by Molson's supporters and those of the Irish labourers. . . . this hurt the pride of the Irish."[27]

At the Viger Market polling booth, the returning officer, P. Beaudry, closed the booth after it was surrounded by "400 ferocious looking fellows" who prevented voters coming forward. Upon his request for troops, two companies of the 43rd Regiment were sent under Col. Sir Charles Gore. The Riot Act was read by Police Superintendent Ermatinger, who, with Chief of Police Alexander Comeau, had kept up a steady round of inspection at the various polling areas. The poll was reopened, but, according to the *Gazette*, "as soon as a vote was polled for Mr. Molson, the voter was literally stripped by the mob . . . while the troops stood by without the power to interfere" because the returning officer did not ask their aid. Similarly the Hay Market polling booth in Queen's Ward was closed by its returning officer, George Brush, on the first day of voting "in consequence of one party [the Drummondites] taking possession . . . to the exclusion of the other."[28]

On the first day of the election, some confusion and antagonism arose between magistrates and military authorities when aid was refused in one case because the requisition was not signed by a returning officer or his deputy. Col. George Wetherall was most careful to issue a statement to the magistrates explaining that the aid was refused because the six magistrates requesting it had not specified the circumstances under which the troops were to be employed. Wetherall warned that the "troops were not to parade the streets to prevent risings, or riots, which might not even be in contemplation; their very appearance might tend to create a disturbance where none was before thought of." Referring to the "misrepresentations that have gone abroad amongst the magistracy, on the subject of affording military aid," Wetherall assured the magistrates that "all riots or overt acts of a mob will be promptly suppressed by the soldiery . . . and even without the presence of a magistrate, if the circumstances should be urgent."[29]

Yet even such assurance left some uneasiness. Magistrates wondered how troops could suppress overt acts of violence promptly if they were still in barracks. Military authorities were rightly reluctant to have troops needlessly called out on civil duty and above all wished to avoid any imputation that the soldiers were acting under partial magistrates. They thus insisted that requests for aid at elections come directly from returning officers or their deputies, rather than from the magistrates only.

On the second day of polling, 17 April, the returning officer for the Hay Market polling booth asked for troops before he attempted to reopen his poll. Some 150 were immediately placed at his disposal and were put under the command of magistrates Charles Tait and Lt.-Col. John Dyde, the latter one of Molson's strong supporters. Brush instructed the troops to form two lines so that both parties could get to the polls in safety. No trouble was experienced until John Dyer, whom the *Pilot* claimed was a violent Orangeman,[30] cast his vote. As Dyer left the poll, he was attacked by a number of men and he quickly returned to the poll to ask for protection. Brush told two policemen to escort him, but as soon as he was beyond the line of soldiers, the crowd assailed him again and he rushed back to Dyde. Dyde advised Dyer to go with Councillor Tully and another gentleman who had offered to take him again safely beyond the crowd, as "Mr. Tully had great influence with the mob." No sooner had Dyer again got beyond the soldiers' line than he was struck down, his clothes ripped off, and he was stunned by blows. When this row broke out, Dyde ran towards the reserve body of soldiers of the 89th Regiment, stationed on St. James Street, and ordered them to advance. Town Major Colin Macdonald reiterated this order, telling the officer to have his men slope their arms and follow the magistrate.[31] The soldiers moved into the crowd, their arms sloped and bayonets elevated, dispersing the crowd by pushing them with the sides of their muskets.[32] At their head was young Lt. Thomas D'Arcy, "a sword in his hand striking left and right, but not raising the weapon."[33]

Chief of Police Comeau galloped ahead, shouting "The troops are coming" in an effort to frighten the rioters. Later he testified that "had the troops intended to hurt the crowd, they could have killed dozens. . . . My impression was that they wished to disperse the crowd with as little injury as possible."[34] In one spot where a fight was going on, one of the combatants, Julien Champeau, grabbed the bayonets of two soldiers as they approached and was stabbed by a third and died three days later. According to one witness at the inquest, Champeau had been trying to rescue Dyer,[35] but as the *Gazette* on 4 May rightly pointed out, such "interference . . . is utterly impossible to permit in a riot. Soldiers must, in such situations, on no account, allow their Arms to be touched." This third day of violence was too much for Molson. He resigned under protest and Drummond carried the day with 1,383 votes against Molson's 463.[36]

On the death of Champeau, the *Pilot*, edged in black, stridently charged on 23 April that "April 17th, 1844, will be remembered by the citizens of Montreal . . . as a day on which murder was committed by Her Majesty's Troops." The extravagant language used by its editor, Francis Hincks, was contradicted by the victim himself who, before his death, made a formal statement describing how he had become involved in a fight, and "seeing the soldiers forcing themselves upon us, I turned about and seized hold of two bayonets in front of me, and then received a stab in the left side from a soldier who came in between the two whose bayonets I had pushed aside."[37]

On 29 April the French-Canadian reform newspaper, *La Minerve*, with more restraint, asserted, "Il faut de toute nécessité que ces meurtres d'élection, commis par les magistrats et l'intervention militaire, aient un terme." A few days later, on 2 May, *La Minerve* listed two outrages committed by soldiers on French Canadians and stated, "Depuis longtemps on se récrie et avec raison, sur l'abus de laisser circuler les soldats dans les rues, jour et nuit, avec leurs armes. Un grand nombre de personnes ont déjà été victimes de cette coutume."

After a three-day inquest into the death of Champeau, the coroner's jury could not agree on a verdict. Four doctors who examined Champeau stated that the bayonet wounds were not in themselves sufficient to cause death, but suggested that the wounds, in combination with the diseased state of his body from tuberculosis, caused death.[38] On 22 October, in a somewhat macabre fashion, the *Gazette* referred to "poor Champeau . . . who some say died of the Doctor, and some of drink and a broken constitution, and some of a blow, and some of a stab, but who, it is our conscientious opinion, was privately strangled in order to make political capital of his martyrdom."

The day after the mixed verdict was announced, on 26 April, the *Pilot* charged, "Those of the men [soldiers] who were Orangemen and political bigots murdered and attempted to commit murder while the majority (no thanks to Messrs Dyde and D'Arcy) were humane and acted with moderation and forbearance." "But," asked the editor, "are the lives of the citizens of Montreal to depend on the humanity and forbearance of irresponsible private soldiers?"

The editors of the *Pilot* and *La Minerve* answered in the negative and, through George-Etienne Cartier, they pressed murder charges against both Lt.-Col. John Dyde and Lieutenant D'Arcy.[39] D'Arcy was released on bail of £500, posting £250 himself, the additional securities being provided by Lt.-Col. Augustus Gugy, the adjutant general of militia of Canada East, and by Montrealer Haviland LeMesurier Routh,[40] an indication of the personal relationship and sympathy that existed between Crown and town forces. The anxiety of the military authorities at the arrest of D'Arcy was indicated by their seeking the advice of Queen's counsel Alexander Buchanan, but he, too, concluded that the depositions were "sufficient to justify the arrest of Lieutenant D'Arcy."[41] However, at the fall session of the Supreme Court, the grand jury, as was usually the case, dropped the charges against D'Arcy and Dyde.[42] Chief of Police Comeau did not survive the crisis. Having testified at the inquest to the good discipline and humanity of the troops in quelling the riots, his resignation as chief was announced, without explanation, on 30 April.[43]

The reference in the *Pilot* on 26 April that the soldiers and officers of the 89th were bigoted Orangemen led the grand master of the Canadian Orange Order, Ogle Gowan, to retort in an evasively rhetorical manner, "Point out a single member of the Regiment from the gallant Bouverie [the colonel] down to the youthful lieutenant who commanded the rescue, from the sergeant-major down to the last recruit who is either an Orangeman or a political bigot."[44] It is unlikely that a formal Orange lodge existed in the 89th Regiment; it was not among those regiments listed in 1830 as having a warrant for a lodge. General orders had been issued several times since 1813 ordering military Orange lodges to dissolve;[45] it is therefore unlikely that a lodge would have been formed in the regiment after 1830. Yet this did not exclude the possibility of some soldiers being Orangemen. The regiment had its depot in Cork, and some of its rank and file may have come from the solidly Orange town of Bandon. Even if some of its soldiers were Orangemen, Hincks's accusation that they acted partially was spurious and irresponsible. Of all election riots over the next ten years in Montreal, the behaviour of the troops at this election was probably the most controlled, moderate, and effective. There was neither an order to charge nor to fire,[46] and as the troops advanced with sloped arms, the crowd dispersed "running . . . in [all] directions . . . [and] the Ward was perfectly peaceable after that."[47] The behaviour of the troops was such as to move George-Etienne Cartier to call for three cheers for the troops whom, he said, "behaved better than the magistrates."[48]

Even while the inquest was in progress, troops of the 89th, along with companies of the 43rd Regiment and the Queen's Light Dragoons, were sent to Lachine where Irish labourers were threatening to destroy the locks on the canal, a move which would have seriously disrupted trade. This new disturbance arose when those of the canallers who had come into Montreal the previous week during the election found "to their immeasurable surprise and indignation . . . that having quitted their work in violation of the terms of their engagement, they [were] . . . not employed again."[49]

In the midst of the furore created by the election, the inquest, the journalistic bombast, and the disturbances at the Lachine Canal, the Amateurs of the 43rd Light Infantry announced a performance of *Two Galley Slaves* and *Birks the Bagman* to be given in the Theatre Royal. Somewhat plaintively, the *Gazette* commented on 25 April, "We trust that the taste for innocent amusement has not altogether passed away in Montreal, and that their [the soldiers'] laudable efforts to add to the stock of public enjoyment will be properly appreciated."

The *Gazette* continued to champion the British soldier. On 8 May it noted "with much pleasure" an address to the officers and men of the 74th Regiment stationed at Laprairie and commented, "Documents such as these are the best replies to the brutal and violent attacks on the character of the British soldiers, such as have lately appeared in the *Minerve*." *La Minerve's* attacks on the military were somewhat out of character and, as in 1832, once the election excitement died down so, too, did the hostile references to the soldiery.[50]

In the fall of 1844 military authorities viewed with some apprehension the coming elections to the provincial Assembly. Lewis Thomas Drummond would again be one of the candidates, opposed to George Moffatt and Clément Sabrevois de Bleury of the Constitutional party, which was campaigning under the slogan Loyal Hearts and Liberal Measures for a British and Monarchial Policy.[51] The attacks on the military by *La Minerve* and the *Pilot* during the spring by-election, and the harassment suffered by D'Arcy when charges of murder were pressed against him, led the military to seek additional advice from Crown legal authorities on the use of military aid at elections.[52] With this advice Sir Richard Jackson issued a circular in late September emphasizing that during elections it was the returning officers and their deputies who were supreme in their respective polls and that the authority of the magistrates was only concurrent with that of these officers when called upon to assist them.[53]

Elaborate precautions were taken by the military to prevent trouble.[54] Capt. Walter Jones's troop of Provincial Cavalry was ordered to Montreal from the frontier. On the day polling began, 22 October, a strong body of troops with a piece of field artillery was stationed in Custom House Square. Troops were posted overnight at the various polls and only drew off towards nine o'clock in the morning for the opening of the polls. The soldiers then formed two avenues through which supporters of either candidate could make their way unmolested to and from the polls. In addition troops were drawn up on McGill Street and Champ de Mars while mounted officers patrolled parts of the city.

Military authorities were not the only ones taking unusual precautions against disturbances. Civil authorities had learned that the Constitutional party "were taking measures to obtain for themselves the protection which he [Mayor Joseph Bourret] and the law were unable to afford" at the last election when the "Constitutional party . . . [were] insulted, beaten, etc. . . . by organized gangs of ruffians."[55] The measures included importing "fighting men hired . . . [in] the city of Quebec, the Gore of Chatham, Rawdon and other parts of the Province."[56] Mayor Bourret, a supporter of Louis-Hippolyte La Fontaine,[57] whom the *Gazette* accused of regarding with the "most entire indifference the numerous breaches of the peace that accompanied [the spring by-election]," ordered the police to arrest the parties coming from Quebec before they landed from the steamer. How efficient the police were in preventing election reinforcements from arriving is indicated by the *Pilot's* complaint that "Dolphins, Dorics, etc. were armed to a man . . . with bowie knives and pistols. . . . Orangemen from Rawdon and sailors from Quebec were supplied with the same deadly weapons."[58] When it came to ruffians, the party of La Fontaine may have been the first to employ them at the spring election, but by the fall the Constitutionals showed that they could play the game as well as, if not better than, their political opponents.

During the polling the most serious disturbances occurred, as usual, at Hay Market in Queen's Ward. The chief returning officer, John Young, accompanied by his legal adviser, tried to prevent trouble. He rode constantly about to inspect the different avenues of approach to the polls. So, too, did Capt. Charles Wetherall with a detachment of the Lachine canal police and Thomas Wily, the newly appointed chief of police. Like the intervention of troops at elections, police surveillance presented problems. Precise instructions had been worked out early in the decade for the conduct of police during elections, and if military authorities showed hesitation about the use of troops during elections, the police were in an even more unenviable position. Police magistrates had been instructed to "prohibit all interference on the part of the Police Magistrates or Police Force, direct or indirect, . . . at elections . . . and that every precaution shall be employed on your part to remove even the appearance of interference . . . [and] that no Policeman can be permitted at the Poll unless such emergency should arise and such requisition be made by the Returning Officer, . . . the men to be provided with no weapons save constables' staves."[59]

These instructions against the use of police during elections were devised to avoid the "imputation of party bias or temporary irritation,"[60] just as military authorities tried to restrict and regulate the use of troops to avoid similar charges. Yet these restrictions on the police put the burden of keeping order on the military force. The Queen's Light Dragoons were posted at various polls and towards evening, when disturbances began to get out of hand at Queen's Ward "with a ferocious attack on the Constitutionals," the infantry and artillery were moved from Custom House Square to Hay Market, their approach being enough to disperse the turbulent crowd.[61]

On the second day of polling, 23 October, the military was again formed up on McGill Street, Custom House Square, and Champ de Mars. As rumours persisted that serious outbreaks were anticipated,[62] military authorities brought in detachments of the 71st and the 81st Regiments from St. Johns and Chambly.[63] Again, it was at Queen's Ward that a fight broke out when the avenue assigned to the Constitutionals was invaded by supporters of Drummond. The deputy returning officer applied for troops and order was restored temporarily by the Queen's Light Dragoons. Shortly afterwards a body of some 300 to 400 canallers arrived from Lachine. They moved up McGill Street in military array, some of them armed. At the top of the street Lieutenant-Colonel Gugy awaited them with the Queen's Light Dragoons. The canallers pelted stones at the cavalry until a party of the 93rd Highlanders was ordered to charge. At this, the ranks of the canallers broke and they fled, pursued by the cavalry who captured thirty and sent them to jail.[64]

The active participation of the military hierarchy in the election was indicated by the fact that Sir Richard Jackson, the commander of the forces, and several of his staff voted,[65] a somewhat unusual step for British officers in colonial garrisons. Their attitude was more frequently that of the officer who said that they "care little about local Colonial politics, the very worst and most complex."[66] Sir Richard's act of voting was described as an "iniquity" by Hincks in the *Pilot*, while the *Gazette* on 25 October defended the right of the military to vote. "Why should not Sir Richard Jackson exercise as well as Sir Richard Anybody-else a franchise acquired in the mode pointed out by law?" the editor asked. "A soldier does not lose his rights as a citizen by being a soldier." Yet, undoubtedly, the vote was exceptional and indicated the still-powerful links between the military command and those Montrealers who had filled the loyalist ranks during the rebellion and still filled the ranks of the Constitutional party.

In spite of their successful efforts to maintain order during the elections, or perhaps because of their success, the military authorities were accused by the defeated candidates, Lewis Thomas

Drummond and Dr. Pierre Beaubien, of "acting under the orders of magistrates known to be active and violent partisans of the opposing candidates . . . and drove electors from the neighbourhood of the polls. . . . that for the two days of polling . . . the city bore all the appearance of being in a state of siege."[67]

The indignant protest was lost in the flood of praise that flowed in from all directions to the military for the way in which the election disturbances had been handled. The chief returning officer, John Young, a liberal stalwart, was the first to acknowledge the "prompt and efficient services rendered to me and to the Civil Authority . . . and that this has been done under very trying and peculiar circumstances without injury either to the inhabitants or to those who came from a distance to create disturbances." Governor General Sir Charles Metcalfe added his praise to that of the chief returning officer. He wrote, "The presence of the troops alone prevented the attempts . . . to disturb the elections . . . and that under very trying circumstances the conduct of the troops was admirable." In his address of appreciation to the troops for their "goodwill and good conduct" during the elections, Sir Richard Jackson especially alluded to the conduct of the Provincial Cavalry under Captain Jones and mentioned "his high opinion of it on former occasions and indeed throughout their whole course of service." His dispatch to the Horse Guards brought eulogies from the Duke of Wellington, Lord Stanley, the secretary of state for the colonies, and finally a letter conveying the approbation of the Queen herself.[68]

An uneasy quiet prevailed during the month following the provincial elections. Troops were stationed in the Irish section of the city, Griffintown in the St. Ann's suburbs, where it was claimed that not only were the Methodist chapel and the Baptist Missionary church attacked and windows broken in the Recollet church, but that fifty houses had been marked "ready" and would have been burned if troops had not been stationed there.[69] In fact a request to have troops posted all winter in the St. Ann's suburbs was made by Mayor Bourret, who assured the commander of the forces that "without such protection loss of life or at all events of propertys [sic] may occur." His request was accompanied by a petition of forty inhabitants of St. Ann's to the governor general.[70]

The third and final election of 1844, that of the municipality on 2 December, was preceded by a riot on 1 December at Hay Market. In requesting military aid to quell the riot, the three magistrates suggested to Sir Richard Jackson that "300 soldiers and two guns will be adequate,"[71] and they were. The following day the most serious disturbances were in Griffintown where one man, John Johnson, a native of Belfast, was shot dead as he and a group of other men attacked the house of Patrick Brennan from which shots had been fired at the polling booth. Troops were called out and arrested nineteen persons who were in the house, and "something like order was restored."[72]

Montreal, suffering perhaps from riot fatigue, did not indulge in disturbances during the municipal election in 1845, but the riots that accompanied city elections in 1846 and 1847 were suppressed by what had become almost a normal military operation during Montreal elections. Reports of the officer in charge of the detachments in 1847 pointed out that "during the whole course of my duty yesterday over nearly the whole of the city, I do not remember having observed a dozen policemen on duty." He went on to report that "ill-disposed persons evaded the authorities by making use of sleighs which conveyed them in bodies to the different places where they had information that the troops were not in charge and thus they were enabled to traverse the city at their will, it being impossible for any but a mounted police to deal with them."[73] For the ordinary officer, the disturbances accompanying municipal elections were dismissed contemptuously. Capt. James Douglas, aide-de-camp to the newly appointed military governor, Lord Cathcart, noted simply in his diary, "Municipal elections going on. A good many broken heads."[74]

Within the Montreal military establishment in 1848, Maj.-Gen. Sir Charles Gore, now commandant of Canada East, was probably the most knowledgeable of local conditions, though Lord Elgin reported to Earl Grey that "it is generally believed that his judgment could not be relied on in difficulties." Gore never outlived his defeat at Saint-Denis. To the new commander of the forces, Sir Benjamin D'Urban, whom Elgin described as "an excellent man . . . but very old,"[75] Gore outlined his plans to secure the city during the approaching elections to the House of Assembly. Warning that "the civil authorities are almost always late in the application for military assistance and expect immediate assistance when called for," Gore suggested that the Provincial Cavalry be moved up from the frontier and stationed at Chambly ready to cross to Montreal "should the river take." He pointed out that Sir Richard Jackson thought that the garrison of Montreal was not sufficient for the "two days' constant work night and day which will be required from the troops, and in the event of fires or collisions between the parties, the duty will be severe in this weather."[76]

The advantages of having the Provincial Cavalry on hand were also stressed by the chief returning officer who wrote, "Their services will be of great avail and attended with less loss of life than those of infantry should they be called upon to act in suppressing a riot."[77] The disadvantages of using a local force had been noted by the *Gazette* editor who wrote on 15 July 1844, "Regular troops act with greater coolness and humanity. . . . A regiment of the line, if it has done any necessary but unpopular work, can be removed and a more popular garrison substituted. But bodies of local [troops] are permanent residents, their individual members are known, and the arming of them is the arming of one class of the same community against another." But in 1848 the advantages outweighed the disadvantages. Troopers under Capt. Walter Jones and Capt. Charles Oakes Ermatinger were ordered to cross the river on 11 January 1848. The difficulty of eighty troopers and a wagon of equipment crossing the newly frozen St. Lawrence was solved when the ferry-keeper agreed to attempt the dangerous task of finding a safe route and making a road across the ice for the cavalry. The troopers were at their posts in Montreal on the morning of the election, 12 January, despite severe frostbite suffered by several troopers during the hazardous journey.[78]

In spite of temperatures of nine degrees below zero, disturbances requiring military intervention occurred at two polls. Details of the riots were reported to Town Major Macdonald by Maj. Graham Egerton, the major commanding the 77th Regiment, who had accompanied a detachment of 100 rank and file to St. James Ward. There, a group of men, armed with axe handles and bludgeons, were being fired upon by men in the Royal Oak Tavern, which was described by the major as "a rendezvous of the Conservative party."[79] The editor of the *Pilot* regarded the Royal Oak as the headquarters of the "Orange bullies . . . brought in from Rawdon." The deputy chief of police, Hippolyte Jerémie, with a party of police and a magistrate, had tried to arrest the men in the tavern, but they were forced to retire "owing to the strength of the party."[80] Troops surrounded the tavern, arrested five men who were sent to jail under military escort, and they then took up a position at the polling booth.[81] Though suffering from the extreme cold, the troops prevented any further serious disturbance in that ward.

A second detachment of the 77th was sent to St. Louis Ward

73

where shots were being exchanged. Upon arriving, an officer saw "a respectable person covered with blood helped into a sleigh." The dilemma of troops being called out during election disturbances was indicated by the major's report. He stated that "large bodies, armed principally with sticks and axe handles, were . . . at the corners of the streets whose object appeared to be to assault the voters. . . . The Magistrate remained wholly inactive, although he had gone through the form of reading the Riot Act." A captain dispersed the crowd without injuring anyone, but as shots continued to be fired, he suggested to the magistrate that steps ought to be taken to arrest the persons firing the guns. The magistrate replied that he had no police and could make no arrests.[82]

Fearing that the troops were being needlessly exposed to danger, an officer sought out Sir Charles Gore, who returned with him to the poll. There they found the troops trying to keep back a large body and "considerable tumult on the spot." The magistrate insisted that he only wished to keep the crowd back, but the crowd vociferated that they were "loyal subjects wanting to vote and [that] the Magistrate [was] a 'Papineau Rebel' using his authority for party purposes." The crowd taunted the magistrate that "although he had now British bayonets under his control, the last time he had felt their influence was when they guarded the gaol in which he was incarcerated as a prisoner for High Treason."[83]

Major-General Gore ordered the troops to fall back to allow free access to the polls. The troops then lined the road into the poll so that supporters of either party could vote without injury or molestation "after which the polling proceeded extremely briskly until its close." Civilities were not entirely forgotten on such a cold day. Major Egerton reported that "an influential Gentleman, on the Conservative side, expressed his wish to the officer in charge to be allowed to furnish the Soldiers with some refreshment." The major hastened to add, "I need hardly say that Captain Forbes peremptorily and indignantly forbade anything of the kind." The same gentleman then pressed five-dollar bills into the hands of a sergeant and a corporal and told them it was given to the men with the sanction of their officers, but the money was surrendered immediately to the officers. The major reported that he believed the "feeling which prompted the Gentleman to act thus . . . was a kindly one, and not intended to seduce the men

74

from their duty, but . . . that he was ignorant of the character of British soldiers in making the attempt."[84]

The election over, military authorities looked forward to a respite from duties in connection with the civil power. Yet Montreal in 1848 was not isolated from the new mode of civil disturbances which broke out in France in the spring and in Ireland in late July. Major-General Gore, on the orders of Lt.-Gen. Sir Benjamin D'Urban, made preparations to meet barricade tactics and incendiaries as those among the Montreal Irish who held militant nationalist sympathies became more vociferous. In April Gore wrote a confidential letter to the officer commanding the Royal Artillery, asking him to supplement the six- and twelve-pounders in garrison by a battery of two nine-pounders and two twenty-four pounders from St. Helen's. He also asked that bags for filling with powder and prepared with a fuse strong enough to force open gates and doorways be made ready for immediate use.[85] To the deputy adjutant general, Gore sent a request for a supply of "good axes, not less than 200, to be kept at Quebec Gate Barracks as well as a supply of large iron hooks and a few cords of ropes with which the troops may remove impedimenta to their progress."[86]

D'Urban had intelligence that St. Helen's Island was one of the "main designs of those who guided . . . the project in the United States for inundating our Southern border with a horde of Irish and other vagabonds." St. Helen's was not only the main depot for ordnance supplies of Lower Canada, but also held reserve supplies for the whole country. D'Urban's information was that the "disaffected in Lower Canada" would attempt to get possession of the "Depots and Magazines in St. Helen's, or, if that should prove impracticable, to set fire to them."[87] He carefully inspected the defences on the island in company with the commanding officer of the Royal Engineers and authorized repairs amounting to £243. 12s. To strengthen security on the island, orders were given that "no person be suffered to land on the island, excepting those belonging to the garrison or departments there, without stating his name and business to the satisfaction of the C.O., and no stranger to be allowed to remain on the island after dark on any pretence whatsoever."[88]

These military apprehensions during the spring and early summer of 1848 were finally allayed after the visit to Montreal of Michael Thomas O'Connor, an Irish delegate from the newly formed Irish Republican Union in New York. O'Connor reported

to his colleagues in New York that "the love of monarchy did not
. . . burn with excessive intensity in the hearts of the British soldiers [in Montreal]." As proof of this he claimed that as he walked
up Notre Dame Street, he saw fifty men of the 19th Regiment and
"singular to say, every man of them took off his cap as he passed."
O'Connor boasted that of the 10,000 troops in Canada "not more
than 3,000 of them would pull a trigger for England."[89]

O'Connor's speech, which was printed in New York newspapers
and reprinted in Montreal, exasperated officers of the 19th Regiment, who asked permission to "give a public contradiction to so
gross a fabrication," which, they said, was intended "for publication not in Canada but at the other side of the Atlantic."[90] Gore
agreed with the officers of the 19th as to the "impression such
false reports may make at Home."[91] On the day that O'Connor had visited Montreal, the "whole of the Regiment was confined to Barracks," wrote Maj. Robert Sanders, commanding the
19th, "and could not possibly have made Mr. O'Connor's acquaintance."[92] The loyalty of the 1,400 troops in garrison in Montreal
was not to be put to the test in 1848, however. The rising in Ireland at the end of July proved abortive and the threats of the New
York Irish to invade Canada came to an end.[93] With regard to the
Irish nationalist sympathies of the 19th Regiment, these soldiers
were men of the Yorkshire North Riding Regiment, which had arrived in Montreal in May 1848 from a tour of duty in Barbados
where it was unlikely that the Irish soldiers of the regiment
would have been subjected to nationalist Irish pressures or
propaganda.

Throughout the decade of the forties, then, Montreal civil and
military authorities had become experienced in matters of riots
and civil disturbances. Procedures had been worked out with
care. Magistrates, militia officers, and regular officers knew each
other socially and as colleagues in difficult times, and many of the
regular general and staff officers had been resident in the city at
least since the early forties. The record of the troops in suppressing civil disturbances was unmarred. Except for the death of
Julien Champeau, which most of the coroner's jury had attributed
to "misadventure," soldiers had suppressed riot after riot with
firmness and without injury, winning the applause of both liberals and conservatives and gaining the acknowledgement of home
authorities.

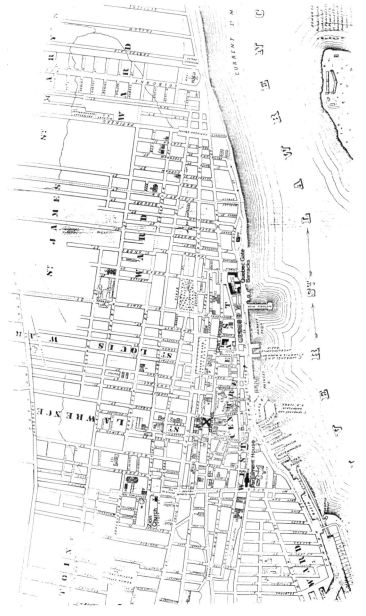

Montreal in the late 1840s. This map shows the location of the Quebec Gate Barracks in relation to Parliament House, Government House, Place d'Armes, and Zion Church.

6. Rebellion Losses Bill Agitation

Neither the garrison nor the inhabitants of Montreal could escape the air of uneasiness that hung over the city below the hill during the spring of 1849 as the House of Assembly debated the Rebellion Losses Bill. Two commissions had been set up to deal with the question of compensation to those who had suffered during the 1837 and 1838 Rebellions,[1] but neither had completed the task. Sir John Colborne had established the first in May 1838 when some seventy-one claims for losses sustained by loyalists had been examined.[2] Of these, fifty-nine were from French Canadians, among whom were the widow and children of Joseph Chartrand, the loyalist volunteer who had been executed after a brief informal Patriote court-martial. Other claimants were Abbé François-Xavier Demers, the curé of Saint-Denis, whose parish funds had been confiscated by insurgents; Madame Georges St. Germain, whose property at Saint-Denis had been commandeered by Nelson and his irregular troops during the battle; and Madame Louis Cheval *dit* St. Jacques, whose home had been attacked by Patriotes in September of 1837.[3]

The first commission awarded £49,015. 13s. to loyalists by June 1840. Few denied that there were many other outstanding claims,[4] some legitimate, others not. There were unpaid bills of £2,000 for quartering troops, claims for losses sustained on property or pillaged goods, and claims for destruction of buildings by fire, whether on the order of military authorities, by volunteers or insurgents, or through private vengeance. Some £2,605 was asked for property destroyed from 1839 to 1843 by, it was believed, insurgents operating over the border from the United States. Others claimed for loss of arms resulting from the disarming policy of the military after the rebellions, and all the horses appropriated by the Glengarry Highlanders, who helped suppress the rebellion in Beauharnois, had to be accounted for.[5]

On 23 December 1845 a second commission began hearings into 2,176 claims, almost all from French Canadians.[6] Instead of the anticipated £100,000, claims soared to £241,965. 10s. Large amounts were asked for by many of those most active in the rebellions. Wolfred Nelson claimed £19,745. 15s. for the burning of his distillery and other property at Saint-Denis.[7] His business partner, H. D'Eschambault, asked for £12,000. William Henry Scott of Saint-Eustache, who had been arrested for high treason, presented a bill for £5,349. 10s. 11d.

Bonaventure Viger, the leader of the initial attack on troopers of the Royal Montreal Cavalry at Longueuil on 17 November 1837, sought £2,000 compensation for his exile in Bermuda. François-Maurice Lapailleur wanted £1,442 for his burnt home, imprisonment, and exile. George Washington Baker, whose home on the Châteauguay had been used as one of the main rebel encampments in the Beauharnois area, claimed £983. 15s. The leader of the rebels at Baker's Farm, James Perrigo, asked for £253 for his imprisonment and the burning of his home, and François-Xavier Provost, in whose tavern some of the Beauharnois loyalists had been imprisoned, sought £1,147. 3s. 8d. Perhaps one of the rebel claims that galled the loyalists most was that of publisher Louis Perrault. Perrault had gone over the border in 1837 and was among those proscribed by Durham. He asked for £500 to cover his "absence in the United States" and another £1,105 for "loss of business" during his exile.

With such soaring claims and from such sources, it is not surprising that the Draper conservative ministry took no action, even though the commissioners assured the government that the claims, when closely examined, would come closer to £100,000 than £240,000. The report of the commissioners was an unwelcome legacy to the new liberal administration under Louis-Hippolyte La Fontaine. La Fontaine and his provincial secretary, James Leslie, a son of Capt. James Leslie of the 15th Foot who had served as Wolfe's deputy quartermaster-general at the siege of Quebec, had been among the moderate wing of Papineau's party in 1837. After the military engagements of 1837, La Fontaine left the country just in time to evade a warrant for his arrest on high treason. Undoubtedly the grounds to arrest La Fontaine were questionable, but the charge left a taint on his name.[8] Among La Fontaine's most influential supporters in 1849 were such prominent former rebels as Dr. Wolfred Nelson, George-Etienne Cartier, Etienne-Paschal Taché, Augustin Norbert Morin, and Dr. Pierre Davignon. These men were to help La Fontaine promote the passage of the Rebellion Losses Bill through the Legislative Assembly and Council, and to promote it in such a manner as to induce observers as far away as England to comment on the "rough manner and crowing tone which the present . . . Ministry . . . have exhibited . . . while urging on the measure."[9]

An American observer in Buffalo commented, "The measure of Rebellion indemnification has seemed to me from the first an anomalous and unparalleled outrage on all that can be called decency, consistency, law and order, a bare-faced, shameless insult from a rude majority."[12] Another American temporarily living in Montreal, Congregational minister William Rufus Seaver, completely sympathized with the British party. To his wife in Brimfield, Massachusetts, he wrote, "We are on the Eve of another rebellion, not however a French Canadian Revolt, but a Rebellion of quite another stamp, and I have no doubt but that . . . I shall have to tell you of martial law, and fires & blood and murder." Seaver was furious at Jacob DeWitt for supporting the Rebellion Losses Bill. DeWitt was a Montreal businessman of American ori-

As the Rebellion Losses Bill continued to be debated with much acrimony in the House of Assembly and local newspapers, the temper of Montrealers became more uncertain. The former captain of the Royal Montreal Cavalry, Sydney Bellingham, wrote, "It naturally caused intense dissatisfaction as it taxed the loyal inhabitants to pay compensation to the authors of the rebellion." Bellingham did not deny that the "burnings had been excessive," but he felt that as they were part of the military operations, the damages should have been borne by the imperial government.[10] This view was shared by the London *Spectator*, which said that the question of compensation to rebels, "like the question of war and peace, belongs to the Imperial Government . . . but Lord Elgin appears to have treated it as a mere local question, leaving it to be handled by the Local Administration as they pleased."[11]

gin who had long been associated with the reform movement in the city, so much so that he was suspect during the rebellions. Indignantly, Seaver wrote, "He [DeWitt] ought not to be called an American, for I hate to have one of the nation so disgrace it as to sanction such a bill."[13]

If such were the feelings of outsiders who had not filled the ranks of the Montreal volunteers during the rebellions, the indignation felt by those who had been volunteers can be more readily understood. Tory editors did not hesitate to publicize the names of the claimants and amounts of the claims or to point out that the bill reminded "us that this is the triumph of the rebels of 1837 and 1838 over the loyalists of those times; that they are not only riding rough shod over the men who were then called upon and armed by the Imperial Government to assist in upholding Her Majesty's authority in Canada, but that they are assisted and abetted in their nefarious designs by the Imperial Government itself." The new editor of the *Gazette*, James Moir Ferres, thundered, "It is the principle of this scandalous measure that is causing all the irritation, and rapidly and fatally cooling the devoted attachment of the British colonists to the Government of England. It is because the loyalty—the fidelity to their oath of allegiance, which these colonists so conspicuously displayed, during those trying times, is now declared, by legislative enactment, to have been tyrannical and vexatious, it is because this faithful attachment to our Sovereign is ridiculed and insulted by the Home Government, that there is a deep and abiding feeling of resentment fast spreading among the British population of Canada."[14]

To soften the resentment over the Rebellion Losses Bill, the ministry agreed that those who had been convicted before the courts or who had confessed their guilt could not claim indemnities. This would, it was thought, have eliminated the claims of Nelson and Viger, since they had acknowledged their guilt when they accepted exile in Bermuda. It was expected also that the fifty-eight rebels who had been tried by courts-martial and sentenced to exile in New South Wales would be excluded from compensation. Yet La Fontaine was ambiguous. He contended during the debates that the courts-martial which condemned the rebels to exile were illegal and that the sentences had thus been illegal.[15] Similarly, it was argued that the eight exiles to Bermuda were entitled to claim compensation because their banishment had been declared illegal by the imperial government. With such manoeuvring about the claims of the more notorious of the former rebels, the legitimate claims of numerous habitants who had suffered, some of them "wantonly and cruelly" as both Lord Elgin and the ministry frequently and somewhat offensively suggested,[16] were pushed into the background of the debates and almost forgotten.

British regulars in Montreal had been acutely aware of the growing tension over the Rebellion Losses Bill. They had initiated or had shared with the volunteers much of the burning, pillaging, and destruction of property, the payment of which was now causing such uproar in the provincial Assembly. When aspersions were cast on the volunteers for their part in the rebellions, regulars felt themselves tarred by the same brush. Nor were individual British officers immune from personal censure. Maj.-Gen. Sir Charles Gore's action at Saint-Denis was referred to in such scathing tones by members of the La Fontaine party that Sir Allan MacNab felt obliged to come to his defence and specifically deny that Gore had acted out of a spirit of revenge.[17] This protection of regular officers by militia officers within the House of Assembly was reciprocated by the military hierarchy. When the Executive Council asked military authorities for dispatches relative to MacNab's actions in Norfolk in 1837 "as the Council . . . have occasion to refer to them," Deputy Adj. Gen. George Wetherall replied glibly, "After a minute search, no documents could be found in the Adjutant General's office relative to Colonel MacNab and the disturbances of 1837."[18]

Despite the bitter session of the provincial Assembly, army authorities in Montreal felt no undue alarm during the spring of 1849. The strong garrison of the 19th Yorkshire West Riding Regiment and the 23rd Royal Welsh Fusiliers kept the Montreal station up to strength, even though the total force in Canada had been reduced to under 7,000 in keeping with the imperial policy of reducing overseas garrisons.[19] Senior staff officers had fought against any reduction of the Montreal station and were doing their best to retain the Provincial Cavalry on the imperial budget, despite the pressure of colonial reformers in England.[20] The Provincial Cavalry, which had reduced desertion from the Montreal station to a bare trickle by the end of the decade, was described by senior British officers as "being in excellent order, equal perhaps to the same number of any Cavalry in the world,"[21] an opinion in which Lord Elgin, the governor general, entirely concurred. When asked by Earl Grey privately about taking the cavalry off the imperial budget, Elgin emphatically replied, "The

Provincial Cavalry can very ill be spared. . . . I would rather part with two Regiments."[22] The Provincial Cavalry was thus still on the frontier in the spring of 1849, easily available to the British military command should civil tensions in Montreal erupt. The 71st Highland Light Infantry was stationed at nearby St. Johns, with one company in Montreal and another at Chambly. In Montreal itself, with a population of about 50,000, there were 1,435 regulars in garrison.[23]

With the stormy but successful passage of the Rebellion Losses Bill through the Assembly and Legislative Council by 15 March, tension seemed to subside somewhat. The opposition firmly believed that Lord Elgin would not dare to sanction the bill himself, but that he would send it to the home government in Britain where, they were sure, it would be shelved indefinitely. Yet on 16 April, five years almost to the day since troops had bayonetted Julien Champeau at Hay Market, some forty youths, bent on mischief, erected a barricade at the entrance to Place d'Armes. The disturbance was created partly because of rumours that the governor general intended to sanction the bill and perhaps partly in imitation of Toronto troublemakers, who paraded with images of Attorney General Robert Baldwin and Solicitor-General Hume Blake and demonstrated outside the house where William Lyon Mackenzie was staying.

A hundred soldiers of the 19th Regiment were ordered out under Police Magistrate Charles Wetherall to destroy the barricade or to "take it at the point of the bayonet." The troops pulled the barricade down without opposition and remained under arms until four o'clock in the morning in what proved to be but a preliminary skirmish to far more serious disturbances.[24]

La Fontaine and his provincial secretary were at a disadvantage when faced with this deteriorating civil situation because of their lack of rapport with the senior army command in Montreal and their distaste for calling out troops. Therefore, as tension in the city increased, they fell back on local forces to maintain internal order, a step which the army hierarchy had been constantly urging. The civil force at their disposal was a police establishment of seventy, appointed and paid for by the city, and two police officers, paid for by the provincial government. Their alternative, other than recourse to military aid, was to swear in special constables under the high constable or to create a provincial force.

Elgin's delay in sanctioning the bill kept tension boiling. Finally Francis Hincks, the minister of finance in La Fontaine's administration, went to Monklands on the afternoon of 25 April 1849 to urge the governor general to settle the matter quickly.[25] Elgin agreed. Accompanied only by his personal aides-de-camp and servants, he rode into town at an unusually late hour. He then gave royal assent to thirty bills, including the controversial Rebellion Losses Bill. No special provisions for security had been made as neither the police nor the military had been informed of the governor general's intention to sanction the bill, nor, indeed, had the speaker or members of the Assembly.[26]

The first intimation of trouble reached Police Superintendent William Ermatinger at about half-past five in the afternoon after the governor general had hurriedly left the House, amid cheers mingled with groans and hisses and some eggs "pelted by a dozen blackguards."[27] Ermatinger rushed to Parliament House, located in St. Ann's Market at the corner of McGill and Commissioners Streets, where he was given instructions to find out who the "dozen blackguards" were, a task he found "impossible to accomplish as it is seldom one can be found . . . to point out and identify individuals actually engaged in such acts."[28]

The mood of the city was apparent to members of the Assembly as they returned to the evening session on 25 April. Sir Allan MacNab found the streets filled with people, bells ringing, and "everything denoting the probability of a row." He urged the government to send for troops but was informed, "Your Party call out the troops; we never do."[29] Yet within an hour, as news of a mass meeting of the Constitutional party spread, it was Hincks who left the Assembly about eight o'clock to find Ermatinger to tell him to call out the troops immediately. Hincks was careful to add that he had "no wish to prevent the meeting." Ermatinger told Hincks that were he to go to Major-General Gore with "no more ground for alarm than his suspicion, he would only be laughed at, that there must be something to go upon before he could get troops."[30] Ermatinger, however, consulted with Chief of Police Thomas Wily and instructed him to collect the constables and to proceed to Parliament House. This involved gathering the men from three different stations and from their beats, a task that could not be accomplished in less than half an hour.[31]

Meanwhile Ermatinger hastened back to Parliament House where he consulted with Attorney General La Fontaine, who agreed with him that troops must be called out. The police superintendent then began the formal procedures to obtain troops.

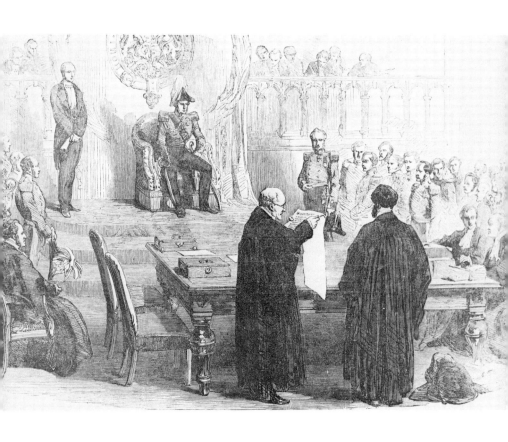

Lord Elgin giving assent to bills in Parliament.

The burning of Parliament House, 1849.

First, he had to hurry to the home of Mayor E.-R. Fabre to have him sign the requisition. From there he had to go to the home of Gore, where he arrived a little after nine o'clock. Gore gave his approval for troops, and directed Ermatinger to apply for them through Town Major Colin Macdonald. It was while Gore was accompanying Ermatinger to the home of the town major that they saw the blaze of the fire from Parliament House.

Gore's first thought was for the safety of the governor general. He ordered Lieutenant-Colonel Antrobus, the provincial aide-de-camp, to Monklands to alert the governor general and the guard there. Shortly afterwards he detached a company of the 23rd to reinforce the guard at Monklands, as it was rumoured that rioters intended to go there. Gore and Ermatinger hurried to the Quebec Gate Barracks, but before they arrived, 100 soldiers of the 19th Regiment had already been ordered out by the commandant. Gore ordered another two companies of the 19th to reinforce the picquet at Parliament House, but by the time they arrived, the building was fully ablaze. Their main job was to hold back the crowds from the burning building and assist city firemen in preventing the fire, fanned by a brisk breeze, from spreading to houses facing the north side of Parliament House.[32] Before the night was out, Parliament House with its valuable library, valued at a price far beyond that which the Rebellion Losses Bill proposed to pay to claimants, was gutted.[33]

The military was criticized for not arriving until the building was in flames, but they, like civil authorities, had not been forewarned that the governor general had intended to sanction the bill,[34] and were unprepared for the suddenness of the outbreak. Major-General Gore praised the troops. "They turned out at a moment's notice and conducted themselves in a most orderly manner and to my most perfect satisfaction."[35] Town Major Macdonald was on the spot at once, and several other regular officers volunteered their services to Gore, who reinforced the main guard at Nelson's monument and posted a captain's guard at the Château Ramezay where the Executive Council continued in session all night.

The next day, 26 April, troops were pressed into the unpopular duty of escorting to jail five prominent Montrealers who had taken a leading part in the meeting at Champ de Mars shortly before the burning of Parliament House. Among those arrested on charges of arson and held without bail for two days was the editor of the *Gazette*, James Moir Ferres. Carried off to jail also were lawyer Gordon Mack, the corresponding secretary of the Montreal branch of the British American League, and Augustus Heward, an insurance broker and son of Stephen Heward, registrar of the Probate Court of Upper Canada from 1818 to 1828. Augustus Heward's uncle was Chief Justice John Beverley Robinson, and his brother Charles was one of those implicated in the attack on William Lyon Mackenzie's press in 1826. The other two men arrested were Hugh Montgomerie, a merchant and captain of the Montreal Light Infantry, and Alfred Perry, a volunteer fireman and engine manufacturer.[36] The *Gazette* assistant editor remarked tartly, "It was a new feature to see British troops conveying to prison (surrounded by 2,000 cheering men) men who had fought and suffered for the Queen, and that, too, under the directions of a dominant French faction, whom those very loyalists had put down twelve years ago."[37]

At the Château Ramezay a crowd of 500 to 1,000 were "hooting, jeering, and jostling" in such a threatening manner that La Fontaine, in consultation with Gore, readily agreed to have a strong guard of soldiers posted on Notre Dame Street.[38] Every now and then the soldiers cleared the way by marching to and fro with fixed bayonets, "the people always retired before them, cheering and laughing, as there was, of course, no ill feeling between them and the soldiers."[39]

Because of this apparent goodwill between the crowd and the soldiers,[40] the government was accused of "leaving the city in the hands of a mob, though a powerful military force only waited the requisition of the civil authorities to turn out and maintain the supremacy of the law."[41] Yet this was hardly the case. Gore was somewhat adamant about formalities, even in the midst of tumult, and this possibly explains why Montreal magistrates tried to circumvent the strict regulations regarding the request for troops. When Parliament House caught fire, for example, the magistrate went straight to the Quebec Gate Barracks and secured a detachment of 100 rank and file directly on the orders of the Montreal commandant. Later when Magistrate Monteith also applied for troops directly to the Montreal commandant, he was reprimanded by Gore who pointed out that Monteith should have applied to him and that "troops would not be granted unless I am aware of the object for which they are required or that a riot actually exists."[42] Yet Gore was no fool. He knew Montreal and its citizens well. He reinforced the military guards at the jail, at Bonsecours Market Barracks, and the Court House, and ordered that

Five gentlemen arrested: (*clockwise from top*) J. M. Ferres, Augustus Heward, Alfred Perry, H. E. Montgomerie, and (*centre*) W. G. Mack.

The attack on Lord Elgin.

a picquet of 100 men be always in the barracks square ready to turn out at a moment's notice.

The next night a mob began to attack the Quebec Hotel where some liberal members of Parliament dwelt. Ermatinger requested troops, but before they arrived, the crowd had moved off to Beaver Hall Hill to smash the windows of Francis Hincks's home. Ermatinger applied to Gore for another picquet of troops, which he brought to Hay Market only to learn that the rioters had moved off in the direction of the St. Antoine suburbs where La Fontaine had lately acquired a new home. Here the mob gave vent to its fury by burning the stables, smashing dishes and furniture, and destroying La Fontaine's library before the approach of the troops sent them scurrying away.[43] Ermatinger marched the troops back to Hay Market where they were cheered by a crowd collected there. He continued with the troops to Craig Street where he met Sheriff John Boston with another detachment of soldiers drawn up in front of the home of Solicitor-General Lewis Drummond, who had taken the precaution to have a guard stationed there.

The day after the burning of Parliament House, La Fontaine and Leslie urged Mayor Fabre and Police Superintendent Ermatinger to enrol "a sufficient number of citizens to act as Police Officers." When this proved unsuccessful, La Fontaine undertook to have the former deputy adjutant general of militia, Lt.-Col. Etienne-Paschal Taché, organize "a special police . . . and to furnish Colonel Taché with police arms," an unusual step in a city which never had an armed police.[44] Taché set about mobilizing reliable members of the Montreal militia as special constables. This force, supplemented by other Montrealers friendly to the government,[45] and "armed with 172 swords, 161 scabbards, 189 pistols . . . and fifty sets of carbines, pistols and swords, all from the Ordnance store" was stationed at Château Ramezay.[46] One of Lord Elgin's aides-de-camp commented privately, "These blockheads of Ministers got in such a funk about themselves that they must needs swear in and arm about 500 French Canadians as special constables with pistols and cutlasses, which exasperated the British party more than ever."[47]

News of the arming of the special constables so infuriated the disaffected elements in the city that they began to march to Bonsecours Market where "Colonel Taché, commanding the armed constables, was drilling them by lamplight. . . . So full of martial ardour was he, that it was difficult to persuade him that it was better to house them, armed as they were with cutlass and pistol

. . . than to provoke an attack on them by the opposing party, all ready for a fight as they were."[48]

Military authorities were far from sanguine that the mob could be controlled and took the initiative in turning out the garrison. A guard was thrown across Notre Dame Street, with a company of troops at its rear, and Government House was barricaded. At Dalhousie Square the entire garrison was under arms, ready to move with artillery.

For Ermatinger it was a fearful day. "The slightest collision with troops or with the newly armed [police] force must have produced the most dreadful results. Masses numbering two or three thousands advanced as far as the old Court House . . . [where] they halted and were harangued by some gentlemen [Lieutenant-Colonel Gugy and Major-General Gore] who, after great trouble, dispersed them gradually and by midnight the town quieted down."[49] It was only with Gore's assurance that "the arming of the constables had been a mistake, and that they would be disarmed," that the crowd agreed to disperse.[50] Had the special constables been supported by troops, civil order might have been more quickly restored, but as tension increased, La Fontaine, pressured by George Moffatt and other leaders of the Constitutional party, backed down and disarmed the special constables.[51] Thus the initial efforts of the provincial government to assume responsibility for the maintenance of internal order were defeated, owing partly to the criticism of senior army officers who spoke out sharply against "arming one portion of the people against the other."[52]

Not only did the government dismiss the special constables, but it also released the five men who had been arrested for arson, much to the disgust of Solicitor-General Blake of Canada West, who told La Fontaine he had "disgraced himself forever and rendered the gov^t contemptible . . . in deserting the Govr after his sticking to them." As the prisoners were released, they were greeted by a crowd who cheered them all the way through the Quebec suburbs, the cavalcade growing larger until it arrived at Orr's Hotel. There Moffatt urged them to be peaceful and assured them again that the "French Canadians had been disarmed and the safety of the city confided to the soldiery." Moffatt added, "All knew the gallant feelings of the soldiers, and that everything would now go right." Moffatt, like Gugy and Gore, kept a constant vigil, urging the angry crowds to disperse and attempting to allay violent feelings.[53]

Moffatt was not only head of the Constitutional party, but he was now chairman of the recently formed Montreal branch of the British American League and, as such, still possessed immense influence over the British element in Montreal. It was he who was spokesman for the "gentlemen leaders of the Conservative party who pledged themselves to use all their influence to prevent farther riots."[54] Yet, having given La Fontaine his word that the crowd would be controlled if the new police were disarmed, Moffatt faced grave responsibilities.

Knowledge that the commander of the forces had ordered the 71st Highland Light Infantry and the Provincial Cavalry to the city to help quell disorders tended to dampen ardent mischief-makers,[55] but Lt.-Gen. Sir Benjamin D'Urban took no chances. He privately alerted Sir John Harvey, the governor of Nova Scotia and commander of the forces there, to hold the 97th Regiment ready to move to Montreal. By 1 May he had Harvey's assurance of the "prompt and essential measures taken to reinforce the troops here if it should be necessary."[56]

The Queen's Light Dragoons rode into town from the border on 28 April 1849.[57] Its captain, Walter Jones, and other officers commanding regiments in Montreal, were briefed by D'Urban, who instructed them to be "lenient with the mob and not, if possible, shed blood . . . [for] if you do, I cannot say when we will be able to stop it as our force is so small."[58] Precise written instructions on how the cavalry was to act in concert with the infantry were given to Captain Jones,[59] the cavalry as usual to charge rioters in an effort to disperse them while the infantry would fire only if all other methods of control failed. The instructions stated, "Should the officer be directed to fire by the Magistrate, he will not do so, should he be able to disperse the Rioters, without resorting to the last act."[60]

These instructions were rigorously followed, both by the cavalry and by the infantry. When Lord Elgin came into the city on 30 April to receive an address of confidence from the Assembly, he was personally escorted to and from Government House by Captain Jones and sixty-three armed troopers of the Queen's Light Dragoons.[61] The popular 71st Highland Light Infantry, under its colonel, Sir Hew Dalrymple, was drawn up in front of Government House to protect Elgin.[62] Before leaving Government House, Elgin, in consultation with military and civil authorities, agreed to take a different route back to Monklands to avoid the crowd,[63] but even as he stepped out of the building, a shower of

stones was thrown at him over the heads of the soldiers. Behind
the line of soldiers, Magistrate Ovide Leblanc read the Riot Act
and ordered Dalrymple to fire. Judging that the situation did not
warrant such action, Dalrymple ordered the soldiers to charge
the rioters, "who fell back on either side of the troops and good-
humouredly gave them three cheers." This was the usual tactic of
the rioters. One eyewitness described how amusing it was to see
"the manoeuvres of the military and the mob at this time. When
the military moved, they moved, following every motion. Gibes
were played off at no small rate by the crowd on the soldiers, who
seemed to take it in good part."[64]

Lord Elgin and the viceregal party did not fare so well. As the
party galloped away up St. Lawrence to Sherbrooke Street to take
the road across the mountain to Monklands, "the people were so
savage," according to Elgin's aide-de-camp, Capt. F. A. Grant,
"that they jumped into cabs and went as hard as they could to a
place they knew he must pass and gave us a tremendous shower
of stones from both sides of the road; poor Bruce got a nasty cut
on the head, the carriage is badly damaged and the Dragoons
[Queen's Light Dragoons], Kerr [Lord Mark Kerr, Elgin's other
aide-de-camp], and I were all hit. The poor horses got some very
hard hits too."[65] Among the injured were Captain Jones and Police Superintendent Ermatinger. Elgin was so shaken by the
events of the last week of April that he did not go into Montreal
during the next four months,[66] preferring to remain at Monklands, guarded by troopers of the Queen's Light Dragoons and the
Royal Montreal Cavalry.[67] So anxious was he to avoid being the
occasion of a conflict "in which lives might have been lost" that he
was gently rebuked by Grey for remaining shut up at Monklands.
Grey wrote, "I should myself be inclined to think you have carried forbearance too far . . . [and] that you ought to have gone
into Town as usual, taking care to meet any attempt at violence
by prompt and severe measures, and the free use of the Troops if
necessary."[68]

Elgin and La Fontaine were still reluctant to make free use of
the troops and, indeed, military authorities shared their reluctance. Yet it was evident to them that if order was to be maintained without the constant use of troops, there must be a local
force to take the place of the dismissed gendarmerie. At the suggestion of Capt. Charles Wetherall, La Fontaine decided to raise a
fifty-man armed mounted force on the model of the Royal Irish
Constabulary—soon derisively dubbed "Elgin Guards" by the

British party.[69] To supplement the mounted police, a foot police of 100 men was also to be raised, all to be paid for by the provincial government.[70]

Earl Grey congratulated Elgin on this move. "I am very glad that you are going to organize a regular Police in Montreal, . . . the more so as I am compelled to send out orders by this mail to D'Urban to reduce the Garrison of that Town." Somewhat smugly Grey added, "It strikes me it may not be a bad punishment on Montreal for its misconduct, depriving it of the Expenditure of a Regiment."[71] This particular form of punishment, however, was not immediately inflicted. As the mounted constabulary could not be organized, trained, or equipped quickly, the government had to rely on troops.

Captain Wetherall was appointed to take charge of the security of the city and faced the task of organizing the new force.[72] To avoid delays in securing the use of troops, Wetherall was given new instructions. If an emergency arose, he could apply directly for troops from the field officer of the week or from Town Major Macdonald. Yet, such was the state of the city and the instability of government measures concerning the raising of the new police that Wetherall's first request to the ordnance for "50 carbines, 50 pistols, 50 scymetars [sic], 50 sets of saddlery complete, and 500 rounds of Pistol Cartridge" was followed immediately by his resignation.[73]

Cautiously, Capt. Vesey Kirkland, the military secretary, asked Wetherall for an explanation. Kirkland assured Wetherall that "the commander of the forces had ordered the arms and ammunition to be issued to him without hesitation, because in the letter of requisition, it was stated that *you* were charged with the *organization* and equipment of the Mounted Constabulary Force. . . . He hopes therefore that this is essentially the state of the case (viz) that the selection of officers and men who are to compose it, has been placed in your hands." To avoid all misunderstanding, Kirkland went on, "Otherwise, warned by the two apparently abortive attempts by the authorities of Montreal recently made to form a foot Police, he would have assuredly paused upon the issue of these arms and equipment." Kirkland told Wetherall that "His Excellency trusts to your well known Judgement and discretion that, as these arms and equipment are to be issued to *your order*, you will not suffer them to be delivered to any persons whom you do not feel confident or duly qualified to be entrusted with them."[74]

It is not surprising that military authorities were overly cautious about the reissue of arms to another incipient police force. Nor is it surprising that Captain Wetherall trod warily. His appointment to this delicate post was due largely to his connections with the high military command and his impeccable loyalist stance. His brother was the affable deputy adjutant general, Lt.-Col. George Wetherall, who had been idolized by the British party ever since his success at the battle of Saint-Charles. Not without reason did Lord Elgin refer to Capt. Charles Wetherall as "a person enjoying in a high degree the confidence of the Tory Party."[75]

Yet the task of organizing the new police force and the responsibility for the security of the city proved too exhausting for Wetherall. He fell ill and was persuaded to continue in the post only on condition that two other magistrates share with him the responsibility of the peace of the city. By the end of May William Ermatinger and William King McCord were named to act with him as special magistrates through whom the military was to be contacted in case of disturbances. These magistrates estimated that there were "3,000 organized and armed malcontents" in the city, and they asked the commander of the forces to permit troops to be quartered in different areas of the city to discourage the disaffected. The military opposed this move because "it would expose troops to be overwhelmed and destroyed in detail," whereas the "troops in their present Barracks are centrally posted and prepared to move promptly." Captain Kirkland assured James Leslie, the provincial secretary, that, in addition to the picquets of soldiers that were held in readiness to turn out at a moment's notice in aid of civil power, "strong moveable columns, consisting of cavalry, artillery and infantry, each under an able and experienced officer, had been formed and duly instructed, to act against any mob."[76]

New instructions for getting military aid caused alarm among the Montreal magistrates when they received them in late May. Requests for military aid had to be signed by two of the three special magistrates, either Wetherall, McCord, or Ermatinger. McCord protested immediately to the military secretary against the arrangements, as "from various causes, it might be impossible, on a sudden emergency, to procure the signatures of any two magistrates . . . if riots should occur in different parts of the city requiring the presence of one of the magistrates at each." He also warned that "two or even three of the magistrates might receive such bodily injury as would incapacitate them from signing such a requisition" or that there might be a difference of opinion among the magistrates as to whether military aid was really needed.[77] His objections, however, were overruled when his two associates failed to reinforce his stand.

The training and arming of the new mounted constabulary was not without difficulties. Wetherall insisted that the force not be given arms until "they are sufficiently well instructed in the use of them and are able to act so efficiently in a body as to resist any attempt by the mob to disarm them." He urged that the force be allowed to occupy the military barracks and stables at Laprairie and "that an Officer with a few N.C.O.'s of Cavalry be permitted to instruct the force in the usual cavalry exercises and stable duties."[78] Yet the provincial secretary urged the military secretary to release arms and ammunition to Wetherall. It may have been that the provincial authorities, anxious to get arms and equipment immediately from the ordnance, seized upon the device of appointing Wetherall as a special magistrate in whom the army authorities would have complete reliance and to whom they would issue the equipment.[79] Once having secured the equipment by way of Wetherall, they would then assign it to the officer appointed by Lord Elgin to command the force, Maj. R. B. Johnson, an appointment not approved by Wetherall. Johnson had been one of the rural police magistrates under Gugy and had succeeded Wetherall at the difficult post of Laprairie. Though not a military man, he was obviously qualified to undertake a post of higher command in the police.

To Kirkland's anxious queries about who was organizing the constabulary, Wetherall explained testily that as the "Governor-General has been pleased to appoint an officer as the Chief of that force, I feel that the responsibility of selecting the junior officers and men legitimately belongs to him." He assured military authorities, "I have given that officer all the assistance in my power by recommending to him such N.C.O.'s lately discharged from the Service as would be likely to assist him in the organization of the force." He again urged that the mounted constabulary be moved out of the city for training at Laprairie, as "the total absence of such a force from the city would, I conceive, be infinitely less disadvantageous . . . than its defeat by the mob." Undoubtedly Wetherall had grave doubts about the new force. Yet, by the end of May the constabulary and foot police were sufficiently organized to begin training at Laprairie. The military command ordered a regular officer, a sergeant of cavalry, and two gunners of

Above: The tory press pokes fun at La Fontaine's new mounted police.
Below: Lt.-Gen. Sir Benjamin D'Urban, commander of the forces in Canada during the Rebellion Losses Bill agitation.

the Royal Artillery to Laprairie to help in training. Wetherall considered this "absolutely essential as the officer appointed to command the force is not a military man and consequently not competent to undertake these duties.[80]

The new force seemed ill-starred from the beginning. It was mainly the creation of this provincial police force that provoked the resignation of Montreal's chief of police, Thomas Wily, "badgered," according to *Punch in Canada*, "by civic authorities . . . into resigning a duty ably discharged by him for upwards of five years." In explaining why he resigned, Wily left no room for doubt. "I could not allow myself to be made use of in forming a purely partisan force, paid by the government, recruited by well-known partisans, and attempted to be amalgamated with the City Police—a force which it has ever been my pride to make strictly impartial."[81]

The mounted police were lampooned unmercifully in the pages of *Punch in Canada*. When City Councillor John Tully of Griffintown, a strong liberal supporter, chose to make his tour of inspection of the police on 18 June, the anniversary of the Battle of Waterloo, *Punch* had a field day. As orders had been received from England that the anniversary of Waterloo was no longer to be celebrated, *Punch* lamented, "Cheerless passed the Day of Memories in thy Colonies. In the City of the Royal Mount, Rowan of the cocked hat forbade his warriors to gather. Peppered, said he, were the Gauls, but are our warriors therefore to be mustered? And the warriors remained within their tents in the City of the Royal Mount." But, *Punch* asked, "Who cometh from the Town of Griffin, with a peacock's feather in his hat? Tully of the terrible countenance, eminent in Council . . . on his own hook, he goeth forth, as a mighty general. Let the warriors of the Royal Mount, said he, slothful snooze in their camp. I will raise the war-cry in the ranks of the Mounted Police. Come, O Fortin! Gather thy warriors for the inspection of a mighty leader!"[82]

The *Gazette* on 15 June was less amusing in its attack. When it was reported that the foot police of the new force was to be disbanded, the *Gazette* demanded, "Let them dismiss the horse portion too. . . . The men were fools to enlist in such a service. . . . It is madness to keep up irritation by threatening a quiet people with a troop of raw levies, not equal to any 50 Montreal mechanics."

By mid-summer much of the pent-up fury had run its course and would-be rioters, aware of the elaborate military and civil measures to deal with disturbances, assumed a more docile stance. The sudden death of the commander of the forces, Sir Benjamin D'Urban, at the end of May had the effect of quietening discordant forces within the city. D'Urban's funeral was attended by 10,000, and, as a display of military and civil power, it was a silent warning to troublemakers.[83]

The respite from civil tumult was welcomed by the military. The increase of troops in the city had caused serious inconvenience in barrack space, but more serious than the crowding was the state of the Water Street Barracks where the 19th Regiment was quartered. This building, originally constructed as a store, had been hired in 1846 at an annual rent of £250 from Baron Grant to serve as barracks when the provincial government resumed occupation of the Queen's Barracks in the old jail.[84] Some £1,168. 9s. 10d. had been spent converting the store into barracks, but the unsuitability of the building with its low ceilings and a yard so confined that "effluvia from the privies [were] offensive in summer" was soon apparent.[85] Lt.-Col. Charles Hay of the 19th complained, "My Regiment has suffered more from sickness in these barracks than at any time [during] the last six years, which embraces the whole period the Regiment was in the West Indies." Hay rightly protested that the makeshift barracks were "located in the dirtiest part of town where spirits can be procured for 2 shillings a gallon."[86] Before he died, D'Urban had pressed for the removal of the 19th from Montreal because of the lack of proper barrack accommodation, but Earl Grey now advised the new commander of the forces, Maj.-Gen. William Rowan, to retain the 19th "if necessary for the peace of the city." Grey instructed Rowan that if the regiment was kept in Montreal to aid civil authorities, the military "must apply to Canada the rule observed in this Country . . . [that] the Provincial Government or the City of Montreal . . . defray the expense of quartering the regiment."[87]

The 71st Highlanders, who had been brought in from St. Johns at the height of the disturbances, was lodged in quarters almost as inconvenient as the Water Street Barracks. It was quartered in Bonsecours Market where the want of privies and cooking facilities, as well as the excessive heat of the compartments as summer wore on, proved not only unpleasant but unhealthy.[88] An outbreak of cholera among the troops in garrison brought the quartering difficulties to a crisis. The commander of the forces immediately consulted the governor general about reducing the

Montreal garrison to one regiment by returning the 71st to St. Johns and moving the 19th out of the city. Lord Elgin was adamant about not removing troops "to a distance from Montreal." Rowan did the next best thing to ensure the health of the troops. He stationed the 19th Regiment on St. Helen's Island "where it remained until October enjoying perfect health."[89]

So anxious were provincial authorities to retain two regiments in Montreal that they went to considerable expense to refit the Bonsecours Market barrack accommodations, but a Board of Ordnance officers reported it doubtful that the market, even with the improvements, could be used for winter quarters. The government then offered to hire and fit up any building which the ordnance might consider suitable. This was the same government that a few months previously had taunted that they, unlike their political opponents, never called out the troops. The shoe was firmly on the other foot by August of 1849. Not only were La Fontaine and his supporters wresting from the loyalists of 1837 their monopoly on loyalty, but they were breaking into the closed circle that had bound the garrison and the British party since 1832.

With the 23rd Regiment and the Provincial Cavalry in garrison and the 19th encamped on St. Helen's Island, the city remained tranquil until 15 August 1849. On that day, the government, after an investigation conducted by Clerk of the Crown Alexandre-Maurice Delisle,[90] arrested nine men in connection with the burning of Parliament House.[91] One was John Orr, a native of Ireland, who was captain of the Montreal Volunteer Fire Battalion and a member of the Royal Arch Chapter of Masons. Orr had crossed swords with the radical reformers as far back as 6 November 1837 when he was shot at by the Patriotes during the first major street fight before the outbreak of the rebellions. His fashionable hotel on Notre Dame Street, which solicited the patronage of "officers and commercial gentlemen," was frequently the location of the Constitutional party election meetings.

Another of the arrested men was John Dier (Dyer), a tavern keeper and senior district master of the Provincial Grand Orange Lodge, likely the same man who had been beaten up by the Drummondites during the 1844 by-election. The others were Joseph Ewing of the grocery firm of McGibbon and Ewing; Robert Cooke, a bootmaker and shoemaker; Alexander Courtney of Notre Dame Street; a grocer named Jamieson; James Bone, a labourer; Robert Howard; and James Nelson.

As soon as news of the arrests became known, the executive of the Britons Club issued a proclamation calling its members to be ready to act at a moment's notice to meet any emergency.[92] All troops were confined to barracks from seven o'clock in the morning, and a picquet of 100 rank and file guarded Government House where the arrested men were to be assembled.[93] Half the Provincial Cavalry was saddled and ready to ride, for rumours were rampant that the house of Attorney General La Fontaine would be attacked that night.[94] La Fontaine, well aware of what a mob could do, took the precaution of sending a note to Police Magistrate Wetherall asking him "to be good enough to be on the alert," as he had information that "my house will be visited by the Boys."[95] He also sent messages to several friends to ask their aid in defending his house, but he made no effort to seek help from the city police, then under his political foe Mayor Fabre.[96]

Government authorities were anxious to make use of the new mounted constabulary, which had been in training at Laprairie all summer, but Wetherall considered this unwise.[97] La Fontaine relied, therefore, upon the friends to whom he had sent a personal appeal for help and upon several others who arrived of their own accord "to protect the house in case the military did not arrive in time."[98] By nine o'clock there were about ten men in the house, including Lt.-Col. Etienne-Paschal Taché, Dr. Wolfred Nelson,[99] and, most likely, George-Etienne Cartier. Coroner Charles-Joseph Coursol, a close friend of La Fontaine, was there early in the evening but claimed to have left before the mob arrived.[100] For Nelson and Cartier, the situation must have held strange memories. Twelve years before they had stood, musket in hand, ready to shoot down both British regulars and local volunteers. Now they anxiously awaited the appearance of the regulars and the Provincial Cavalry to help them repulse an attack by English-speaking Montrealers.[101]

When Wetherall received La Fontaine's note at about half-past six in the evening, he immediately alerted the military authorities, and then sent scouts to keep a lookout for any movement of the mob towards the St. Antoine suburbs.[102] So serious did the commandant, Lieutenant-Colonel Hay of the 19th, consider the situation that he hastily sought reinforcements from St. Helen's Island by firing a signal rocket. This brought a detachment of 100 men of the 19th Regiment to the Quebec Gate Barracks in less than an hour, though their commanding officer later somewhat peevishly complained of their being called out "without sufficient cause." He was rebuked by the Montreal commandant who informed him that it was not his "prerogative to consider whether the riot he is called out to quell is a great, or a small one."[103]

Disturbances began on Notre Dame Street near Orr's Hotel, whose owner had been one of those arrested earlier in the day. A crowd of some 300 began to collect there in the early evening, probably by design, to distract the attention of the military from the projected attack on La Fontaine's house. A barricade was erected of building stone, planks, and ladders across the street where the crowd had cornered City Councillor Tully. Tully sought shelter in a nearby tailor's shop, and although all three magistrates were on the spot with police, they could not control the mob. Wetherall got 100 rank and file of the 23rd Regiment on the move, but their captain refused to disperse the crowd unless Wetherall read the Riot Act. The crowd temporarily scattered as the troops knocked down the barricade.[104]

Taking advantage of the lull, Police Magistrate McCord went to his office at Government House at about 8:45 P.M. Here he found La Fontaine's note which Ermatinger had left for his perusal. Scarcely had he read it when a scout came rushing in to tell him that the mob had moved off in the direction of La Fontaine's house. McCord quickly signed the requisition for troops and took it to the commandant. Close to an hour elapsed from the time he got a detachment of fifty soldiers until he reached La Fontaine's house, a distance of about a mile. He passed some of the crowd still mingling near Orr's Hotel on Notre Dame Street who "received me handsomely by yells and screams." The mob, heading for La Fontaine's with fife and drum and the Union Jack carried aloft, outdistanced McCord and his troops and crashed through the iron gates of La Fontaine's house shortly after nine o'clock. Inside the unlighted house La Fontaine and his friends waited silently as the mob outside shouted, "Hang La Fontaine. . . . Burn the d——d house."[105]

Swept along by the crowd were a number of youths, one of them eighteen-year-old William Mason, a son of veterinary surgeon James Mason, a former trooper of the 1st King's Dragoon Guards who had taken his discharge nine years earlier to settle in Montreal. Before Mason had time to throw a stone, a volley of stones burst through the windows of the house followed by several shots fired by the mob. The men inside, most of whom were lawyers, were armed with pistols and muskets. With a whiff of buckshot, they put the mob of some 200 to 300 to flight, wounding about five, one of them the young Mason, who died the next day. Before he died, Mason had bemoaned the fact that he had lingered with the mob at Orr's Hotel instead of continuing on to visit the young lady to whom he was paying his addresses, as had been his intention.[106]

Captain Wetherall received news of the intended attack on La Fontaine's house from one of his scouts. With a party of the Royal Montreal Cavalry he started off, overtaking McCord and his detachment of infantry, and galloped ahead as shots were heard in the distance. They arrived to find "not a soul save Mr. La Fontaine and some of his friends, their muskets and pistols piled in a corner in a backroom."[107]

In spite of constant vigil by the police magistrates and preparedness on the part of the military, a mob in motion could confound the best-laid plans, and the leader of the government thus found that his most dependable source of protection was personal friends. The delay in getting troops in motion meant that they arrived too late; yet had they been ordered to La Fontaine's before the attack, likely no attempt would have been made on the house and the magistrates would have been open to the charge of calling out the troops unnecessarily.

McCord, with his long experience as a police magistrate in Quebec City, was sure that he could have "with 20 efficient police, such as in Quebec, . . . defied that mob to have come up the lane, if they were unarmed."[108] Yet this was an armed mob.[109] Wetherall was less sanguine. He was convinced that even with troopers of the Provincial Cavalry he could not have held back the mob.[110] The government press was also certain that if the mounted police had been brought to the city from Laprairie in time, it "could have been promptly moved to the spot . . . to surround and capture the assailants in the very act."[111] The two police magistrates tended to hold civic authorities responsible for not "taking proper precautionary measures," and Wetherall obliquely criticized La Fontaine for not having applied to civic authorities for protection. A few men of the mounted constabulary were ordered to cross the river by bateaux the day after La Fontaine's house was attacked, but as the men awaited their horses which were being ferried over by another steamer, they were stoned on the wharf by a group of men and young boys.[112] The constabulary fired warning shots and as the *Transit* pulled into the wharf, the mounted police were ordered to return to Laprairie. The *Gazette* on 18 August remarked smugly, "Thus ended the first day of the Prairie Hens with a 'Montreal Mob.'"

Wetherall was convinced that only martial law could save the city from a fratricidal *émeute*, but, unable to persuade Lord Elgin of the need to declare martial law, he threw up his appointment as police magistrate on 18 August after he had been assaulted by a mob.[113] In his letter of resignation he warned that the constant use of the troops "in support of the inadequate Civil Force" would end in direct collision with the mob and great loss of life. Lord Elgin kept a cooler head. Embarrassed by Wetherall's resignation, he feared that any attempt to appoint a successor would lead to fresh outcries against the government, but he was confident that the government could "rely on their military force" if all other efforts to preserve peace failed.[114]

An inquest into the death of young Mason began at the Cyrus Hotel on 17 August. When troops were pressed into guard duty, the *Gazette* on 18 August complained that such a use of the troops was "unprecedented in history." Nevertheless, a sergeant, corporal, bugler, and twenty-five privates were posted at various entrances to the hotel and in the room where the inquest was being held. On the third day of the inquest, the military guard was doubled,[115] but this did not prevent the hotel from being set on fire just as La Fontaine was about to give his testimony.[116] The soldiers began to rush out, but were ordered back by their officers whose coolness kept the staircases from being blocked up. The officer in charge, Capt. A. Hamilton, described the confusion as "coroner, jury and spectators all made a rush to get out. . . . I got my men out as quick as I could . . . and was ordered to escort the Hon. Mr. LaFontaine to Government House."[117] An attempt to injure La Fontaine was made even in the midst of the confusion.[118] La Fontaine, in generously acknowledging the services of the soldiery, said it was "owing to the care and management of the military . . . that the lives of all present were saved."[119]

To cope with the continued disturbances and incendiaries the troops were again confined to barracks on 20 August, while troopers of the Provincial Cavalry under Capt. Charles Oakes Ermatinger were saddled and ready to turn out during the night. The guard at Government House was increased to 50 soldiers and another 150 rank and file were ordered from St. Helen's Island.[120]

The inquest continued on 21 August at the main guardhouse opposite Nelson's monument on Jacques Cartier Square where, it was presumed, the most intrepid of the ill-disposed would not interfere. Like Julien Champeau, the French-Canadian casualty of the 1844 election turmoil, William Mason, before his death, had set the record straight. He told his father and Dr. Arnoldi that the mob had attacked La Fontaine's house first. This information, given by the victim's father at the inquest, was conclusive. The jury prudently agreed that Mason came to his death by a gunshot "fired by one of the persons, to us unknown, assembled for the purpose of protecting Mr. LaFontaine's property."[121] Throughout the inquest witnesses refused to identify the men whom they saw at La Fontaine's. Taché had no reluctance to admit he had helped defend the house, but stated, "I do not think myself bound to give their names . . . because of threats uttered against them."[122] The identity of the men remained uncertain, and for some time it was believed that troops or the mounted police had been involved, even though La Fontaine specifically denied this.[123]

By the end of August of 1849 Elgin's efforts to persuade civil authorities to assume responsibility for the peace of the city bore fruit. He insisted that "nothing is to be hoped for . . . until . . . the citizens feel that they have nothing to rely upon but themselves." Elgin was right. Both military and police forces had been unable to wipe out the urban disorders associated with the political tensions that had gripped the city since April. Tranquillity returned only after the city corporation began swearing in "upwards of 200 gentlemen, many of the highest respectability and of every shade of political opinion" who pledged themselves to maintain public order. Town Major Colin Macdonald was able to rest from his labours. On the last day of the inquest, 25 August, he informed the military secretary, "Everything is apparently quiet in this Garrison and its neighbourhood. . . . No military aid has been called up since August 23rd."[124] The government press, the *Pilot*, confirmed this on 25 August. "The City has continued in a state of tranquillity . . . and peaceable Citizens can now move about without apprehension of being assaulted by the mob who have of late infested our streets."

The British party made a last effort to drive a wedge into the relations between the military and liberal administration which were assuming such a friendly air, with La Fontaine publicly praising the troops and the military doing its duty in protecting the head of government. While the inquest was in progress, the *Gazette* published on 22 August an affidavit of a carriage-maker named Peter Groome. Groome had sworn on 14 May before Magistrate McCord and Clerk of the Crown Delisle that he had seen an officer of the 23rd Regiment, dressed in mufti, at the meeting on Champ de Mars on 25 April and that the officer had incited the mob to go to Parliament House. Publication of this affidavit, which obviously had been smuggled out of Solicitor-General Drummond's office, produced a minor tempest when the commander of the forces, Major-General Rowan, expressed his "surprise and regret that any officer of the Government should have had a document in his possession for more than three months containing a charge of so grave a nature against an officer in H.M.'s service, without submitting it to His Excellency."[125]

The *Gazette*'s attempt to stir up trouble failed, for Drummond assured Rowan that Groome had admitted his error about the identity of the officer and that the authorities had disregarded this part of Groome's deposition,[126] though they had used his testimony in their case against the Montrealers who had been arrested for arson on 15 August.[127] Groome's charges against those arrested on 15 August were not adjudicated in court. Groome absconded, possibly through fear for his personal safety.[128] It may well be that the inquiry conducted by Delisle had uncovered the ringleaders in the attack on Parliament House and that, on the whole, the guilty parties had been arrested. Securing witnesses and evidence sufficient for a conviction was more difficult and Crown officers may have relied too heavily on dubious depositions in making the arrests. In any event, the individuals who attacked Parliament House went unpunished, for the government did not proceed with the charges at the fall assizes.

An uneasy calm ensued as the city took stock of the past six months of tension. A new balance of forces had emerged, disrupting the old alliance between the garrison and the British party that had begun in 1832 and matured in the rebellion years. The firmness of the stand by the old Patriote guard at La Fontaine's house against the same forces it had faced twelve years earlier demonstrated anew to both sides that some issues were not negotiable. The stand evoked both admiration and respect from the military and a grudging admiration from the physical force wing of the British party. Faced with buckshot from muskets in the hands of veteran Patriotes, who were about to be reinforced by British troops, the tory physical force wing gave way. Some, like the Patriotes of 1838, returned to conventional politics. Others turned to annexation, thus giving their old Patriote opponents a chance now to label them "rebels."

The provincial secretary, James Leslie, lost no time in sending off dismissal notices to one militia officer after another of the Montreal district who signed a manifesto favouring annexation

107

to the United States.[129] The Provincial Cavalry, which had been on duty for the past six months in Montreal, also fell under a ban. When the home government decided to remove the Provincial Cavalry from the imperial budget,[130] the provincial government refused to undertake the financing of the force that had grown out of the rebellion and whose elite corps, the Queen's Light Dragoons, had never quite lived down its Doric Club origins. The British garrison viewed these moves with concern. Without the Provincial Cavalry on the border, desertions soared,[131] and with both the city police and the militia officer corps demoralized by the events of 1849, the garrison stood alone in the event of renewed civil tension. Even the controversial mounted constabulary was phased out in the fall of 1850,[132] so that the garrison had neither Provincial Cavalry nor mounted constabulary to call upon for support in 1853 when Father Alessandro Gavazzi paid a visit to the city.

7. The Gavazzi Riot of 1853

If the Rebellion Losses Bill agitation tended to discredit the British party in Montreal, the Gavazzi riot shattered the entente cordiale that had existed between the garrison and the British party since the election riot of 1832.[1] Alessandro Gavazzi, an apostate Italian priest, arrived in Montreal on the morning of 9 June 1853 accompanied by armed friends from Quebec City. He was met not only by Presbyterian minister Robert Campbell and the minister of the Wesleyan St. James Street Church, J. Jenkins,[2] but also by a party of the Montreal police under Superintendent Lt.-Col. William Ermatinger. Civil authorities had been warned by government officials at Quebec City that Gavazzi's appearance in Montreal would likely produce disturbances.[3] His lecture a few days earlier at the Presbyterian Free Chapel in the normally tranquil city of Quebec had ended in a brawl during which Gavazzi had warded off irate Irish Roman Catholics by swirling a stool over his head until he was tossed from the pulpit onto the heads of the congregation below.[4] It was, therefore, with mixed feelings that the clerical and police delegations awaited his arrival in Montreal and escorted him to St. Lawrence Hall.

Later in the day a handbill was distributed announcing that Gavazzi would lecture that night at Zion Congregational Church, located at the corner of Radigone and Latour Streets near Hay

Market, a distance of about half a mile from the Quebec Gate Barracks. Ermatinger conferred with Mayor Charles Wilson about the best means of securing the peace of the city. Wilson was a Roman Catholic whose wife was a sister of Daniel Tracey and whose grandfather was Captain Monteith d'Ailleboust, an officer of the French army who entered the British service after the Conquest.[5] He was one of those Montrealers with family connections in every direction and who, because of these ties, was caught in the cross fire whenever cultural, linguistic, or religious tensions arose. Wilson had been elected mayor in March of 1851 amid turbulence and gunfire.[6] Once in office, he and his reform administration pledged themselves to ending the riotous proceedings in the city.[7]

Wilson ordered the new chief of police, Capt. Charles Oakes Ermatinger, the former captain of the disbanded Provincial Cavalry, to have fifty constables at Zion Church. As the high constable was able to secure only ten men as special constables,[8] it was decided to supplement the city police by eighteen Water Police,[9] a force recently organized by Police Superintendent William Ermatinger. Composed largely of discharged soldiers and former members of the Royal Irish Constabulary, the Water Police was a thirty-man corps of well-drilled and well-disciplined men whose main job was to protect the wharves and canal shipping, but who could be pressed into general police service when emergencies arose. Even with this combined force of some eighty men,[10] authorities were far from confident that the police could prevent disturbances at the lecture. They therefore took the precaution of applying in advance for troops.[11]

The military hierarchy was not unduly alarmed about Gavazzi's arrival. No major civil disturbances had occurred since 1849 and under Mayor Wilson city authorities had made serious efforts to curb riotous tendencies. During the three-year tour of duty of the 20th Regiment of Foot, the garrison had slipped back into the comfortable days of the prerebellion era. Fancy dress balls, mock ice battles on the St. Lawrence "witnessed by General Rowan and numerous spectators from the City," and temperance lectures were more usual than charging rioters.[12] The more serious-minded officers of the garrison attended public meetings to discuss "what would tend so much to the health, comfort and happiness of the community"—plans for an eighty-foot broad boulevard around the upper part of Mount Royal. One of these officers, Sir James Alexander, who undertook to survey the mountain, knew Montreal in all its moods. He regarded the invitation to Gavazzi as highly injudicious. Having seen the city in the midst of the Rebellion Losses Bill riots, Alexander felt that under the calm of 1853 there was still "a strong leaven of party spirit which it was dangerous to rouse into action." When he saw the notice of Gavazzi's lecture, he took the precaution of reconnoitring the ground about Zion Church "to consider how troops could be placed to the best advantage in case of serious riot."[13]

Other officers showed less concern. They were occupied with the duties involved in a change of regiments. On that very day the 20th Regiment was being replaced by the 26th Cameronians, freshly arrived from a tour of duty at Gibraltar, "a very quiet place where there were no riots," as its colonel was later to recall somewhat wistfully.[14] So popular had the 20th Regiment been in Montreal that the *Transcript*, in bidding farewell to the regiment, spoke of the "high moral tone which so happily prevails among . . . our friends, the N.C.O.'s and privates of the gallant XXth." The editor congratulated them on their temperance, attributing the £2,259 that the men saved while in Montreal to their record of sobriety.[15] The relief of the 20th Regiment was no less welcome. The Cameronians had a record for steadiness in the army, and when it left Gibraltar for Canada in May 1853, a highly complimentary general order had been issued to the men. Two-thirds of the men were Protestant and one-third Catholic; its officer corps was largely Presbyterian.[16]

It was with some surprise that the newly arrived officers of the 26th received a visit from Mayor Wilson and Police Superintendent Ermatinger on the afternoon of 9 June with a request for troops to be available at half-past six that evening. The new commandant, Lt.-Col. A. T. Hemphill of the 26th, said he would consult Lt.-Gen. William Rowan, but he told Mayor Wilson that if the troops were granted, they should be placed under cover and not stationed in Place d'Armes as the mayor had suggested. Police Superintendent Ermatinger and Mayor Wilson made arrangements for the troops to be placed in the fire engine house at the corner of Craig Street and Hay Market, a distance of about a quarter of a mile from Zion Church.

The anxiety of the police superintendent and mayor was increased by the fact that the previous night they had refused the aid of a number of Protestants who had offered to be sworn in as special constables.[17] Ermatinger adamantly opposed such aid. He recalled that on the occasion of a previous election "both parties swore themselves in as special constables and, armed with sticks, began the row." Wilson feared a "collision between persons of different religions."[18] Before the visit of the Protestants, Wilson had received a deputation of "20 to 30 Catholic gentlemen, both Irish and French," who protested strongly against Gavazzi's being permitted to lecture in the city concert hall.[19] On Wilson's refusing the use of the concert hall for the lecture, he received the assurances of the Catholic gentlemen that they would use "all their influence to prevent those who might dislike the lecture from coming up to Zion Church."[20] Sir James Alexander realized how serious the situation was. After the Protestant delegation's offer of services had been rejected by the mayor, one of the delegates told Alexander, "We will be prepared in the church to meet force with force."[21] This was no idle boast. Fowling pieces, pistols, clubs, and a double-barrelled shotgun were piled in the basement of Zion Church.[22]

Mayor Wilson, having arranged for the troops to be placed in the engine house, returned at six o'clock to the Quebec Gate Barracks with Police Superintendent Ermatinger where they pressed the commandant to hasten the movement of troops. Wilson was anxious to be "on the spot at the Zion Church previous to the commencement of the lecture" and was "rather uneasy . . . as it took considerably more time to prepare the troops for marching . . . than I had expected."[23] The commandant felt some uneasiness, too, at his regiment being pitched into duty in aid of the civil power so soon after its arrival in Montreal. His officers did not even know which gate to take to get the picquet out of the barracks, let alone how to get the men to Hay Market. To make matters worse, all the senior staff officers who knew the city, including the commander of the forces, Lt.-Gen. William Rowan; his aide-de-camp, Sir James Alexander; the military secretary, Maj. H. S. Rowan; the deputy quartermaster-general, Lt.-Col. W. J. D'Urban; and Town Major Colin Macdonald, were at the wharf bidding farewell to the 20th Regiment.

Still, 100 men were on the move in less than half an hour, having been "well warned not to take any orders but from their officers." Each man carried the usual ten rounds of cartridge and marched off briskly, commanded by Capt. Charles Cameron and Lts. Robert Quarterley and Richard Chute, all of the 26th Regiment. Their lieutenant-colonel, George Hogarth, who had spent thirty-six years in the army, joined them en route and took command of the picquet. Mayor Wilson directed the officers to march their men by way of a side road to avoid creating any excitement, although Captain Cameron considered the ruse a failure as "moving through these by-lanes attracted more attention than if we had marched boldly through the main street."[24] When they reached the engine house, the Cameronians were within a stone's throw of the spot where British troops had marched into the city for the first time less than a hundred years ago. A little to the south were the ruins of Parliament House, a silent reminder of what an angry Montreal crowd could do.

But the men of the 26th Regiment were innocent of Montreal's past tensions, having arrived in the city within the last forty-eight hours. They piled their arms and, to keep from suffocating, threw open all the doors and windows of the small house. The evening was so hot and sultry that even those in Zion Congregational Church felt the oppressiveness of the thunderous skies as Gavazzi lectured to them on the "errors of Popery," clenching his fists and "occasionally flinging the loose folds of his gown over one shoulder whilst his hair at times streamed over his face," altogether a scene which "must have been startling to those with weak nerves" as one British officer later confessed.[25]

For the 100 soldiers cramped in the small engine house, the heat and dust were excessive. One soldier had to be excused from duty and escorted back to the barracks. Their colonel walked up towards Hay Market with Mayor Wilson and Police Superintendent Ermatinger so as to become familiar with the locality. It was then that Wilson took the opportunity to ask his advice about the procedure to be followed if the troops should be called on to fire, "as I did not know how these things were conducted." Lieutenant-Colonel Hogarth assured him that the men, if ordered to fire, "would shoot by twos or threes or fives."[26]

Surrounding the church were about eighty policemen, some of whom were well experienced in the art of quelling riots. Their chief, Capt. Charles Ermatinger, had had ample riot experience during the thirteen years he had served in the Provincial Cavalry. High Constable Benjamin DeLisle, who was on hand with his ten special constables, had been present at almost every riot in Montreal since 1832. Sgt. Wylie Hutchinson had spent seven years on the Liverpool police force before coming to North America. He then served four years with the Boston police before joining the Montreal force in 1852.[27] Since then he had twice helped suppress riots in Griffintown.

Armed only with their batons, the police tried to keep the

Above: The interior of Zion Church. *Below:* British regulars used as riot control police.

largely Roman Catholic Irish crowd, estimated at between 200 to 300,[28] from gaining entrance to the church, but with each burst of applause from within, the crowd outside became more agitated and began to hurl stones at the police. Captain Ermatinger tried to arrest one man whom he regarded as a leader of the rioters, but he was stunned by stones.[29] The Water Police, seeing Ermatinger surrounded by the crowd, managed to get through to him, aided by some of the city police, and Ermatinger was helped to a nearby dispensary for treatment. His brother, Lt.-Col. William Ermatinger, was so severely stoned about the face and body that he, too, was stunned. An Irishman in the crowd came to his support, saying, "Lord, Colonel, are you hurt? I am sure it was never intended for you."[30]

The difficulties faced by the police were numerous. Before they were stationed at Zion Church, their chief had urged them to do their duty well and "in the performance of that duty, we shall not know Catholic, Protestant, Jew, or any other religion."[31] Yet undertones of religious antagonism within the police ranks were evident. Samuel Medill of the Water Police, a force which was mostly Protestant,[32] testified that Deputy Chief Eugene Flynn, a Roman Catholic, cautioned him not to use a baton against one of his assailants, that it was "more prudent to flatter the mob than use violence." Medill implied that the police were prevented from quelling the riot by "Constable Flynn finding fault with him [Medill] for doing so." It is unlikely that Flynn was derelict in his duty. The more moderate *Transcript* described Flynn as one of the "men who could not have exerted himself more bravely."[33]

The police were also confused by the fact that while they were trying to keep the crowd back from the church, armed men came out of the church and fired into the crowd, killing one of the leading rioters, James Walsh, and wounding two others. Some of the police regarded this as aid, testifying that "if it had not been for the help we received from the church, we would have been beaten."[34] Others regarded the armed intervention as something of a mixed blessing. Constables Jean-Baptiste Simard and Michel Renaud discussed arresting the man who had shot Walsh, but decided if they tried to do so, they themselves would be shot.[35]

The troops remained under cover well over an hour before they heard shots being fired and saw Mayor Wilson running down the hill towards them, waving his hat in an excited manner, and shouting "to turn the men out."[36] The men fell in, one soldier asking Captain Cameron whether he should load. Captain Cameron, who had twice helped suppress riots in Ireland, said, "No, decidedly not!" but Lieutenant-Colonel Hogarth, on the advice of the mayor, ordered the men to load and prime, an unusual step as the act of loading and priming in front of a riotous mob was often found effective in dispersing a crowd without resorting to firing.[37]

The men marched off, the mayor urging them to run as, he said, the police were being murdered. When Captain Cameron asked Lieutenant-Colonel Hogarth if he should order the men to double, the lieutenant-colonel told him, "No, keep your men cool, and see that no one obeys any order except mine." The soldiers were met by Police Superintendent Ermatinger, who urged the mayor to bring the troops quickly, as "a regular firing was now heard between the parties."[38] The troops were halted at the foot of Hay Market, facing up Radigone Street towards Zion Church. With their appearance, the crowd temporarily quieted. Town Major Colin Macdonald, who had been attending to the embarkation of the 20th Regiment, arrived and conferred with the mayor as to where to place the troops. They were joined by Sir James Alexander, who had earlier reconnoitred the ground. Alexander suggested that one party of troops be brought up the hill beyond Zion Church so that they would face down towards the front of the church.

On the advice of the mayor, however, the troops were marched nearer Zion Church and posted in two divisions, one facing up towards the church, the other facing towards the engine house where the crowd had rallied after being driven back by the armed church party. The two divisions of troops stood back to back about fifty paces apart, their colonel standing about midway between them. The men were at ease, their arms sloped. Captain Cameron and his subaltern, Lieutenant Chute, stood in front of the division facing the church, while Lieutenant Quarterley was with the lower division that faced Craig Street. The police, who had been beaten back from the church by the mob, rallied with the arrival of the troops. Their chiefs, the two Ermatinger brothers, were so injured that they were being treated by Dr. Robert MacDonnell at his nearby dispensary. On the church steps were some of the congregation who had helped drive back the crowd. As they saw the troops approach, they began to "hurrah for the 26th, the gallant Cameronians."[39]

At the close of the lecture as the congregation began to come out of the church, stones were thrown and shots fired from the direction of the weigh house directly opposite the church. Some of the congregation began to move towards the troops, presumably for protection, and tried to move into the space between the two divisions of soldiers. Others who passed the line of soldiers and were moving off towards Notre Dame Street were attacked by the crowd that had gathered near the engine house. Neither the mayor nor the troops had any way of knowing whether the people moving towards them were ill-disposed or not. Mayor Wilson shouted to them to keep back and told Lieutenant Quarterley that "a violent mob was coming down upon us . . . [and] that he would read the Riot Act, after which they must be repulsed."[40]

Although the rank and file were standing steady with their arms sloped, few of them felt at ease. They were total strangers to the city. Above them they could see that the police had been beaten back from the church and were caught between the fire of an armed party from the church and the rioters; below them a disturbance broke out near the engine house and a mob began to rush towards them firing shots. All the men on duty that day were soldiers of over three years' service, many of them veterans of nineteen or more years and some wore medals won in the Chinese campaigns.[41] It must have seemed to them as crowds were moving in from both directions that they were facing a Six Mile Bridge affair, a riot that was the talk of every canteen and mess in the British army. This riot occurred in 1852 during the County Clare elections in Ireland when a detachment of two officers, two sergeants, and forty rank and file were ordered out to protect voters going to and from a poll. When the party was attacked and stoned by a riotous crowd, the soldiers fired into the crowd without orders from their officers. According to the testimony of their commanding officer, they did so in defence of their lives. Although indictments were preferred against those who fired, the bills were thrown out by the grand jury. Thus a precedent was set that soldiers on duty could, even without the command of their officers, fire in self-defence against rioters.[42] The troops of the 26th Regiment that were lined up back to back on Hay Market Square in Montreal on that muggy evening of 9 June 1853 were well aware of the precedent set in Ireland the previous year.

Mayor Wilson was not so knowledgeable of recent military developments as far as riots were concerned. As he saw the troops being surrounded by the crowd, he lost his composure and quickly read the proclamation of the Riot Act:[43] "Our Sovereign Lady the Queen chargeth and commandeth all persons, being assembled, immediately to disperse themselves, and peaceably to depart

117

to their habitations or to their lawful business, upon the pains contained in the Act made in the first year of King George the first, to prevent tumults and riotous assemblies. God Save the Queen."[44] Scarcely had he finished when he heard the words "Fire, Fire" and, to his astonishment, the lower division of troops fired.[45] Lieutenant Quarterley's impression was that the mayor shouted the command to fire and the men obeyed.[46] Quarterley ordered his men not to fire again and reprimanded them for firing without an order from an officer. One soldier replied that it was high time to fire, as a bullet had passed close to his head. Another answered that he had seen officers obey the orders of the mayor and thought that they should fire when the mayor so ordered them. Other privates thought that it was Lieutenant-Colonel Hogarth who gave the order to fire,[47] but one private later testified that it was Lieutenant Quarterley who gave the order.

Lieutenant-Colonel Hogarth was startled by the sudden irregular fire of the lower division of troops and rushed towards it shouting, "Cease firing." As he did so, he was even more astounded to hear the upper division fire. Captain Cameron, who was standing directly in front of his men, was no less astonished. He had deliberately taken this position as, from the excited manner of the mayor, he felt that the mayor "had lost his presence of mind and that a great responsibility rested with me . . . to prevent accidents." Shots had been fired towards the upper division of troops, but the men remained calm when Cameron had called to them, "Don't move, men, keep steady." Then, a few seconds afterwards, the lower division fired and within a minute or so the upper division broke into an irregular file firing.[48]

Rushing along his division, Captain Cameron threw the firelocks up into the air to stop the fire, bullets flying under his arm and over his head. When he asked his men how they dared to fire without the orders of their commanding officers, two or three of them pointed to the mayor and exclaimed, "Why, sir, that little Civil Magistrate that is with Col. Hogarth, told us to fire—not once, but twice." Police Superintendent Ermatinger had just come out of Dr. MacDonnell's dispensary when he heard the troops firing. He ran to the mayor and shouted, "Great God, what is this all about?"[49]

It was sheer luck that Town Major Macdonald, Sir James Alexander, and Capt. George Cressigny of the 20th Regiment were not shot when the upper division fired. A few paces in front of the division, Macdonald was urging the gentlemen leaving the church to get the women and children away "as soon as they could." Near him were Sir James Alexander and Captain Cressigny, who were also urging the men and women "to get out of this" when a cry went up that the troops were going to fire. Alexander pushed the people back against the wall of a house just as the firing began. Some laughed, saying, "It is only blank cartridge," but Alexander shook his head, "They don't fire blank cartridge now-a-days in riots." Nearby they saw a boy of eight fall over, his leg smashed by a bullet.[50]

Turning to Cameron, Macdonald exclaimed, "In God's name, what is this?" Cameron, who was in the act of throwing up his men's muskets with his sword, retorted, "I am doing my best to prevent this."[51] Haviland LeMesurier Routh, the Montrealer who in 1844 had put up part of the bail for Lt. Thomas D'Arcy of the 89th Regiment after the bayonet death of Julien Champeau, was one of the most irate against both civil and military authorities. Seeing men and children fall around him from the fire, he rushed towards the mayor and demanded, "What, in the name of heaven, could have induced you to give the orders to fire on innocent and inoffensive citizens?"[52] A number of other gentlemen, who were crowding around the mayor, accused him of murdering the people and shouted that he ought to be hanged.[53] Even Joint Coroner Charles-Joseph Coursol was so unnerved that he accosted the mayor angrily, "In the name of God, how is it that citizens are shot down like dogs?"[54]

The mayor, as much astonished as everyone else, withstood the onslaught of indignant men, Catholic and Protestant, French and English, gentlemen and tradesmen, who were reproving him in such violent language and gestures that Alexander feared for his life. Alexander remonstrated with the shouting men, and taking the mayor by the arm, he placed him among the soldiers and warned him, "On no account allow the crowd to close round you."[55]

The firing from the lower division had mortally wounded James Macrae and Thomas O'Neil, and that of the upper division had killed four men and mortally wounded three.[56] One was Daniel McGrath, son of the former chief of police. Another was the son of City Councillor Charles Adams. Every man in the upper division fired, and those who deliberately fired high tended to hit people in the distance who were already partly up Beaver Hall Hill. Thus many of the twelve or more wounded from the soldiers' fire were struck in the legs.

Shortly after the firing occurred, the deputy quartermaster-general, Lt.-Col. W. J. D'Urban, son of the former commander of the forces, arrived on horseback. Having just finished his duties in connection with the departure of the 20th Regiment, D'Urban immediately assumed command of the troops. Members of the congregation who had remained in Zion Church asked him for military protection to get home. He arranged an escort for them and ordered a detachment under Captain Cameron to escort Father Gavazzi back to St. Lawrence Hall. As shots continued to be fired from the direction of McGill Street, D'Urban placed himself at the head of the troops and patrolled along St. James Street and down McGill Street, the crowd dispersing as the troops approached. The shooting was heard as far away as Sherbrooke Street where the commander of the forces, Lt.-Gen. William Rowan, lived. He immediately rode to Hay Market, accompanied by Major Rowan, Capt. Fane Keane, and Lts. W. H. Noble and W. J. Lambert, his aides-de-camp. The presence of the commander of the forces gave an air of reassurance to the civil and military forces. When a reinforcement of 100 soldiers arrived from the barracks, 50 were stationed with some police near Zion Church to prevent it from being set on fire. The others were placed in the engine house where the final disturbance had broken out. Mayor Wilson, worn out with almost twelve hours of constant duty trying to secure the peace of the city and abused by many of the crowd, was escorted home by Macdonald and Ermatinger.

The day after the riot, the city had all the appearance of martial law. Picquets of soldiers were posted overnight at the mayor's home, St. Lawrence Hall, the engine house, and Zion Church. Capt. G. Rotton of the Royal Artillery with twenty-two gunners, two sergeants, and a trumpeter acted as a cavalry patrol in the area of the riot. Police Chief Charles Ermatinger and Dr. Walter Jones must have viewed the makeshift cavalry with some misgivings.[57] One charge of the Queen's Light Dragoons into the crowd on Great St. James Street the previous night would likely have sent the rioters fleeing, and the regulars would not now be facing the somewhat hostile and puzzled English-speaking population in Montreal.

While the joint coroners for the district of Montreal, Charles-Joseph Coursol and Joseph Jones, began initial preparations for an inquest into the deaths of those slain during the Gavazzi affair, the military authorities prepared their first reports of the shooting for Horse Guards. Lt.-Gen. William Rowan, the commander of the forces, whose service in Canada extended back to 1832 when he acted as Sir John Colborne's civil and military secretary in the upper province, wrote, "It is greatly to be regretted that from insufficient police arrangements, the Queen's Troops have been constantly called upon by the magistrates to aid in putting down tumultuous assemblages. . . . Every precaution has been taken by myself and my predecessors in the command to guard against the actual collision between the troops and any part of the inhabitants, so much so, as to have incurred the reproach of unwillingness to resort to extreme measures, even when considered to be necessary."[58]

Some 400 Montreal voters called a public meeting at which they formed the Committee of Vigilance, which was sent to ask the commander of the forces if the military intended to hold an inquiry. The deputy acting adjutant general, Capt. Frank Griffin, informed the committee that the "Lieutenant-General conceives that . . . the investigation now being made by the Coroners of Montreal . . . will be the one most likely to be satisfactory to the citizens of Montreal."[59] The Committee of Vigilance then called upon Mayor Wilson, who was holding a special council meeting to discuss the affair. F. W. Torrance, the secretary of the Vigilance Committee, asked what steps city council would take to preserve peace should Gavazzi lecture again that night. City Clerk J. P. Sexton frankly told him that the corporation "will do everything in their power to preserve peace, but are unable to give any guarantee that their efforts will be successful." The council admitted that they would have to call upon the military for aid if Gavazzi persisted in lecturing.[60]

Demands for a *gens d'armes* police system which would make military intervention during riots unnecessary were pressed on city authorities from several quarters. On 13 June the *Gazette* commented tartly, "If we required an example, one has been furnished which the present generation is not likely to forget, showing how imperfectly troops can be made to perform the duty of the Police." On 14 June the editor of the *Transcript* added his voice to those demanding an increase in the size of the police force, saying, "There ought to be not less than 200 regular police." The police committee of city council recommended that the force be increased to 100 men and be paid three shillings and ninepence a day instead of three shillings, "the men to be furnished with firearms and bayonets and drilled to their use."[61] City council agreed to increase the size and pay of the police, and ordered that they be supplied with "fusées or light muskets and bayonets, to be used in cases of great emergency."[62] The council tried unsuccessfully to buy arms from the ordnance stores. At first the commander of the forces agreed to allow arms for the police to be bought from military stores, providing the governor general issued the order, but this decision was reversed, ostensibly because arms could not "be spared from Ordnance."[63] The military command, recalling, perhaps, that most of the pistols issued to special constables during the riots of 1849 had not been returned to military stores and suspecting that some of the shots fired by the Gavazzi rioters had come from these very pistols,[64] were reluctant to issue more arms.

With the prudent retreat of Father Gavazzi to the United States at dawn on 11 June 1853, a semblance of calm returned to the city, although few of the civil or military authorities slept easily. So tense were feelings in the city that Councillor Charles Adams, whose son had been among those slain by the troops, demanded that the portrait of Mayor Wilson, which had been purchased by public subscription, be removed from the city council room until, as Adams somewhat acrimoniously remarked, "the Mayor could return honorably to the seat which is now vacant." Marchand, one of the city councillors who had favoured permitting Gavazzi to speak "to maintain the right of free discussion," chided the councillors for their harshness, and reminded them that "it was a boast of English liberty, that every man was innocent up to the moment that he is proved guilty."[65] Council decided to let the portrait of the mayor hang. Other more militant Montrealers decided otherwise. The mayor's portrait was slashed to bits by unknown parties.[66]

Rancorous feelings were not confined to the person of the mayor. Men of the 26th Regiment were waylaid and beaten, and when the surplice of the garrison chaplain, David Robertson, was found "covered with mud and impurities of other descriptions," the *Transcript* implied that the desecration was the work of soldiers of the 26th. The editor pointed out that the key to the chapel of the military cemetery where the surplice was kept was in the safekeeping of the noncommissioned officer on guard. The *Transcript* commented, "The 26th Regiment is certainly achieving for itself a most unenviable notoriety."[67]

The inquest began the day after the disaster, 10 June, and continued until 11 July. The sixteen-man jury listened to some 107 witnesses.[68] They included the five British officers in charge of the troops, a number of the privates and sergeants of the 26th Regiment, the two police chiefs and a number of constables, as well as Mayor Wilson, Joint Coroner Coursol, and numerous citizens who had attended the lecture or had been at Hay Market on the night of the riot.

Each group involved in the riot sought legal advice and protection. The soldiers were represented by advocate Gordon Mack, one of the men who had been arrested in 1849 during the Rebellion Losses riots. The officers were represented by Henry Stuart. Bernard Devlin was named to represent the interests of the Irish Catholics. The trustees of Zion Church named G. Robertson as their advocate, and William Badgley, a member of the provincial Parliament, watched the proceedings on behalf of the Crown. The Committee of Vigilance appointed John Ross and Francis G. Johnson as its lawyers. Mayor Wilson was represented by Christopher Dunkin. With such an array of legal talent present, the joint coroners began the proceedings with some trepidation.

The jury recommended that the proceedings of the inquest should not be published or commented upon in the press until the end of the inquest, but as the weeks wore on, such garbled versions of testimony were printed that on 20 June the coroners lifted the ban, "as it was infinitely better that the public should know, by responsible reporters, what was said, than gather the reports from mangled conversations."[69]

Testimony concerning the order to the troops to fire was completely contradictory. Several privates swore that Lieutenant-Colonel Hogarth gave the order. Two said it was Captain Cameron. Lieutenant Quarterley testified that the mayor gave the order, but both the mayor and the military officers denied that they gave the order to fire. Town Major Macdonald, who was standing near Captain Cameron in front of the upper division of troops when they fired, stated with some asperity, "I do not believe there is any officer in any army in the civilized world who would give an order to fire upon officers belonging to his own force." Near Macdonald at the time of the firing, though not directly in front of the troops, were Sir James Alexander and Captain Cressigny, both in undress uniforms. The town major, who stood six foot four in his stockings, remarked drily, "I am not such a small body that they could mistake me."[70]

Yet there was no doubt that the order to fire had been given. Numerous witnesses testified to hearing "Fire, Fire, there is no time to be lost,"[71] and several soldiers swore that they also heard the usual command of "ready, present" before they fired.[72] The only plausible explanation came from Margaret Brown Parker, a widowed schoolteacher who had recently arrived in Montreal from Upper Canada. Identifying herself as the "daughter of one who commanded in the 42nd Regiment," she claimed that a man in the crowd shouted the "words of command as well as Lieutenant-Colonel Hogarth could." She said she was standing close to the man, "a common Irishman . . . who wore a blue coat, made in the real old Irish fashion, and corduroy moleskin pantaloons that came to his boots, and a home made straw hat . . . not tall enough to be in a grenadier company, but tall enough to be a common soldier." When she taxed the man with causing trouble, he retorted, "Nineteen years Pat has served for a louzey [sic] shilling, now it takes Pat to suck Sandy." Another Irishman told her, "It was the Virgin Mary who gave the commands to fire," and then the two men disappeared into the crowd.[73]

Regardless of the identity of the person giving the command to fire which resulted in the lower division firing, no order was given to the upper division. Their firing was undoubtedly a gross breach of discipline.[74] These soldiers were facing the Unitarian Church where there was no riotous assembly. The people leaving Zion Church were standing about chatting, and in some cases were moving towards the troops and trying to stand between the two divisions while the mayor was ordering them to move along.

Unlike the police, whose two chiefs and one constable had been felled by stones, the soldiers had neither been stoned nor attacked, although immediately before their firing, two shots fired by the mob on Great St. James Street sped past the soldiers of the lower division and three shots were fired from the area of the church in the direction of the upper division. Yet these shots did not provoke the firing of the troops, for, after the incident, Captain Cameron ordered his men to be steady and they were. The firing of the upper division was taken up irregularly a few minutes after the lower division fired. Their firing was, as their colonel, their captain, and Town Major Macdonald frankly described it, "a bungling act."[75] Cameron denied that they fired in self-defence as had been the case at the Six Mile Bridge affair. Cameron admitted that even had Hogarth given the order to fire to the lower division, "My division would, most decidedly, not have been entitled to take up the firing from them."[76]

In answer to Haviland L. Routh's accusation that "a very great part of the slaughter would have been prevented, had . . . the officer in charge shewn that presence of mind and judgement which one holding so important a charge should have shewn," Hogarth replied that "one unsteady man will set a whole regiment to fire." Hogarth felt the criticism keenly. At the inquest he remarked that "Mr. Routh cast . . . a great slur on my character as a military man, for not ordering the men to cease firing sooner. . . . It is very difficult to cause troops to cease firing when they once begin. It is only by bugle it can be done." As Hogarth truly stated, the firing from both divisions had lasted only a few minutes, and before it ended, the bugler had sounded cease fire.[77]

It was part of the tragedy of the affair on 9 June that members of the military family abused each other. Routh, a Montrealer of military background, was one of the most outspoken in his criticism of the military. Town Major Macdonald, a military man raised from the ranks, who knew both townsman and soldier intimately and strove to keep the two in harmony, minced no words in his condemnation of the action of the troops. The soldiers were questioned closely by the officers' lawyer as to their drinking the night of the riot. The soldiers' lawyer reciprocated by asking officers whether they had drunk "champagne or wines or liquors . . . with the officers of the 20th previous to going on duty that night."[78] Both soldiers and officers denied that there had been any drinking. Even had there been any, the men and officers had been on duty since six o'clock and the firing did not occur until some time after eight, presumably time enough to sober up.

The English-language press, especially the *Gazette* which had invariably in the past championed the military, lashed out on 15 June at troops, police, and mayor with equal vigour, asserting that "the blood shed at Zion Church cries for justice." The more moderate *Transcript* was no less outspoken. On 11 June the editor asked, "Under what orders . . . we should like to know, was it that the gallant Regiment of Cameronians signalized their first landing in this Colony, by their uncalled for butchery, of which no man in office dares to take responsibility?" On 10 June the *Gazette* softened its tone a little by praising those soldiers who raised their muzzles when they fired, "seeing nothing but a peaceable congregation before them quietly moving off to their homes, else the consequences would have been still more terrific."

Newspaper accounts and some witnesses tended to emphasize the "peaceful" character of the congregation. Yet this image hardly accords with the facts. Arms had been stored in the basement of Zion Church, and armed members of the congregation left the church twice to ward off attackers and engaged in a running exchange of gunfire with the crowd outside. Two men of the attacking crowd, James Walsh and Michael Donnelly, were mortally wounded by gunfire from the church party before the troops fired. Thus, although those who were near the church at the moment that the troops fired may not have been among the armed members of the congregation, the picture of a peaceable congregation wending its way homeward after a peaceful church lecture is inaccurate.

The *Gazette*'s suggestion on 13 June that the disaster might have been "avoided by ordering the troops to charge instead of firing" was out of step with current military policy on riot control. After the bayonet killing of Julien Champeau in 1844, military authorities in Montreal had issued confidential instructions that "especial care must be taken not to allow the Troops to come into contact with the people—they must be held at arm's length. The Bayonet is very good when opposed to a regular Enemy, but it would be sacrificing much to attempt to use it when Hundreds are opposed to Thousands." The instructions emphasized that "Officers must at all times recollect that the two most important advantages possessed by Regular Troops over a Mob are Discipline and Fire."[79] In the Gavazzi riot the military lacked the first and employed the second.

After a month's investigation the coroners' inquest ended in a divided jury. Eight jurors, all English and Protestant, including the foreman, Henry Mulholland, decided that Mayor Wilson had given the order to fire. They expressed their regret "that any body of Her Majesty's troops should be found so wanting in discipline, as to fire without the lawful order of their officers." The jurors reprimanded the officers as well, stating their regret "that any circumstances of assumed urgency should have induced the officers in command to have departed from the ordinary practice of directing the soldiers to load in the presence of those on whom it was intended to fire, and that the soldiers had not been instructed, previous to their coming on the ground, as to how they should act in such an emergency."[80]

A minority report was presented by seven Catholic jurymen, including four French Canadians. This report, more moderate in tone, stated that the order to fire was "uttered by a person unknown, other than Col. Hogarth, Captain Cameron, Lieut. Quartley [*sic*], or other officer in command of the said troops."

The reprimand of the military was less severe than that of the solidly British party report. The minority report read,

> Although the undersigned Jurors do not reproach the military with having acted against the rules of military discipline, they nevertheless think it their duty to express themselves strongly against the precipitation with which the various orders and consequent movements are made by the military on like occasions, and would earnestly recommend that if unfortunately the services of the military should again be required for any similar purpose, the intervals between such different orders should be made long enough to admit of an opportunity to persons likely to be exposed to the fire of the troops to get safely out of reach.

Their report ended with the suggestion that "it would be desirable in future to rely rather on an armed police, than on the military for the suppression of dangerous riots."[81] A further divergence of opinion was recorded by three other French-Canadian jurors, who stated their general agreement with the minority report except for the paragraph respecting the armed police.

When the verdicts of the coroners' inquest were announced, English-language newspapers were not slow to criticize those jurors who did not agree with the majority in condemning the troops. On 16 July the *Gazette* testily commented that it was thought that "the Romanist jurors would view the evidence as all men of intelligence out of the jury did, and condemn them [the military]." Neither the men nor the officers escaped the *Gazette*'s condemnation. "Even if the soldiers had received word to fire, they are guilty . . . because at the time they fired upon the men, women and children before them, there was nothing to justify the act. The officers of that Regiment are, to civilian eyes, no credit to the service, in having a Regiment so defective in discipline, and the men of that detachment insult the memory of the enthusiastic Cameronians, who so profusely shed their blood, in defence of their strong Protestant principles." On 13 July the *Transcript* observed, with less censure on the troops, "The verdict delivered is . . . no verdict at all. . . . It was a most extraordinary caricature of English jurisdiction. . . . The jury divided according to their religious creeds. . . . Everybody knows that no justice is to be had in the matter, nor can anyone tell when it will end."

As soon as the coroners' inquest closed, military authorities ordered a court of inquiry to "investigate and report upon certain points connected with the apparent neglect . . . of the detachment of troops employed in aid of civil power . . . and the apparent want of discipline and steadiness manifested by the soldiers on that occasion." The court began its inquiry behind closed doors 18 July and recommended that Sgt. John Conner and the privates who swore that they received the order to fire from their officers be tried by court-martial, "thus affording them an opportunity of proving their charge." Lieutenant-General Rowan wrote to military authorities in England that he would not take any steps "with reference to the conduct of the officers and soldiers . . . without . . . receiving instructions [from Viscount Hardinge, commander-in-chief of the army]."[82]

No action was taken to hold a court-martial because civil authorities proceeded with indictments for murder against Lieutenant-Colonel Hogarth, Lieutenant Quarterley, and a number of privates. Not only were officers and soldiers indicted, but so, too, were Mayor Wilson, Augustus Heward, Murdock Morrison, and seven other Montrealers, including Robert Cooke and Alfred Perry,[83] both of whom along with Heward had been arrested in 1849 during the Rebellion Losses riots.

To ensure that disturbances would not accompany the trials of the soldiers and Montrealers charged with the deaths, Lieutenant-General Rowan, who was acting as administrator of government during Lord Elgin's absence from the country, decided to bring 200 enrolled military pensioners to Montreal during the session of criminal court "to act as a local Police Force . . . under the superintendence of B. C. A. Gugy."[84] The need for such an external force was evident from the experience of Samuel Medill of the Water Police. During the inquest Medill had identified several of the leaders of the crowd that attacked the church. From that time Medill believed he was a "marked man."[85] At one time it was reported that he had been murdered, but later it was learned that "he had skipped town to avoid it." The *Orange Lily* of Bytown, commenting on Medill's experience, claimed that the "Water Police were the only legal force in Montreal at the time of the riots which did their duty."[86] It may have been that such praise coming from such a source eventually led to the demise of the Water Police, for within six years the force was disbanded,[87] both the city corporation and the Harbour Commission refusing to continue to finance it.

At the fall session of Supreme Court, the grand jury threw out the bills against the officers and soldiers, as well as the charge against the mayor. Once the civil charges against the soldiers were dropped, military authorities went ahead with a general court-martial "for the vindication of Military Discipline." It was proposed to try several of the soldiers "for having . . . fired off their muskets loaded with Ball Cartridge, towards a crowd of people . . . without having received any orders so to fire . . . from Brevet Lt. Col. Hogarth . . . or from any other of their Superior Officers . . . such conduct being insubordinate, unsoldierlike and to the Prejudice of good order and military discipline." Doubts were expressed by some of the officers as to whether the soldiers could be legally tried by a military tribunal "for a crime which, though intended to be strictly a military one, so closely merges on the more serious offence of felony."[88] The military hierarchy sought the advice of Attorney General Lewis Drummond, who gave his opinion that the proceedings were legal. The court-martial assembled 17 November 1853 with Col. Plomer Young as president and Capt. J. R. Michell, Royal Artillery, as judge advocate.

Pvt. James Macullock was brought before the court first. His lawyer, Gordon Mack, who had also represented the soldiers at the coroners' inquest, objected to the court-martial itself on the ground that the civil court had acquitted the soldier.[89] The officers, still dubious about the legality of their proceedings, adjourned the court-martial to await further advice from the attorney general. In an unusual move Mack, supported by lawyer Henry Stuart, appeared before Judge Thomas Cushing Aylwin of the Supreme Court on 22 November to argue against the competency of a military tribunal to try the soldiers.[90] Mack used the argument that had been presented by Joint Coroner Joseph Jones in his charge to the jury at the close of the inquest when he emphasized that the soldiers were "merely armed citizens and may like citizens interfere to repress an affray or riot, and if resisted are justified in killing the resister, and like other citizens are subject to the law and its punishments."[91] This surprising interpretation could apply only to soldiers who happened as individuals to be in the area where a riot was occurring. It could hardly apply to armed soldiers, deliberately marched to a scene of riot on the orders of their officers and accompanied by a magistrate. In the latter circumstance the soldiers were under military discipline when it came to the use of firearms. Mack argued that the soldiers "had orders from the Civil Magistrate [Mayor Wilson] to fire, that a soldier never ceases to be a citizen, and is bound to obey the order of . . . the Mayor, in quelling a riot." He then asked, "How was he amenable to a military court for performing his duty as a citizen?"[92] Stuart based his argument against a court-martial on the ground that in this particular case the charge of felony could not be separated from that of a breach of military discipline and that such a charge could only be tried in a civil court.

As the civil authorities had already acquitted the soldiers, the defence lawyers evidently expected that by insisting that the offence of the soldiers, if any, was a civil offence, the soldiers would be exonerated completely without a court-martial. Attorney General Drummond, appearing for Lt.-Col. A. T. Hemphill, commandant of the Montreal garrison who had ordered the court-martial, spoke forcefully in favour of the court-martial procedure. He argued that "the real liberty of the subject depended upon the proper discipline of the Soldiers . . . were it permitted to men with arms to fire, without receiving proper instructions, an end would soon be put to that liberty of the subject."[93]

Judge Aylwin, in an another surprising development, decided that the court-martial was not competent to hear the case. In a powerful charge, he stated that if a "soldier is tried for disobedience of orders in firing among a crowd, . . . and makes out a justification [that he was] obeying the civil magistrate, . . . he is liable to be indicted for murder . . . and if in his capacity as a citizen, he obeyed the Mayor's order to discharge his musket, he violates military discipline. This would be placing the soldier in the most dangerous position and, to avoid this, the law ordered the . . . party to be brought before the civil tribunal."[94] He therefore recommended the attorney general to bring Private Macullock before the next session of Supreme Court. Drummond, somewhat stymied, declared that the civil authorities had nothing against the soldier.

Military authorities were only too well aware that public opinion was still focused on the events of 9 June. The trials of two of the church party, Augustus Heward and Murdock Morrison, for murder, and of Garrett Barry, Michael Devaney, Michel Moses, Pierre Brouillet, and Thomas Patton for riot and assault, were still going on,[95] while the military party seemingly was let off. The trials ended with the acquittal of Heward and Morrison, and the cases of those charged with riot and assault were pushed ahead to the next spring.[96] On 4 November the editor of the *Transcript* asked somewhat caustically, "Where are the guilty? On whose heads rests this unavenged blood?" The answer of the commander of the forces was to go ahead with the court-martial in spite of Judge Aylwin's charge.[97] Another private was brought before the court on the same charge as Private Macullock, but the court decided to transmit the judgement of Judge Aylwin to Horse Guards "to receive the opinion of the highest authorities on its legality."[98] The court then adjourned.

Whether civil and military authorities were simply stalling for time until public resentment should die down is difficult to know.[99] The soldiers had been brought before civil authorities who had acquitted them; the attempt to have the charge of military insubordination tried in a military tribunal was thwarted by Judge Aylwin's opinion that such a tribunal was not competent to deal with the case. In January 1854 when it was announced that the Cameronians would be transferred to Quebec, the *Transcript* observed pointedly on 24 January that as "the catastrophe of June 9th remains to be farther investigated at Horse Guards, this will, we suppose, obviate all possibility of interference from the Judges of the Civil Courts." The taunt was not lost on the officers of the 26th. They requested a general court-martial to "investigate their conduct on that occasion," and steps were put in motion to reassemble the general court-martial that had adjourned 28 November. By 10 March, however, military authorities changed their minds about a general court-martial and announced simply, "It has not been considered advisable to revive the inquiry into that unhappy business." Instead, the commander of the forces, in a harsh general order, reproved both officers and soldiers of the 26th. In the order Rowan expressed "his deep regret that in consequence of a total disregard of H.M.'s Regulations for the Guidance of Officers commanding detachments proceeding to suppress riots and disturbances, a gross breach of discipline occurred on the 9th June last, which has not only tended to impair the unanimity and good understanding which should exist between officers and soldiers of a corps, but has brought discredit on the previous high character of the 26th Regiment for discipline and subordination."[100]

This reproof was not sufficient for the more bitter of the English newspapers. The editor of the *Herald* spoke of the "disgraceful defection of the officers" and asked why they had not put the men under arrest if they had fired without orders, and if the officers gave the orders, why the officers had not been cashiered.[101] The editor of the *Transcript* confined his rebuke to the individual regiment, rather than abusing the garrison generally, and on 24 January announced "with much pleasure that the 26th will be relieved by our old friends, the 66th, whose verdant facings will be once more welcome to our eyes."

At the spring session of Supreme Court in 1854 no charges were preferred against the soldiers by Crown authorities, and no evidence could be found in military records of any further action by military authorities. Except for a few letters and references in general orders, military records are silent on the subject of the Gavazzi riot, and it may be that most of the records relating to the affair were returned to Horse Guards at the same time as Judge Aylwin's judgement. The cases of the civilians charged with riot were adjourned to the fall session of Supreme Court in 1854 when all were acquitted.[102] Thus, neither civilians nor soldiers suffered any legal penalties in connection with the Gavazzi riot, but the affair seared the traditionally amicable relations between the garrison and civilian population and within the English-language community.

How deeply the men and officers of the 26th Regiment felt the reproof of the commander of the forces and the hostility of the city can only be hinted at. Sir James Alexander came to their defence. "The men fired from misapprehension . . . and I am sure they regretted extremely, as we all did, the innocent people who fell by that fire. There was much to be said in excuse for the men . . . [as] many . . . fired high on purpose, else the loss of life would have been much greater."[103] Captain Cameron, who had run along the front ranks of his division throwing up the soldiers' muskets at the risk of his own life, felt the censure keenly. He retired from the service by the sale of his commission.[104] Lieutenant-Colonel Hogarth, who had served for thirty-six years in the army, died suddenly on the eve of the departure of the regiment for Bermuda in the fall of 1854.[105]

The only positive result of the Gavazzi riot was the realization on the part of civil authorities that troops made indifferent policemen. A gesture towards the police was made in the form of a pay increase from three shillings to three and ninepence, but the force remained underpaid and undermanned until the sixties.

With the unsung departure of the 26th from Montreal in the spring of 1854, coupled with the exigencies of the Crimean War, the garrison for the first time in a hundred years was reduced to less than half a regiment.[106]

Soldiers as Firemen

If military aid to the civil power during riots was the most onerous and least popular of garrison duties, military aid at fires was probably the function of the garrison most appreciated by the townsmen. In the early forties protection against fires in the city was afforded by a volunteer fire department, flanked by elaborate regulations and by-laws. The enforcement of the fire regulations, as well as inspection of buildings and chimneys, and the general supervision of the fire companies were under the control of the Fire Society, established under an ordinance passed by the Special Council.[1] When the city was incorporated in 1841, this ordinance continued, the Fire Department coming under the control of the Fire Committee of city council.[2]

Heading the Fire Department was a paid staff composed of an inspector, superintendent–chief engineer, and one or more overseers of sweeping. The various companies of twenty to twenty-five volunteers were each officered by a captain and a lieutenant. Captains were responsible for the equipment and discipline of the men of their company, and were required to keep an up-to-date roll of the names of their firemen, together with their residences and occupations. Firemen were paid for attendance at fires only, captains receiving ten shillings, lieutenants seven and sixpence, and volunteers five shillings.

In the early forties there were five fire stations and seven companies, including one hook and ladder company and one hose company,[3] totalling about 150 volunteer firemen. By the time of the burning of Parliament House in 1849, there were ten fire stations and companies and about 200 men under John Perrigo as inspector and chief engineer.[4] For ordinary fires these volunteers were adequate. From the early forties they were regularly drilled and, in 1846, despite some opposition, the fire companies were organized into a militia infantry battalion, the Montreal Fire Battalion, by order of Lord Cathcart, the commander of the forces and governor.[5] The adjutant general of militia of Canada East, Lt.-Col. Augustus Gugy, opposed this move,[6] for he believed it was done simply to give a lieutenant-colonelcy to the mayor, James Ferrier. Councillor Benjamin Lyman was made major of the battalion, and two of the fire captains, John Fletcher and Alexander Bertram, were made lieutenants.[7] The militia volunteer fire companies drilled without arms during the winter in the Bonsecours Market Hall, and as many of the volunteer firemen came from the more affluent sector of society, they supplied their own infantry uniforms, the cost of which ranged from twenty-four to seventy dollars. By 1849 the Fire Battalion had outdistanced the fire companies in enrolment. In the annual militia returns for July 1849, there were five militia fire companies of 461 volunteers,[8] but the regular fire companies numbered about 200.

Partisan feeling and activity in municipal institutions were more likely to be found within this volunteer Fire Battalion than among the city and canal police. The latter, as full-time paid servants, had to be more circumspect in the expression of political sympathies. The firemen, as volunteers, could be independent. At the time of the Rebellion Losses riots, for instance, it was the firemen's ringing of their engines through the streets that brought the crowd to Champ de Mars.[9] Two officers and one fireman were among those arrested on charges of riot, but they were not convicted.[10] Again in 1853 two officers of Hero Fire Company were identified by police as leaders in the Gavazzi riots.[11] Although arrested, they, too, were subsequently acquitted.

Yet, despite political and religious tensions among the various fire companies, the volunteer firemen served well, calling on the military only in fires of grave dimensions. In a city largely of wooden houses, built close together in narrow streets, the possibility of fire was always present. In winter the stove used for heating was a wood-burning oblong type with three pipes called "gallow pipes" placed on top of the stove to throw out more heat. These pipes became very hot in a few minutes but cooled off quickly unless a brisk fire was kept up, "and not infrequently the pipes took fire and then set the chimney on fire."[12] Curiously enough, the gravest fires occurred, not in winter when these heating stoves were all ablaze, but in summer. The advantage of fewer stoves being in operation in summer was offset by the dryness of the wooden houses and the lower water supply.

One of the first serious fires requiring troops occurred in Griffintown on 4 October 1845.[13] Mayor Ferrier requested troops at about four o'clock in the morning, as the fire was rapidly spreading. Two companies of the 52nd Oxfordshire Light Infantry and the 93rd Sutherland Highlanders were sent immediately, and as the fire became more extensive, the commandant, Lt.-Col. R. Spark, followed with four additional companies, "part of them with arms for the protection of property, the rest without arms to assist the firemen." The mayor thought it necessary to blow up two brick houses to prevent the fire passing to an adjoining part of the city, and a party of the Royal Artillery used a barrel of gunpowder to effect this. The fire levelled thirty-six houses and left 109 families homeless. The commandant reported that the "officers and soldiers exerted themselves to the utmost in saving property and assisting the Fire Companies, the inhabitants standing by idly." City authorities lost no time in expressing their appreciation to the troops. At the first meeting of the corporation after the fire, they passed a resolution of thanks to Lieutenant-Colonel Spark "for having permitted troops to assist and for having himself remained during the whole period of the disaster, directing their well-timed and energetic exertions."[14] Mayor Ferrier also expressed to Governor General Metcalfe "his very high sense . . . of the services which [the soldiers] rendered."[15]

The military faced a delicate situation in 1848 with regard to fires. Intelligence of the activities of Irish nationalists from the United States among the Montreal Irish was causing some concern, especially as it was believed that "fires were wilfully resorted to for the purpose of distracting the attention of the military."[16] A series of fires in March and April lent credence to the fear that the fires were being deliberately set as a diversion to an attempt to get possession of the depots and magazines on St. Helen's Island or to set them on fire.[17] On 2 March 1848 troops were called to a fire on Craig Street where nineteen wooden houses were burned,[18] and, again, on 26 April troops were called out by Mayor Joseph Bourret and City Councillor Benjamin Lyman to assist at a fire at the east end of the city. A detachment of 138 troops under Major Granville, including an armed party of thirty privates, helped put out the fire, which destroyed thirty homes.[19] The day following this fire, the commander of the forces, Sir Benjamin D'Urban, alarmed at the frequent calling out of the troops, issued confidential instructions against the use of troops at fires, leaving it to the discretion of the officers on duty to determine whether the fire was serious enough to warrant the furnishing of troops.[20]

Early the next morning, 28 April, a fire broke out in Griffintown. Lyman, in urging Maj.-Gen. Sir Charles Gore to send troops, told him the fears that "the whole of that suburb would go." The mayor sent a "pressing message for assistance as the firemen were positively worn out."[21] Gore sent both a messenger and his aide-de-camp to make sure that the fire was accidental before he ordered Captain Chester and 100 soldiers of the 23rd Royal Welsh Fusiliers out. But by the time the troops arrived, the fire had been extinguished and the troops returned to barracks.[22] Gore received a testy reprimand the next day from the commander of the forces for having sent the troops. In a somewhat petulant tone, Gore replied by outlining the dilemma that field officers now faced when asked for troops in aid of fires. He pointed out that "in the confidential instructions, I am informed that the precautions [to discover if the fire was legitimate or deliberate] are to be taken without ostentation. . . . had I refused to give the troops on this occasion, pressed as I was by a member of the Corporation and the application of the Mayor, it would have been immediately noticed in all the papers, and as assistance has always been given on the application of the Mayor or Corporation, in fires, I thought it prudent and judicious to do so."[23]

No further requests for troops were made during the summer of 1848. On 27 November when the mayor again applied for troops to aid in arresting a fire on Bonaventure Street, 150 men without arms and 50 with arms under Lieutenant-Colonel Hay of the 19th Regiment were sent immediately, although they arrived after the fire was put out.[24] In December the military had its own incendiary problems when the prison on St. Helen's Island burned down.[25] The prison had housed military prisoners from the Montreal district who were sentenced by district or garrison courts-martial for periods longer than forty days. The forty-five prisoners "behaved in an exemplary manner" during the fire, assisting their comrades-in-arms in every manner. When the fire was put out, all prisoners were present.[26] The problem of finding a new prison in mid-winter was solved temporarily by sending them to the Quebec Gate Barracks. Major-General Gore was "anxious not to send any Prisoners to the gaol of this City, if it can possibly be avoided," and he asked permission from the commander of the forces to have ten cells at the cavalry barracks at Hochelaga prepared as a district military prison.[27] To remove the "slight coating of ice" that covered the walls of the Hochelaga Barracks, a few fires were lit in stoves and the Royal Engineers made some minor repairs before the military prisoners moved to their new quarters, a number of them having been pardoned "because of their good behaviour during the fire."[28]

Military aid to the city fire companies took an unusual turn in the spring of 1849. When Parliament House was put to the torch on the evening of 25 April, Capt. John Fletcher was on duty at Protector Company Fire Station on Notre Dame Street. As soon as the alarm sounded, he had his firemen at the scene but the crowd shouted at them, "Take the engine away, boys" and "no attempt was permitted the firemen to save the Legislative Building."[29] An urgent request for troops to aid the firemen was sent to the commandant of the garrison and he detached 100 men of the 19th Regiment.[30] On their arrival at about nine o'clock, the troops helped to hold back the crowd, while an armed party was placed near the fire engine to allow the firemen to work it and armed sentries were posted to protect firemen. Thus troops undertook the unusual chore of guarding firemen from fellow citizens intent on preventing them from putting out a fire. So intense was feeling against the firemen for attempting to do their duty that they were assaulted going to and from fires during the summer by "roughs prowling about."[31]

Newspapers observed that the "troops which have often turned out at an ordinary fire were not on the spot at the Parliament House till the mischief was done, and it was too late to be of the slightest service."[32] This was true of the burning of the Parliament Building itself, but it was only with the arrival of the troops that the firemen were able to work at all and to prevent the fire from spreading to the Grey Nunnery and to the houses on the north side of Parliament House.[33]

The assistance of the troops was sought again on 23 August 1850 when fire threatened to get out of hand on Craig Street. At the request of the mayor and magistrates, an armed party of 100 men of the 20th Regiment aided firemen, while Councillor Lyman authorized Royal Artillerymen to blow up a range of brick buildings belonging to Perrault and Perrault Company to halt the spread of the fire.[34] This fire, aggravated by a low water supply, led to the construction of an aqueduct which, it was hoped, would provide an adequate supply of water in summer.

For both regulars and Montrealers the summer of 1852 was by far the most distressing with regard to fires. Two occurred in the heart of the city, and before they were finished, the centre of Montreal was all but destroyed. Soldier and townsman worked until they dropped from fatigue trying to control the fires that engulfed some 1,400 houses and left 8,000 homeless,[35] including the officers of the garrison whose major lodgings at Cornwall Terrace and Durham Place were wiped out.

The first fire broke out in a carpenter's shop on St. Peter's Street about six o'clock in the morning of 6 June. A high wind carried sparks to the roof of the Custom House, and fire swept down St. Paul Street destroying nearly a whole block of buildings. Magistrate J. Beaudry, in a scribbled note to the commandant, stated tersely, "The city is now in [sic] fire in its most valuable part and this request is to ask the assistance of the military."[36] Two hundred men of the 20th Regiment rushed to Custom House Square where the fire was raging. A detachment of troops helped civilians carry sick people from the nearby Hotel Dieu, while another detachment of twenty armed soldiers stood guard over property that had been carried for safety to the King's Wharf.[37] Before it was spent, the fire had consumed some thirty buildings.

Scarcely a month later the city was devastated by another fire of such magnitude that city authorities took stringent measures to enforce the law against the construction of wooden buildings in the centre of the city. At this fire the entire military establishment on Dalhousie Square was threatened. The fire began at a baker's shop on St. Lawrence Main at nine o'clock in the morning of 8 July. Little or no water could be had because new pipe arrangements were being fitted up in the city reservoir subsequent to the disastrous fire of 6 June.[38] A brisk westerly breeze carried burning shingles from one wooden rooftop to another along the entire area from St. Lawrence to St. Denis Streets. Even stone buildings with tin roofs did not escape as their wooden gutters took fire. Temperatures soared to ninety degrees in the shade as blankets of flames several hundred yards wide leaped fifty feet above the tallest buildings and sent flaming shingles as far as St.

Helen's Island where "the greatest watchfulness was necessary . . . on account of sparks and burning shingles flying across and alighting about the large magazine."[39]

Troops were rushed to St. Dominique Street where the married officers' quarters were in flames.[40] Maj. Sir James Alexander, who was among those residing at Cornwall Terrace, and Lady Alexander had just left on a journey to Galt, Canada West, leaving their two young sons in the charge of maidservants. The children were saved from amid burning flakes by Maj. J. W. Mitchell of the Royal Artillery who carried them to his own home. Alexander, learning of the disaster while at Hamilton, returned to Montreal to find that he, like most of the officers, was bereft of all "my swords, belts, best books, guns and rifle, gymnastic apparatus, and trophies of the chase in Africa. . . . those of my effects which were not destroyed or stolen were scattered, though the horses, carriage and sleigh were saved . . . and, thankful that no lives were lost, we tried to make the best of our position, others having suffered as much as we had."[41]

The city presented a fearful sight as distracted inhabitants ran to and fro with bags of hurriedly gathered up clothing. Thieves made off with chests of plate, jewellery, and cash boxes that were never seen again. Priests and nuns devoutly sprinkled holy water around in the hope that the flames would not envelop their cathedral and bishop's palace.[42] By five o'clock in the evening the fire had reached the open square of Viger Market. Firemen and troops pulled down the market while the Royal Artillery, with the consent of the mayor, blew up buildings near the market to increase the area of open space.[43] Fears were felt that a fire raging on Craig and St. Lewis Streets would threaten the military offices, but Maj. Hugh Crofton with a large party of the 20th Regiment worked a town fire engine manually and managed to subdue the fire. Another company of the 20th succeeded in saving Campeau's building where they were quartered. By seven o'clock in the evening the fire, having nothing more to feed upon in the open space of Viger Market, abated. Troops were withdrawn and, like their civilian firemen comrades, retired exhausted to barracks.

In less than two hours the alarm sounded anew. Flames broke out at the rear of Durham Place on St. Lewis Street just north of Dalhousie Square. Within a short space of time Durham Place, the other major officers' quarters, was in flames and the fire spread rapidly to Hays Hotel[44] on Dalhousie Square and to another building on the square used as officers' quarters. The fire raced down St. Mary Street into the Quebec suburbs beyond Dalhousie Square, destroying not only all the officers' quarters, but also the Royal Artillery and Engineers' mess, with its wine supply, and offices of the military secretary and Royal Engineers' headquarters. Only the books and papers of the Engineers' office were saved through the exertions of the clerk of works, P. Hanlon, and his staff.[45]

To save the infantry and the artillery barracks at Quebec Gate Barracks, two adjoining buildings were blown up by the Royal Artillery while Major Mitchell rigged up a water supply from the river to keep a continuous stream of water drenching the roofs of the barracks.[46] The Quebec Gate Barracks were saved even though the gutters and rafters were smoking at times from the heat. The fire, having swept as far as the jail at the eastern boundary of the city, raged all night and left a trail a mile and a half broad of blackened and crumbling walls and "tall chimneys standing in all directions like gigantic tombstones."[47] In the morning the commissariat fuel yard east of the barracks took fire and continued to burn for two days "carefully watched" by the military.[48]

Severe as was the loss to the military, with all the officers' quarters and their effects burned, the Royal Artillery and Engineers' mess destroyed, as well as the fuel yard and several hired offices, it was nothing compared with the devastation suffered by the city generally. Estimates placed those homeless at between 8,000 and 12,000.[49] Military authorities erected tents to house the homeless,[50] and others were temporarily cared for in the emigrant sheds at Point St. Charles. As in 1844 when troops quelled election riots, praise flowed in from all directions to the commander of the forces and the soldiers of the 20th Regiment. City councillors conveyed their thanks directly to military authorities and expressed to Lord Elgin their appreciation of the services of the troops.

From Horse Guards, Lord Fitzroy Somerset wrote that "the Commander-in-Chief [the Duke of Wellington] had derived great satisfaction from . . . this report of the praiseworthy conduct of the officers and men composing the garrison of Montreal." The officer most knowledgeable of the exertions of the troops, Major Crofton, spoke in the highest terms of the efforts of Lord Mark Kerr and of the officers and men of the 20th Regiment. Yet his report carried the usual bite of military men against civil authorities. He censured them for the failure of the water supply and observed that "there was no concert amongst the authorities or fire companies." The efforts of the military deserved and received praise, and when fire broke out at St. Helen's Island a month later, city firemen tried to reciprocate. Ten men of the Hook and Ladder Company "very materially aided by their exertions in pulling down the beams on fire in the stables and afterwards turning the straw with their hooks."[51]

In the period from the 1837–38 Rebellions to the Crimean War, the regulars in garrison played a variety of roles in aiding the civil power at fires. They provided help to worn-out city firemen in arresting the flames; they protected firemen when civil tension was so high that irate citizens prevented firemen from approaching the burning Parliament Building; they blew up buildings at the request of civil authorities in an effort to prevent the spread of fires, and, above all, they provided armed detachments to guard private property from looters. In the most devastating fires, when the city water supply failed, Royal Engineers were able to organize a makeshift water supply from the St. Lawrence River. The city expressed its gratitude generously and sincerely, and it is not surprising that the 20th Regiment, which saw the city through its most devastating summer of fires, received from its inhabitants such cordial expressions of friendship when it left the city in 1853 to make way for the newly arrived troops of the 26th Cameronians.

Part

The Cultural Dimension of the Garrison

The officers of the local garrison with their
bright uniforms and gentlemanly manners were
an acquisition to Montreal society, literary, social, and artistic, and to whom, apart from their
extravagances, the colony is largely indebted for
its heritage of culture, literature and art.
William H. Atherton, *Montreal, 1535–1914,* ɪɪ

The Soldier at Leisure

Unlike modern army establishments that tend to be so hidden away that the civilian population is hardly aware of their existence, the British garrison in Montreal was so involved in a multitude of social activities, sports, religious functions, and fraternal and cultural relationships with townsmen that the townspeople seldom went a day without encountering the military at some level. Whether it was a brilliantly uniformed officer adding a touch of colour to the pageantry at the opening of the Legislature, or a somewhat less than sober private helping to fill the coffers of an unlicensed grogshop in Griffintown, or even a Cameronian bent over a candlelit school desk at Quebec Gate Barracks as he learned to read from a locally hired teacher—all found their way into the lives of Montrealers.

The rebellion era had tended to unsettle routine patterns of life in the city, so much so that the Baptist minister-historian Newton Bosworth regretted to find that "the passions drawn forth by rebellion not only diverted Montrealers from their regular course of action, but have introduced a martial and unsettled spirit which has operated unfavourably upon a large portion of the community." With misgivings he noted that "many of the regular troops are from time to time seen reeling on the streets, to the interruption of that good order which their services are so efficient in pro-

145

moting; and that intemperance has increased among the volunteers since they received pay."[1]

The charge of drunkenness against the soldiers and their influence in encouraging others to drink has been repeated by both the British and French Canadians. Robert Jones in his *History of Agriculture* suggested that it was the large demands of the resident soldiery that were responsible for the breweries and distilleries that sprang up in the early part of the nineteenth century. E.-Z. Massicotte, in deploring the decline of athletic prowess among French Canadians at the end of the nineteenth century, blamed the military for introducing "l'usage des boissons contenant un fort pourcentage d'alcoöl . . . parmi nous. . . . comme la jamaïque et le whiskey se vendaient à un prix dérisoire, ils pénétrèrent partout. . . . Les soldats anglais . . . ont été témoins de formidables orgies. Les cultivateurs cependant, échappèrent plus que les autres à la contagion."[2]

The military command did not believe that the corruption was entirely one-sided. Maj. John Richardson noted that "drunkenness pervades almost all classes of people, and is the besetting sin of the country . . . which naturally extends itself to the soldiers who are invited to spend their money in that manner." Drinking was such that another contemporary observed that "he was considered a moderate man who does not exceed four glasses of whiskey in the day."[3]

Attempts to control the intemperance of soldiers and young officers and to protect them against corrupting influences of the city were made by senior officers, who assumed an almost paternal attitude towards their men. The lieutenant-colonel of the 19th Regiment complained that his men were located in the dirtiest part of the city where liquor was cheap and easily procured.[4] He urged that his men be moved from the Water Street Barracks to other quarters. In the case of a young aide-de-camp who persisted in frequenting the company of "some French and Polish refugees . . . drinking and smoking with them . . . and running down the English service," the commander of the forces wrote to the young miscreant's father, a fellow officer, explaining the circumstances and the decision to close "his life of idleness and dissipation" by getting him away from Montreal society and returning him to his own regiment, "decidedly the best school for young officers."[5]

Senior officers did what they could to protect younger officers whose behaviour sometimes left something to be desired, but the patience of senior officers wore thin in the case of chronic offenders. Then punishment was sure and swift. Ensign J. E. W. Hussey of the 39th Regiment was brought before a general court-martial for being drunk at a public dinner at Donegani's Hotel. He was found guilty and given a severe reprimand which carried with it a form of public disgrace. It was ordered that the reprimand be read at the head of "every Regiment in this Command . . . to remind young Officers that their conduct and character are not exclusively their own, they belong to and must always materially affect the discipline and character of the service of which they are members."[6]

So prevalent had drunkenness become in 1840 that the commander of the forces issued a general order about the care of drunken soldiers, as, "to his regret," he had "reason to believe that instances of such extreme drunkenness sometimes occur, as to render a man liable to sudden death." Sir Richard Jackson ordered that "in every case of this beastly nature, the stock, shirt, collar and waistband of the Drunkard may be loosened, and that he may never be placed in a situation where he will be removed from the observation of an N.C.O. who will apply for medical assistance if necessary."[7] But other influences were at work in the city to counter the prevalence of drunkenness. This was the decade of Father Charles Chiniquy whose crusade for temperance attracted tens of thousands of Montrealers, including soldiers from the Quebec Gate Barracks. Soldiers were also among those who attended the temperance lectures given by Phineas Taylor Barnum when he was in Montreal with General Tom Thumb. Another temperance lecturer, J. G. Gough, a son of a pensioner of the 52nd Regiment, was invited to give a special lecture to the garrison where the soldiers "heard him with great attention; he made them laugh one minute and they were sobbing . . . the next. Of their own accord they asked him to lecture again; many took the pledge and kept it."[8]

In looking for causes of dissipation among young officers, senior officers pointed with some justice to the mess. Even the central army bureaucracy located at the Horse Guards in London was concerned about the influence of the mess on the junior officers. In a confidential memorandum, the Horse Guards urged officers commanding in Montreal to inculcate "an early economy, frugality and careful watchfulness over the social habits of young officers" by limiting subscriptions to mess funds and by cautioning them against taking credit from mess men. Horse Guards attributed to the "habits of luxury which prevail in those messes . . . many instances of young officers . . . becoming involved in inextricable financial difficulties." The commander-in-chief deprecated the mess equipment in most regiments as "wholly unsuited to that simplicity and absence of ostentation which ought to characterize such an establishment as the British Army." He declared that "the purchase of rich services of plate and glass must be discouraged . . . [and] that whatever is too costly to be attainable by the poorest members of the Regiment without deranging their finances, must be considered luxuries."[9]

For both officer and townsman, the military mess was not always regarded as a place of pleasure. When Edward Hale, a member of the Special Council in 1840, and his brother-in-law, Charles Montizambert, the provincial assistant civil secretary, were invited to dine at the Royal Artillery mess at Dalhousie Square, Hale confessed that "though I got away by nine o'clock (we went there only at seven) . . . the noise of the mess was such that I woke during the night with a bad head-ache."[10] But the mess was not to be avoided either by staff officers. When it was reported to the Horse Guards that one senior staff officer at Montreal made it a habit to decline all invitations to dine at regimental messes, the commander of the forces was instructed to urge all general officers to "avail themselves of such . . . invitations . . . so as to see how the messes are conducted and to observe the tone and character of the officers."[11]

Just as the army command tried to protect its young officers from financial difficulties, intemperance, and the lures of Montreal social life, so, too, it attempted to protect the rank and file from some of the more harmful temptations of garrison life. Some thousand or more soldiers were quartered in Montreal each year from 1839 to 1854, only 6 per cent of whom were allowed to receive army rations and barrack lodgings for their families.

Strict rules existed governing the behaviour of those wives entitled to barrack space. The standing orders of the 23rd Royal Welsh Fusiliers stated that "no woman is to be allowed in barracks who objects to mak[ing] herself useful in the Regiment, in washing and mending, in cleaning rooms, assisting the cooking, and attending the sick women when occasion requires." The women of the regiment were expected "when they appear out to be clean and respectable, and regular in their attendance at their respective places of religious worship on Sundays." Expulsion from the corps altogether was the price paid by any woman caught bringing "spiritous liquors into barracks or quarters of the men" or infringing upon the orders of the regiment in any way. Even the choice of a wife was not left entirely to the soldier. Before he married, he had to apply for permission from the captain of his company, who "will make all inquiry as to the character and usefulness of the woman" before the application from the soldier was forwarded to the commanding officer for a decision.[12] Few married men could afford to bring their families to Canada and provide for them at their own expense. Thus most of these soldiers, unless they chose to lead a somewhat monastic life, found their way to a favourite tavern once their afternoon duties were over and remained there until tattoo beat a return to barracks at eight o'clock.

The army command had no illusions about the manner in which the soldier spent his leisure time. Even in 1851, when the 20th Regiment was earning a reputation for its sobriety and devotion to temperance, which resulted in an increase in its regimental savings bank account, the commander of the forces still described the common soldier as "a creature of routine" who had "no occasion to think for tomorrow . . . [and] no recreation but sensuality. His general haunts are the Grog Shop and Brothel, and the monotony of his daily life makes him susceptible to change [desertion]."[13]

To what extent the soldier promoted grogshops and brothels in Montreal can only be hinted at. As early as 1816 a visitor noted as he walked down Notre Dame Street and observed the buildings that "the first six were taverns, all opposite the Barracks."[14] By 1844 there were 182 taverns in Montreal,[15] not counting the unlicensed ones, and copious as may have been the soldiers' appetite for drink, soldiers could hardly have been the sole patrons of all 182. Just as the grogshop needed both buyers and sellers, so, too, did the brothel. Efforts of the military authorities to keep the soldier out of the brothel were aided by the Roman Catholic hierarchy, the church's efforts being directed to protecting young girls and women from prostitution. In 1844 four nuns, two English and two French, were brought to Montreal from Le Havre to take charge of a house of refuge for "unfortunate females." It was located in the Quebec suburb, which was not only the location of the main British barracks but also the most populous suburb in Montreal. Part of the new establishment was to be a "retreat to preserve the innocent and destitute from pollution."[16] The Roman Catholic hierarchy was not alone in this indirect aid to the military. Police authorities made efforts to suppress brothels in 1849 when seven women and five men with their associates were arrested and brought to trial charged with "keeping disorderly houses."[17] Promiscuity, however, was not confined to brothels. One regular officer remarked that "in every town in which the troops are quartered, the utmost difficulty exists in the management of female servants, who caught, as well as their mistresses, by the glittering bait of a scarlet coat, fall victims to their seducers, and neglect their duties for the pleasures of criminal indulgence."[18]

Military authorities feared the grogshop almost more than the brothel, as the tavern not only encouraged drunkenness but was the usual source of the temptation to desert. To "keep soldiers out of the public houses, the fruitful source of all their crimes," by which the commander of the forces meant the crime of desertion, he urged the construction of fives courts and cricket grounds at all Montreal barracks. He suggested the adoption of a "game . . . called Bowling . . . which is very popular with the lower class of men in this country . . . [and] which can be enjoyed during the most severe weather." Lt.-Gen. William Rowan sought permission from Horse Guards to have bowling alleys built at the various barracks "before the arrival of the two Regiments from the West Indies when we may expect the usual amount of desertion." Above all, he urged that "barracks be better lighted and rendered more agreeable during the long evenings of a winter of six months."[19]

Criticism of the Quebec Gate Barracks cropped up with increasing frequency during the decade of the forties. As army regulations for barracks became more stringent, officers tried to make the lot of the common soldier more palatable and thereby discourage the "disgrace of desertion . . . as discreditable to our Country as it is disheartening to Officers in Command of Corps on this Station."[20] Complaints about the Quebec Gate Barracks ranged from the lowness of ceilings, which did not allow the cubic feet per man laid down by barrack regulations, to a lack of ablution rooms, which forced men to wash in the open yard, an act "severely felt in winter . . . and caused men to neglect cleanliness."[21] Although Lieutenant-General Rowan had arranged some married quarters in Bonsecours Market,[22] there were no "separate accommodations for married men in the Quebec Gate Barracks and the places allotted them are very unsuitable, possessing no convenience for cooking."[23]

The routine of barrack life with reveille at six o'clock in the morning and tattoo at eight in the evening put limitations on a soldier's nocturnal pastimes at the grogshop or brothel. He could obtain late-night passes for specific purposes such as the theatre, exhibitions, or other entertainments, but these were limited. If any ill-feeling existed between townsman and soldier, night passes were absolutely forbidden.[24]

The introduction during the forties of garrison libraries, schools for both soldiers and their families, and regimental savings banks was designed to improve the quality of life of the soldiers and, indirectly, to thwart desertion, even though some officers thought such innovations more likely to produce the contrary effect. Maj. John Richardson was convinced that the introduction of libraries "by no means, in many instances, select . . . in the several corps . . . and the direction of the minds of men to subjects utterly unsuited to their position" tended to induce desertion because in "expanding his intellect, these tended to give the soldier—especially if he be a young man—an unduly exalted opinion of himself, and to induce a contempt for the position he occupies."[25]

In spite of these objections, by 1845 libraries were established at Montreal, St. Helen's Island, Chambly, and St. Johns. Allowances were provided for a military librarian and for supplies of books sent from England. Before the founding of garrison libraries, most regiments had their own collection of books which had to be transported whenever the regiment was transferred. With the establishment of permanent libraries in well-lighted and attractive quarters in the major garrisons, the regimental libraries became redundant and were allowed to expire, thus relieving regiments of such "encumbrances and the soldier from the expense of supporting them." With the demise of regimental libraries and the growing sophistication of those of the garrison, officers sought to become members, but the War Office forbade such a practice because the new libraries were "expressly established for N.C.O.'s and soldiers."[26] Not all soldiers would prefer the library to the grogshop, but undoubtedly establishing a properly lighted library where they could read, and providing teachers and classrooms if they were unable to read, kept some soldiers out of less desirable locales during their off-duty hours.

School classes for both children and adults proved so popular at the Quebec Gate Barracks that additional rooms along with extra candles for lighting had to be allotted.[27] For example, some 72 children and 280 adults, both soldiers and their wives, took advantage of the school provided for the 26th Cameronians, the children attending during the day and the adults from 5:15 to 7:30 in the evening. When it was proposed that soldiers' children might attend city schools in order not to "segregate military school children from civilian," the commander of the forces considered it "injudicious as some of the Parents would not like the children to attend with those of civilians, from the impossibility of dressing as the children of civilians are generally dressed in this country, or [it] may put the Parents to extra expense in dress for their children."[28]

The maturing of military policy on the literacy of the rank and file was indicated by the gradual shift from schooling being a bounty, provided by the army, and voluntarily undertaken by the soldier during the forties to its becoming a compulsory duty in the fifties. By this time, "every soldier, after being dismissed from drill, shall attend school as a duty, until he is reported upon as sufficiently advanced in reading, writing and arithmetic. . . . Commanding officers [are] to arrange duties so as to give men at least four hours' attendance each week." Promotion was to be dependent on literacy along with the usual qualifications of courage, tact, and moral influence.[29]

This developing interest of the military command in education for the children of soldiers, and for the soldiers themselves, also provided teaching jobs for Montrealers, who eagerly competed for them.[30] In the early forties a regimental schoolmaster was selected, usually from among the noncommissioned officers, and was paid an extra allowance for teaching the children. As more and more adults became involved in the learning process, teachers were sought outside the military establishment. The new educational policy had its complications. Fears were expressed by the Roman Catholic hierarchy, especially in Ireland, about military schools where Catholic children would be taught. Cardinal Paul Cullen estimated that nearly half the British army consisted of Catholics, and he asked how many Catholics "will be employed in superintending the education of these Catholic children." Cullen answered his own question. "The Catholic soldier . . . persisting in the defence of his country bequeaths his children to her care; she places them in schools maintained by funds collected from Protestants and Catholics alike and honours the father's service by robbing them of their Faith."[31]

The charge was not entirely without foundation. In Montreal, for instance, "six cases of religious books were to be distributed in the Command" by the Board of Ordnance and the Committee of the Naval and Military Bible Society in 1845.[32] Undoubtedly such books had not been selected for their suitability for Roman Catholic soldiers and their children. Yet the importance which the military hierarchy placed on schooling, discipline, and religious observances was inspired more by the desire to instil religious principles as a means of improving the character and the life of the soldier than by the desire to change religious beliefs. In any event, in Montreal, a largely Catholic city, counter influences to Protestant proselytizing efforts within the army existed in abundance.

Both the Church of England and the Church of Scotland owed their establishment in Montreal to the British soldiery who formed the garrison after the Conquest and who, on leaving the army, stayed in the city. The original congregation of Christ Church Cathedral was gathered together by army chaplain John Ogilvie of the 60th Royal American Regiment before his return to New York in 1764.[33] Disbanded soldiers of the 78th Fraser Highlanders and the 42nd Black Watch formed the nucleus of the first congregation of the Scotch Presbyterian Church organized after the American Revolution by army chaplain John Bethune of the 84th Highland Emigrants Regiment.[34]

The continuing influence of the garrison on the development of the Church of England in Montreal was indicated by a £3,000 subscription from the military chest towards the construction of Christ Church on Notre Dame Street in 1814.[35] A yearly stipend was allotted to the rector on the understanding that the church and rector would provide for the spiritual needs of the resident soldiery as well as for parishioners. The influence of the military was also apparent in the founding of several other Anglican churches in the city. In 1822 Brooke Bridges Stevens, military chaplain at St. Helen's Island, founded St. Stephen's Church in Lachine as a chapel of ease to Christ Church.[36] Six years later he formed the nucleus of the parish at St. Mary's at the Cross in Hochelaga. A small stone church was erected there by 1830 and became, after 1837, a garrison church for troops stationed at Hochelaga Cavalry Barracks.[37] Trinity Church on St. Paul Street near Bonsecours Market was built in 1840 through the munificence of Maj. William P. Christie,[38] a son of Gen. Gabriel Christie, who was with Wolfe at Quebec. Built close to the Quebec Gate Barracks, Trinity Church drew many of the fashionable military to its pews. The wife of publisher John Lovell mingled there with

"Colonel Wetherall and his distinguished wife, also Colonel Gore and his family. . . . Captain Maitland, retired from the army, was church warden."[39] In 1834 army chaplain David Robertson organized an evening service in a room over a store on Wellington Street for Anglicans in Griffintown.[40] This grew into St. Ann's Chapel, which ultimately formed the congregation of St. Edward's Church.

Christ Church, however, remained the garrison church. It was the repository of military records of births, marriages, and deaths. Its rector continued to receive a stipend of £300 annually as chaplain to the forces, even when he no longer performed any services for the troops himself but was content to let his assistant, David Robertson, do the work at the much lower salary of £150 a year.[41] Although the Church of England, as the established church, received the deference due to it from the military, gestures towards other denominations were made in the form of small stipends for Church of Rome and Church of Scotland clergy who ministered to the soldiers. Roman Catholic priests in Montreal and neighbouring villages received stipends ranging from £25 to £40 a year.[42] Church of Scotland clergy had to fight for their share of the military bounty, for although freedom of worship had been established by the Duke of York as early as 1802, military authorities sometimes found it inexpedient to provide chaplains for both Anglicans and Presbyterians if one clergyman could do for both. For example, when a clergyman of the Church of Scotland wrote to the commander of the forces to seek pay for performing a "separate service for Presbyterian soldiers at La Prairie," he was informed that this was not possible, "as the regulated allowance is granted to the minister of the Church of England where the 74th is now stationed."[43]

Presbyterian ministers did apply for and receive allowances of seven shillings a week for visiting soldiers of their flock who were in hospital.[44] And the Presbyterians had their own methods of circumventing military orders that interfered with the religious observances of soldiers of their faith. For instance, the colonel and most of the men of the Highland Regiment then quartered in the city were Scotch Presbyterians. When general orders were issued for all troops to parade to Christ Church, the Highlanders paraded to Christ Church, entered the front door on Notre Dame Street, marched through the church to the back door that opened onto St. James Street, and kept on marching to the Scotch Presbyterian Church just a few paces away on St. Gabriel Street. The colonel and his officers took their usual place in pew number fifty-eight which "was placed at their disposal."[45]

Relations between the military hierarchy, Presbyterian soldiers, and the local Presbyterian church may have had a somewhat uneven course. Relations with the Methodist church were limited entirely to the voluntary attendance of individual soldiers. When Reverend John Leach of the Panet Street Methodist Church applied for an allowance from the military chest because "a number of troops attend public service," he was informed that the "Regulations of the Service make no provision for such a case as the one presented by you . . . the Churches of England, Rome, and the established Church of Scotland [being] the only ones recognized, in reference to an allowance."[46]

The military hierarchy constantly sought to develop congenial relations with the major religious community in Montreal, the Roman Catholics, who numbered 25,699 out of a population of 40,290 in 1842.[47] Sir John Colborne had been partially successful in securing the goodwill of the clergy, particularly that of the superior of the Sulpicians, Joseph Quiblier, and the Sulpicians paid visits to "les casernes."[48] Other senior officers such as Maj.-Gen. John Clitherow, Maj.-Gen. Sir James Macdonell, himself a Catholic, and Lt.-Col. Charles Grey took every opportunity to visit with the Sulpicians, to pay their respects to the Sisters of the Congregation of Notre Dame, and to allow regimental bands to play at Roman Catholic festivals and services.[49] Lord Cathcart, when he was both commander of the forces and governor general in 1846–47, was particularly careful about relations with the Roman Catholic hierarchy. Priests were frequent guests at his dinner table. When he was unable to attend a prize-giving ceremony at Saint-Hyacinthe, he sent Lady Cathcart and his son-in-law, Capt. James Douglas, who reported that "the Priests were particularly civil to us. . . . we visited several missionaries and had luncheon at the Seminary . . . and visited every Priest's house on our way."[50]

Army regulations were adamant on the observances of the military towards the ceremonies of the Roman Catholic church, particularly that of the procession of the Host. The uncovering of the head, if not the bending of the knee, was rigorously enforced by officers serving in any country in which the Roman Catholic religion prevailed, and Canada was no exception.[51] Thus, in the early 1840s when Montreal, in common with other areas, began to experience a hardening of denominational tension, some Brit-

155

ish officers spoke out against "violent sectarian sermons" which they heard in the city. Lieutenant-Colonel Grey described one minister as "one of the class of men who do so much mischief both at home and abroad. . . . after attacking the Catholic Religion, in a Catholic Country, in as violent a manner as was possible, he laid down forbearance towards those who differed from us."[52]

Regular British officers were discreet enough to keep away from militant Protestant groups in the city such as the French Canadian Missionary Society whose proselytizing efforts among Roman Catholics brought to the surface latent French-Canadian fears that "le dessein de protestantiser les Canadiens français était ancien: il datait de la Conquête."[53] The fact that the society was headed by Maj. William Christie and Lt.-Col. Edward Wilgress,[54] both retired military men, created suspicion towards the military on the part of French Canadians.

Such activities by Montrealers with military connections made difficulties for the regulars. Other difficulties arose between the military and the Anglican hierarchy over the use of Christ Church by the military. The root of the trouble likely lay in the cantankerous character of the rector, John Bethune, the convert son of the founder of the Scotch Presbyterian Church.[55] The cooling of relations between the rector and the military authorities began with the army's decision in 1842 to make David Robertson, also a convert to Anglicanism from Presbyterianism, the military chaplain in place of Bethune.[56] Robertson had been doing the garrison duty for some time, and military authorities, cognizant of his devotion to the men, decided to increase his stipend and to make him chaplain to the troops in name as well as in fact.[57]

In 1844 Bethune and his churchwardens arbitrarily changed the time of the military service without consulting the commander of the forces. A letter to Sir Richard Jackson simply announced that the change would be effective within the week. Jackson, like his predecessor, Sir John Colborne, was a devout member of the Church of England. Nevertheless, such highhanded methods were not to his liking. He instructed his military secretary to go over the head of the rector and churchwardens and to consult Bishop George J. Mountain to "ensure a proper service being performed each Sunday for the Garrison in the Parish Church," for he saw that "if the Church Wardens, who are appointed annually, can, at their pleasure, alter the hours of Divine Service for the Military without His Excellency's intervention, there can be no security against Church Wardens a subsequent year, declining to give the Church on the Sabbath at any hour for the use of the Military."[58]

The commander of the forces was annoyed about the change on other grounds. The usual hour for the soldiers' service had been set since 1831 late in the day because it was "more beneficial to the morals of the soldier who would be thereby deterred from acts of vice which he might be led into, having the whole day to himself." Jackson warned the bishop that "if the Military can only be accommodated in the Parish Church by sufferance, His Excellency will lose no time in making application to Her Majesty's Government for the restitution by the Rector and Parishioners of the original sum granted . . . in order that a Garrison Church may be erected for the exclusive use of Her Majesty's Troops."[59]

The imbroglio was smoothed over quickly by both sides withdrawing to a comfortable distance as neither parishioners, military hierarchy, nor official chaplain to the troops wished a prolonged squabble involving a reference to the home government. Moreover, military and Church of England activities were too closely intertwined to admit of too much in-fighting. Most parish activities were undertaken with both civil and military personnel. The founding of the Church Society of the Diocese of Quebec took place in 1842 at Christ Church and was promoted by both active and retired British military men.[60] Captain Myers of the 71st Highlanders moved the resolution that twenty-five shillings constitute the annual membership fee. Maj. William Christie and Lt.-Col. Edward Wilgress attended the founding meeting, as did military chaplains David Robertson and James Ramsay, the latter chaplain at St. Helen's Island and Hochelaga. A regular officer, Capt. George Talbot, who was military secretary for much of the forties, was organist and choir director at Christ Church.

Yet uneasiness persisted between members of the military hierarchy and the rector of Christ Church. Bethune's proclivity to controversy was so well known that even his obituary described him as one in whom "the fighting blood of the old royalists flowed." His quarrel with his superiors, Bishops Charles Stewart of Quebec and George J. Mountain of Montreal, over McGill College of which Bethune was principal was finally settled by the commander of the forces, Lord Cathcart. Cathcart, in his role as governor general, was instructed by the secretary of state for the colonies to revoke Bethune's appointment as principal, an act which "extinguished the theological pretensions of the University."[61]

Bethune met his match a second time in a dispute about the

military service at Christ Church when military surgeon James Barry arrived at the Montreal station as inspector general of hospitals. Dr. Barry, who, it was reported after his death, may have been a woman,[62] was so abusive towards Bethune in the presence of both the bishop and clergy of Montreal that Bethune officially protested to military authorities.[63] In this instance Bethune found an ally in the commander of the forces, Maj.-Gen. Sir William Eyre, who reported to Horse Guards that Dr. Barry had been the source of "very extraordinary repeated complaints . . . since his arrival . . . [and] it is only a few weeks ago that he publicly insulted and without any provocation whatever the Dean and Rector of Montreal. . . . More recently he has made a gross and, I believe, most imprudent charge against Col. Cole, Commd. 17th Regiment." Eyre insisted that Dr. Barry "must be removed . . . [because] his uncontrollable temperament . . . renders him unfit for this high position." To Dean Bethune, Eyre expressed his "extreme regret that you should have been subject and so unprovocatively . . . to such an annoyance and that the harmony of our society has been, though I trust, only momentarily, interrupted by such an occurrence."[64]

It was perhaps at funerals that the closeness of soldier and townsman was most undeniably demonstrated. The two largest funeral processions in Montreal in the first half of the nineteenth century were not of local politicians, churchmen, or popular leaders, but of British military figures—one, an obscure dispatch carrier, the other, the commander of the forces hurried to his grave by the anxieties of the agitation over the Rebellion Losses Bill. Undoubtedly both funerals were demonstrations of strength. When the body of the young dispatch bearer, Lt. George Weir of the 32nd Regiment, was discovered on 3 December 1837 under some rocks in a stream near Saint-Denis, the head and fingers badly slashed,[65] the mood of both soldier and loyalist was shown by the size of the funeral. Never before had Montreal "witnessed so solemn and imposing a spectacle. . . . so great was the concourse, that the road from the Quebec suburbs to the burying ground, one half mile in length and of considerable breadth, was occupied by one living mass of men."[66]

On the death of Sir Benjamin D'Urban, the *Gazette* sounded the loyalist tocsin. The old Peninsular veteran had survived nine pitched battles,[67] but he could not survive the tension in Montreal during the spring of 1849 that erupted into violence with the stoning of the governor general and the burning of Parliament House. Just a month to the day after the burning, the commander of the forces was found dead by his son, Lt.-Col. William D'Urban.[68] Few doubted that his death resulted from his efforts to allay bitter feelings and to prevent collisions between the troops and the populace. In phraseology that left no doubt that the tocsin was sounded for those who regarded the commander of the forces in a far more favourable light than they did the governor general, Lord Elgin, the *Gazette* urged the British inhabitants to turn out en masse to "pay respects to a tried servant of our Gracious Queen."[69] Liberal political forces had no intentions of letting their opponents monopolize the funeral. British regulars had helped protect liberal members of Parliament and, in an unprecedented gesture, members of the Assembly and the far from tory city council joined the funeral procession as it moved off from Donegani's Hotel where Sir Benjamin D'Urban had resided.

Many, perhaps, came just to see the solemn and imposing show that the garrison was capable of mounting. All shops were closed from half-past ten in the morning until one o'clock. Sir James Alexander estimated that 10,000 lined the street as minute guns sounded from St. Helen's Island to mark the movement of the cortege to the military burying ground on Victoria Road, now Papineau Street.[70] Soldiers of the 19th and 23rd Regiments lined the streets, their guns reversed, while the muffled drums of their bands rolled as the body passed.

Many Montrealers must have recalled that just two years earlier D'Urban had headed the mourners at the funeral of Mayor John Mills, struck down with typhus while succouring the Irish famine emigrants. Even the funeral procession of Sir Richard Jackson four years earlier could not compare with the impressive display of solidarity between soldier and townsman shown at D'Urban's funeral. Heads of military and civilian departments were followed by members of the Legislative and Executive Councils, judges, officers of militia, city councillors, and even students and professors of McGill College. At the sides of the flag-draped coffin were the pallbearers, including two major-generals, a commissary general, and four colonels.[71]

While soldiers and officers might find themselves berated by irate civilians in times of civil tension, these occasions, being limited in time and scope, were overshadowed by the daily intercourse of soldier and townsman. Whether it was at church, school, the grogshop, or brothel, the men of the garrison made their presence felt, usually in a positive mode, but occasionally, when prerogatives were challenged, the military presence was thrust forward with firmness and determination.

10.

The Soldier on Display

The use of the regulars not only for display purposes at public functions but also as an assertion of British sovereignty in the province was not underestimated by governors or military commanders. Sir John Colborne had been one of the first to emphasize the importance of the presence of regular troops at the seat of government. When troops were being withdrawn from the upper province in 1837, he warned that enough must be left behind so that the "Splendour of the Court and Capital . . . must not be forgotten." Some eighteen years later Sir Edmund Head was even more emphatic. "I believe," he wrote to the great critic of colonial garrisons, Sir William Molesworth, "that the presence of some of Her Majesty's troops at the seat of government has a certain moral force and value, which is not less real because it cannot be precisely measured or stated in words . . . [it] proclaims . . . in the face of the Colony and of the neighbouring States, the relations existing between the Mother Country and the Province. . . . It is an open Profession to the world that the Queen of England is the Head of this Legislature and the acknowledged Sovereign of this country."[1]

At Montreal, the seat of government from 1838 to 1840, and from 1844 to 1849, the display of troops at civic functions was not lessened by either the governors or the commanders of the forces when they acted as administrators of the government in the absence of the governor. The swearing in of Lords Durham, Sydenham, Cathcart, and Elgin all took place at the Château Ramezay with a military guard of honour, heads of military departments, and regimental commanding officers present.

Soldiers provided the fanfare to mark the arrivals and departures of governors and commanders of the forces. In 1843 Lord Metcalfe was met at Lachine by the Queen's Light Dragoons and his arrival in Montreal was marked by a salute of nineteen guns. Troops of the 43rd, 71st, and 89th Regiments paraded in review and lined the streets under the command of Town Major Colin Macdonald while a guard of honour composed of men of the 43rd awaited Lord Metcalfe at Rasco's Hotel where the commander of the forces, his personal staff, and senior staff officers welcomed him.[2]

When Montreal resumed its place as the seat of government in 1844, all senior staff officers and officers commanding regiments in Montreal were required to meet with the commander of the forces "to proceed to Parliament House for the purpose of receiving the Governor-General."[3] It was Town Major Macdonald's duty to see that officers were briefed as to where they were to process and stand during the opening ceremonies of the Legislature. On the right of the throne were Sir Richard Jackson, commander of the forces; his aides-de-camp; Lt.-Col. Sir Charles Gore, deputy quartermaster-general; Colonel Campbell, commanding the Royal Artillery; and Commissary General William Filder. On the left of the governor general were Lt.-Col. George Wetherall, deputy adjutant general; Colonel Holloway, commanding the Royal Engineers; Doctor Shortt, deputy inspector general of hospitals; Lt.-Col. J. W. Bouverie, commandant of the garrison; Major Smyth, commanding the 93rd Regiment; and Town Major Macdonald. As the commander of the forces and the governor general came in, they were preceded by the staff officers and, to add to the impressiveness of the ceremony, a salute of nineteen guns was fired by the Royal Artillery.

Lord Metcalfe's departure from Montreal on a dull November day a year later found the streets lined with troops of the 93rd Sutherland Highlanders and the 52nd Light Infantry. At the wharf city firemen formed an arch through which he passed while his successor, Lord Cathcart; Sir James Hope, the commandant of the garrison; Mayor James Ferrier and city councillors; and senior staff officers bade the ailing governor farewell.[4] A former lieutenant of the 1st Provincial Regiment expressed the sadness of both soldier and civilian on the occasion. "We cannot forget the departure of the Governor-General from our City when . . . broken by disease, he looked his last upon . . . the people he had loved so well. That moment levelled all distinctions . . . [and] he wept in unison with those that followed him."[5]

When Lt.-Gen. Lord Cathcart became both commander of the forces and governor general, the presence of the military at parliamentary functions and social events in connection with legislative duties became even more marked. Conscious always of the importance of timing, Cathcart arrived in Montreal to assume his duties on the eve of the anniversary of the Battle of Waterloo.[6] Officers of the staff and a guard of honour of the 52nd Regiment awaited him at Government Wharf while the Royal Artillery fired the customary salute. Lieutenant-Colonel Gore greeted the new commander as he disembarked and led him to a carriage and pair which took him to Rasco's where another guard of honour of the 93rd Sutherland Highlanders welcomed their countryman.

When Lord Cathcart officiated for the first time at the opening of Parliament, troopers of the Provincial Cavalry were ordered to be on hand at Dalhousie Square to escort him to Parliament while the Royal Artillery fired the salute. At Parliament House he was greeted by a guard of honour with regimental colours and band. Lieutenant-Colonel Gore, with the heads of military departments and officers commanding regiments, preceded him to the robing room.[7]

The presence of guards of honour, heads of military departments, regimental commanding officers, and troops in review lent dignity, colour, and form to such provincial ceremonies. No less impressive were the displays by the military on such national days as the Queen's Birthday and the anniversary of the Battle of Waterloo. Since these days fell conveniently in late spring, field days were held during which the troops in garrison paraded to an old racecourse in Lachine which had been levelled by the military to permit such displays. In 1840, when the garrison numbered 2,826,[8] the troops "formed on the ground at the old Race Course and fired a *feu de joie* in honour of Her Majesty's birthday" and then went through a variety of movements simulating the Battle of Vittoria, "producing a most capital effect and admirably executed."[9] Three weeks later on the anniversary of the Battle of Waterloo, the "whole of the troops in Garrison . . . assembled on the Champ de Mars to do honour to the day," a windy one with occasional showers, "resembling the day on which the battle was fought." According to the *Gazette*, "the spectators on the ground were numerous, and many a loyal heart beat high while reflecting on the events of the proudest day in British history, with the exception of Trafalgar."[10]

Troops newly arrived at the Montreal station always preened themselves for their first review on the Champ de Mars where they not only sought to win the approval of the senior officers of the headquarters' staff, but also used the occasion to put on their best show for the citizens of the city in which they would likely spend the next three years. For instance, when the 93rd Sutherland Highlanders arrived for a tour of duty in May 1844, its performance on the Champ de Mars was "splendid in the extreme." The *Gazette* on 24 May told its readers that "it is as a body that they can be seen to perfection, and that their peculiar dress shows to the highest advantage." Not only was the review splendid, but the "band of the 93rd is one of the finest we have heard in a long time and will be a great acquisition to the evening amusements of our good city."

The regiment that probably did more to heal rebellion wounds than any other was the 71st Highland Light Infantry. It arrived in Montreal just as the first rebellion was over and before the second had erupted, its band coquettishly playing "Voulez-vous danser, Mademoiselle" as the troopship neared the wharf where an "immense crowd on the beach . . . cheered without end."[11] From the moment of its arrival, the 71st Highlanders forged close links with local inhabitants. Its soldiers formed the escort for the eight rebels heading for exile in Bermuda in 1838;[12] they shared in the burnings and pillaging south of the St. Lawrence during the suppression of the second rebellion; and when Beauharnois insurgents were marched to jail in Montreal, it was pipers of the 71st who "annoyed us during almost the whole of the journey with the noise of their bagpipes."[13]

Officers of the 1st Provincial Regiment and the Provincial Cavalry found the pipes something of a mixed blessing. When men of the 71st Regiment arrived at the border to help the frontier forces bring in the New Year, their commanding officer, Sir Hew Dalrymple, being a Highland chief, brought his own piper whom one provincial officer referred to as his "noisy attendant" and considered it "lucky for us that he did not bring five and twenty . . . [since] human nature could not have survived the infliction." Yet the "stirring pibroch" produced by the strutting piper was somewhat softened as Dalrymple distributed a "quaigh to all who desired to drink the New Year in."[14]

Residents of St. Johns had no objections to the pipes. When the 71st Highlanders were ordered to take up quarters in Montreal after a tour of duty at St. Johns, local inhabitants met at Watson's Hall to express their regrets "that the rules of the Service required that Her Majesty's 71st be removed from this garrison." In an address to the officers and men of the 71st, they conveyed their thanks to "Lt.-Col. Charles Grey for his kindness in allowing the excellent Grey Band and Bugler and National Pipers . . . to play for the gratification of the public."[15]

For the Roman Catholic bishop of Kingston, Alexander Macdonell, a Highland Scot, the music of Dalrymple's piper was enough to lure him to St. Helen's Island where, in company with his kinsman Maj.-Gen. Sir James Macdonell, he enjoyed "a Gaelic conversation with the Piper beyond measure."[16] Not only did the bishop help to strengthen ties between regular officers and the Glengarry Highlanders by accompanying Sir James Macdonell on a tour to Glengarry,[17] he also strengthened ties between the military and the Roman Catholic hierarchy in Montreal. He invited Sir James Macdonell and the commanding officer of the 71st Regiment, Lt.-Col. Charles Grey, to join him and the superior of the Sulpicians on a visit to the Sisters of the Congregation of Notre Dame and to dine with the priests at the seminary.[18] It is not surprising, then, that the band and pipers of the 71st would be in demand to provide music on the grounds of the "Gentlemen of the Seminary" during the Grand Rural Festival of the Montreal Horticultural Society or to attend a solemn High Mass at the Roman Catholic church on St. Jean Baptiste Day, at which time they led the French Canadians from their church to the quick step of "Vive la Canadienne."[19]

The ability of the 71st Highlanders to mix with and captivate both British and French Montrealers is demonstrated by the myriad social and sporting events with which they were associated. On St. George's Day it was the band of the 71st that hovered close by at Rasco's Hotel while their officers responded to the "toast to the Army." In 1849, the year that Lord Elgin's name was erased from the membership roll of the St. Andrew's Society, it was the pipers and brass band of the 71st that led the "largest procession of the society ever seen in Montreal . . . to Mack's Hotel" where the new president, Hugh Allen, officiated at the St. Andrew's Day festivities. When city firemen left for their annual picnic at Beauharnois, pipers of the 71st "all plaited and plumed in their tartan array accompanied them to provide the music for the day."[20]

Though far from fluent in French, officers of this regiment accompanied "young ladies belonging to the old French families" in large sleighs on winter picnics to habitants' homes in Varennes.[21] The delight of such picnics was described by Lt. Daniel Lysons. "We used to drive in our own sleighs, each taking a lady—commonly called a muffin—and a share of the dinner.[22] A band was also sent out and there were several good rooms in habitants' houses that were used for the parties. After dinner we danced for several hours, then drove home together on the snow roads, all in a long string of sleighs by moonlight, which was often as light as day. These drives were most charming, and on a still night to hear all the sleigh bells jingling . . . was most fascinating, to say nothing of the young lady who was rolled up in warm robes by your side."[23]

Undoubtedly the band of the 71st Regiment was the most popular of the regimental bands during the forties. But other bands as well brought applause and pleasure to Montrealers during the summer when they performed twice a week at the Champ de Mars or in the barrack yard as officers dined, an occasion described by one Montrealer as "a favourite walk in order to hear the band play." For local musicians, the use of the fine military bands at private balls and parties was looked upon with some resentment. A petition to Sir Richard Jackson in 1843 from eleven musicians, headed by Professor J. Maffre, complained that "in consequence of military bands being permitted to attend at such balls, quadrille parties, public assemblies and at private residences . . . in many cases free of charge, and in all cases at very low rates, advantage thereof is meanly taken by the citizens to the detriment of your petitioners who are wholly dependent on such sources for their livelihood."[24]

Although these men were petitioning in their role as Montreal musicians, their connections with the military had not long been severed. Professor Maffre was "late Master of the Band of the 71st Highland Light Infantry," who was "induced to settle in Montreal" and whose "perfect knowledge of the Pianoforte, Organ, Violin, Viola, Violincello, Clarinet, Flute, Oboe, and all wind instruments" as well as his ability to teach the "elements of singing and thorough Bass, with the Art of Scoring music for orchestra or military band" was matched by his perfect knowledge of the use of military bands at private parties.[25] Despite his protest to Jackson, Maffre was not reluctant to seek the attendance of his former officer of the 71st Regiment for a concert and to advertise it as "coming off tonight under the patronage of Sir Hew Dalrymple."[26]

Military interest in music extended to the encouragement of the Montreal Philharmonic Society. In 1846 Lord Cathcart's aide-de-camp, Capt. James Douglas of the 79th Regiment, attended the "first meeting of the Philharmonic Society" at the home of Capt. George Talbot, the military secretary, where "the music was very good indeed."[27] On a somewhat different level, Montreal military men shared musical interests with French Canadians. Sir Daniel Lysons, who served in the Montreal area during the rebellion, described how he and Lord Charles Beauclerk, together with the military secretary, Capt. Brook Taylor of the 85th Regiment, while fishing on Lake St. Louis, discovered that they had usurped the campground of some French Canadians. Hearing them approach by the sound of "their beautiful Canadian boat songs and the splash of water keeping time to the music," the British officers apologized for "having come to their camp, but the men were very civil." Soon the officers were joining in the singing, Lysons and Brook Taylor doing a French duet "which was highly appreciated." On another occasion when Lysons and the Earl of Mulgrave were moose hunting near Rawdon, they stopped for dinner at "Darwin's Shanty, one of Mr. Price's lumbering establishments" where they heard "great shouting, singing . . . and found a wild, jolly, rough lot and we soon fraternized." The officers were invited to join in a French-Canadian frolic in which a piece of paper was pinned to a man's trousers so as to stick out like a dog's tail. He then began to run from the fireplace, dancing around and singing, "Tu ne me mettras pas le feu à derrière," while another man followed with a lighted cedar trying to set the tail on fire.[28]

Lysons and Beauclerk were among the group of talented officers who in their memoirs and paintings have filled in details and provided intimate glimpses of the social and political life of Montreal and other garrison towns. To their legacy of landscape watercolours, the collector of the 1973 work on Canadian paintings pays unreserved tribute. Michael Bell, in introducing his *Painters in a New Land*, writes, "To these officers we owe most of our knowledge of what the colony of Canada looked like in the eighteenth and nineteenth centuries."[29]

British officers, especially those in the Royal Artillery and Royal Engineers, had the advantage of specialized training in drawing and mapmaking at the Royal Military Academy, Woolwich, where every officer had to try his hand at watercolour painting and to acquire a certificate of diligence from the drawing masters. This training was designed to equip them with sufficient skill to make sketches on reconnaissance and to develop an eye for the country, a capacity for simplification, and an ability to select significant features.[30] For both colonials and the British wishing to secure a commission in the British army, drawing was one of the subjects upon which they were examined.[31]

Lysons was able to illustrate his memoirs with sketches depicting games in Darwin's shanty, his camp in the swamp, a Canadian stage sleigh going over cahots, and with watercolours of his own tandem and Lord Mulgrave's four-in-hand.[32] Lysons was typical, too, of the many regular officers whose skill at map drawing proved invaluable. The absence of reliable maps at the outbreak of the rebellion prompted Lysons to suggest that officers of the line be used to make military sketches of the country. It was from this suggestion that the first map of the Eastern Townships was drawn in 1839.[33] In 1841 Lysons was sent to survey the Niagara District, and his maps provided Sir William Logan and the Canadian Geological Department with the basis for later surveys.[34]

Lord Charles Beauclerk's lithographic views of the attacks on Saint-Charles and Saint-Eustache have remained the most frequently reproduced portrayals of those events. Abbé Emile Dubois chose several of the Beauclerk watercolours to illustrate his book *Le feu de la rivière du Chêne*, as did a more modern historian, Joseph Schull, in his excellent narrative *Rebellion: The Rising in French Canada in 1837*.[35] Undoubtedly it was Beauclerk's portrayal of the dispersal of the insurgents at Saint-Eustache that was the inspiration for the enamel wall mural at the Papineau Metro Station built in 1967 in Montreal.

Of the Royal Engineer officers posted to Montreal during the rebellion period and after, perhaps none surpassed the industry and skill of Lt. Philip John Bainbrigge, whose eye for detail and ability as a draughtsman drew him into the group of regular officers assigned to survey the border. His watercolours of the Protestant and Catholic cathedrals in Montreal, as well as his impression of the old fort and barracks at Chambly and the ruins of Saint-Eustache after the battle, rank him with James Pattison Cockburn, whose prolific output of watercolours of Quebec and Montreal in the 1820s and 1830s made him the best known of the group of painters of the British garrison.[36]

The 83rd Regiment with its mascot descending the Lachine Rapids in 1843.

A pencil sketch of the freeze-up of the St. Lawrence opposite Montreal was done by Capt. Henry Warre of the 14th Buckinghamshire Regiment,[37] who served as aide-de-camp to his uncle Sir Richard Downes Jackson, the commander of the forces. Warre also provided one of the best illustrations of the art of sleighing over cahots. Henry Francis Ainslie's watercolour of a bateau descending the Lachine Rapids, carrying troops of the 83rd Regiment accompanied by their mascot, a black bear,[38] in a glance provides some of the sense of fun that surrounded the extravagances of the troops to which William Atherton referred in his book on Montreal during this period.[39]

It was at the theatre, however, that the garrison's contribution to the artistic life of Montreal was perhaps most pronounced. Regular performances were given by the Garrison Amateurs at the small Artillery Theatre set up at the Quebec Gate Barracks in 1835,[40] but special performances, often for some charitable purpose,[41] were given in the Theatre Royal. These became the highlight of the theatre season, as the governor general and the commander of the forces usually attended with their suites, all in dress uniform. Although the amateurism of the officers prompted the Montreal correspondent of the New York *Albion* to comment somewhat grumpily that "though the garrison amateurs will help enliven the winter . . . it must be confessed that amateur theatricals are a great bore,"[42] still the unpredictability of the military actors lent an air of hilarity to the garrison performances. Such was the case of the colonel who, on forgetting his lines, would walk up to the prompter and ask in a loud, hoarse voice, ".What is it?"[43]

The Montreal garrison was far from insensitive to public relations in the forties. Its coup in persuading Charles Dickens to assist it in several performances on 28 May 1842 gave Montrealers an exciting night at the theatre at which they could see the Earl of Mulgrave and officers of the 23rd Royal Welsh Fusiliers perform *A Roland for an Oliver* and *High Life below the Stairs*."[44] The audience of some 500 included Governor General Sir Charles Bagot, and the commander of the forces, Sir Richard Jackson, and their staffs. Dickens was delighted, writing that "as the military portion of the audience were all in uniform, it was really a splendid scene" with the band of the 23rd playing, and tables of refreshments spread in the lobby and salon of the theatre.[45]

Closely allied to the stimulus given the local theatre by the military was the garrison's interest in the Shakspeare Dramatic

and Literary Club, founded in Montreal in 1843 by recently disbanded officers of the provincial frontier forces. Taking the lead
in the formation of the new club were Lt. Joseph Smith Lee of the
1st Provincial Regiment and Lt. Samuel David of the Royal
Montreal Cavalry. Lee, who was to become one of the "ablest students of Shakespeare . . . whom we have ever had in Canada,"[46]
had already shown his "dramatic craze" while with the provincial
forces in Cornwall where, in imitation of his British comrades-in-
arms, he had organized a small military theatre.[47] When he,
David, and others returned from frontier service to Montreal,
they decided to continue their literary and dramatic activities.

The leaders of the Shakspeare Club unabashedly appealed "to
the officers of the Army and Members of the Legislature" for support, assuring them that their "Institution could not fail to be of
signal advantage."[48] So successful was their appeal that before
the decade was out, the Shakspeare Dramatic and Literary Club
had become one of the most exclusive in Montreal, drawing to its
ranks such prominent military and civilian Montrealers as Capt.
Lord Mark Kerr, aide-de-camp to Lord Elgin; Lt.-Col. Augustus
Gugy, who donated "forty-five volumes of the Encyclopedia Lon-
dinensis" to its library; Maj. J. B. Turner, editor of the Montreal
Courier; William Kingsford, the former soldier who would become one of Montreal's leading historians;[49] Cornelius Krieghoff,
the artist; J. Fennings Taylor, the writer; Lts. W. L. Morrison and
Pasley of the Royal Engineers; and Lt.-Col. William Ermatinger,
the former British officer who became Montreal's superintendent
of police.[50]

Topics such as "Would it be advisable to abolish the punishment of flogging in the British army?" followed by "Ought the
Conveyance and Service of the mails be suspended on the Sabbath?" were debated warmly by both soldier and townsman at the
club.[51] Military men appreciated its growing library, especially
after regimental libraries were disbanded. The sudden demise of
the Shakspeare Club upon the removal of Parliament to Toronto,
when many of its members had to depart for the new capital, left
a gap in Montreal amateur theatricals that was filled by another
part-military, part-civilian group—the Garrick Club. Capt. Robert Lovelace, late of the 19th Regiment, who settled in Montreal
in 1849, took the lead in the new dramatic club which performed
in the Miniature Theatre on St. Jean Baptiste Street.[52] The per-
vasiveness of the military influence was evident even in the back-
drop curtain. This had been painted by Adj. Thomas Wily of the

171

1st Provincial Regiment for one of that corps' performances in Cornwall.[53] The curtain found its way to Montreal, probably brought there by Joseph Lee.

Although the Shakspeare Dramatic and Literary Club throughout its ephemeral existence drew many of the military officers to its meetings, the older Natural History Society of Montreal, though more staid, attracted both officers and soldiers whose interests lay in a more scientific direction. One of the earliest joint ventures between the society and the military was in 1837 when "a series of observations . . . to discover the true mean temperature of this part of British America" was undertaken at St. Helen's Island by noncommissioned officers of the Royal Artillery under the direction of the society's officers.[54]

Regulars stationed at Montreal added exotic items to the Natural History Society's growing museum collection. Col. George A. Wetherall of the Royals donated a Burmese prayer book "beautifully enamelled on a Palmyn leaf" and a bell from a pagoda at Rangoon. Assistant surgeon of the Royals, J. G. Dartnell, gave a specimen of paper "manufactured from the bark of a tree by the natives of Lower Bengal, a copy of an ancient Tamil manuscript from Ceylon, a lock of hair and a toenail of an elephant, and a specimen of water from the salt spring lately discovered at Manitoulin Island."[55] A private of the 26th Cameronians gave the society "11 curious copper coins, one an East Indian of 1835," and Sgt. Joseph Turney of the 20th Regiment donated two copper coins, one of Philip and Mary and a Dutch coin of 1769.[56]

The garrison's relations with the local Masonic Order dated from the Conquest. Seven of the British regiments entering Montreal in 1760 had lodges of Freemasons. Of these, at least two were later to promote the formation of civilian lodges in the city in the 1840s. The 1st Royal Scots, which formed part of the garrison throughout the rebellion period, had a Masonic lodge, "Unity, Peace, and Concord,"[57] attached to the regiment. This lodge was composed of both officers and noncommissioned officers, "all bound in one mystic tie, but entirely apart from any system of equality in duty, obedience or discipline."[58]

Masonic influence within the garrison can only be hinted at since the order is secret, but undoubtedly the assertion by Chasseur François-Xavier Prieur that James Perrigo owed his acquittal on a charge of high treason in 1838 to his making the Masonic distress signal upon entering the court may have been true.[59] His acquittal, otherwise, is difficult to understand, as others who had not been as prominent as Perrigo in the Chasseur ranks were convicted.[60] That the Masonic distress signal was recognized and acted upon was one of the attractions of the Masonic Order for military men. Stories of soldiers receiving aid, even from the enemy, through the use of the distress signal drew military men to its lodges.[61]

When the 1st Royal Scots moved from Montreal in 1840, civilian members who had been attached to the military lodge in the regiment, later formed the nucleus of the petitioners seeking a warrant in 1847 to establish Elgin Lodge in Montreal. The other military lodge which had lasting influence on local Masonry was the lodge of "Social and Military Virtues" in the 46th Regiment of Foot. Although stationed in Montreal for scarcely a year, the Masons of the 46th Regiment established fraternal relations with Montreal Masons and formed part of the procession at the laying of the foundation stone of the new Masonic Hall on Dalhousie Square in 1846.[62] They promoted the founding of the Montreal lodge of Social and Military Virtues which drew to its ranks former military men such as Captain Lovelace,[63] the retired officer of the 19th who was active in the Garrick Club. Military Masons mixed freely with local Masons and took part in their policies and disputes. For instance, when a group of Montreal Masonic masters petitioned the Grand Masonic Lodge of England to have Peter McGill appointed grand master of Montreal and William Henry, those mentioned in the correspondence included R. I. Wilson of the 52nd Regiment and J. L. A. Simonds of the Royal Engineers.[64]

The presence of soldiers and officers at local official functions, their services as mapmakers and portrayers of colonial life, their contribution to musical and dramatic performances, and their eager participation in such local societies as the Shakspeare Dramatic and Literary Club and the Natural History Society showed that the garrison's role as an agency of cultural refinement came close to equalling the importance of its role as a protector and aid to civil power. These were activities in which both soldier and townsman joined, the imperial troops often adding colour, dignity, and talent to the local efforts. Troop reviews and field days were the garrison's own public relations exercises. It was during these garrison displays that the regulars sought to win the goodwill and esteem of the people of Montreal and to set an example of excellence for the local military establishment.

11. The Soldier's Sports and Amusements

If relations between military and Montreal Masons remained clandestine, and the ties between the literary, musical, and theatre-loving soldier and townsman strengthened over the decade of the forties, the links forged between town and Crown forces in the field of sports were, perhaps, the strongest of all. Any sport involving horses drew the soldier from his barracks and the officer from his mess. It is not surprising that Col. Sir Charles Gore should be elected president of the Montreal Turf Club by a joint membership of townsmen and British officers and that he remained president for most of the forties.[1] This club organized the annual three days of races in August at the old Lachine racecourse when townsman and soldier vied for the rich purses, including the Garrison Plate.

In 1840, of the twelve stewards of the club, eight were British officers, including Lt.-Col. John Whyte of the 7th Hussars; Lt.-Col. Johnston of the 66th Regiment; Captain Sandeman, 73rd Regiment; Captain Clitherow, aide-de-camp to his father, Maj.-Gen. John Clitherow; Capt. Brook Taylor, aide-de-camp to Sir Richard Jackson; and Lt. Louis Guy of the 81st Regiment. Serving with the military men were Montrealers Clément Sabrevois de Bleury, François-Pierre Bruneau, Robert Weir, and Charles

Penner.[2] By 1844 the preponderance of military men to civilians shifted somewhat. Charles Penner became vice-president, and Samuel David, the former lieutenant of the Royal Montreal Cavalry, and Police Superintendent William Ermatinger were stewards. Of the nine officers of the Turf Club, only three were regular officers.[3]

Although the races occasionally proved for some young and more exacting officers "very bad" and the second day "even more stupid than yesterday,"[4] for the officers and stewards of the Turf Club the preparations and running of the races year after year brought townsmen and garrison together in what was often the most impressive annual sports event.[5]

The Montreal Hunt brought horse lovers, both military and civilian, together in even more frequent meets. Longue Pointe ws one of the favourite locales for hunt meets, the hounds usually starting off from Elmwood, the farm of Capt. Charles Oakes Ermatinger of the Royal Montreal Cavalry. Here, too, was run on 15 October 1840 the first steeplechase ever held in Canada.[6] The event, competed for by eleven riders, both military and civilians, was won by Lt.-Col. John Whyte of the 7th Hussars, riding his own horse Heretic. A large Montreal audience, including Lord Sydenham, watched the new sport with interest, the *Transcript* commenting on 17 October 1840 that "nothing in sporting has given such general satisfaction." Like the summer races the steeplechase was to become an annual event, almost supplanting the races in popularity, a purse of £150 being the prize.[7]

The races, steeplechase, and hunt were pleasures of the summer. In the hyperborean months, as the military were apt to describe a Montreal winter, the regulars also found means of amusement. With the enlarged garrison of 1838, a "good driving club was established, also a four-in-hand club and a Tandem Club." So popular did the Tandem Club meets become that when members assembled at Dalhousie Square and started off to the sound of the bugle, the sleighs of horses extended from Place d'Armes to Champ de Mars. The president, Sir Hew Dalrymple of the 71st Highlanders, was out in front, driving a sleigh with only one horse, "a perfect beauty." Attached to the front of the sleigh was a large owl, and whenever Sir Hew neared one of the deep cahots formed by the carts of the country people, he "would imitate the screech of an owl," the owl would awaken, spread its wings, and clap,[8] an act which never failed to provide hilarity.

The ranks of sleighs raced over the ice road on the river towards Laprairie where the 71st Regiment was stationed, its officers ready with a grand lunch for members of the club.

Sleighing and driving parties were not without their hazards. Occasionally the less-experienced young officer attempted drives over roads that were too narrow or snow that was too deep for a pair of horses. Then both horses and driver floundered, buried in snow, and as the driver was tightly buckled in, it was no easy matter to extricate himself or his companions.[9] For the officer contemptuous of the severity of a Montreal winter, the results could be disastrous. Capt. Jack Saville of the 7th Hussars donned an English top hat, kid gloves, and common leather boots for his ride over the ice from Laprairie. When he arrived at Quebec Gate Barracks and attempted to get out of his sleigh, he was unable to move. Both hands and feet were frozen, and before he recovered sufficiently to be invalided home to England, he had lost several fingers and toes.[10]

These extravagances of the military, when not accompanied by distressing consequences, kept Montreal society attuned to the bizarre. Capt. Lord Mark Kerr's equestrian pranks more often puzzled than amused. He would ride "his back to the horse's head, with an immense umbrella when there was no sun," so that the villagers of Côte des Neiges thought a circus had arrived. On one occasion he rode his horse straight into the dining room and round the tables of the fashionable Donegani Hotel. Donegani's was frequented by American visitors, who sat stunned while the British officer rode past their tables. As the manager rushed in, Lord Mark Kerr rushed out and awaited the excited man who exclaimed, "Oh, my Lord, this will ruin me!" at which Lord Mark handed him a bill for a hundred dollars. The manager returned smiling to the guests and explained the prank at which "they took out their note-books and wrote it down, calling him Lord Mad Kerr . . . and then wrote him invitations to come to New York."[11]

Although horses and clubs associated with horses provided the most popular of the summer and winter sports participated in by both the military and civilian population, the officers of the garrison also tackled with zest indigenous sports such as snowshoeing. The Montreal Snowshoe Club, like the hunt, tended to draw as many military men and their wives to its meets and races as civilians. Capt. James Douglas of the 79th Regiment seldom let a week go by without a day of snowshoeing. The favourite tramps were across the river to a target butt erected by the Royal Artillery or over the mountain when the outing usually included tobogganing and dancing until midnight.[12] The Snowshoe Club became as well organized as the horse races. Stewards planned annual snowshoe races in March, which always closed with the "half mile garrison race," open only to the military. For Montrealers this race was the highlight of the day when they could watch "the gallant defenders of our country floundering and rolling about, encumbered by those rascally frames of gut and hardwood, christened snowshoes and supplied by the Government to their unsophisticated wearers," an event advertised as "one of the best recipes for the blues."[13]

The garrison has been credited with introducing both curling and hockey to Montreal.[14] Whatever the legitimate claims for the military origins of the game of hockey, undoubtedly the military fostered curling. By 1840 the city had two curling clubs—the Montreal Curling Club, presided over by Lt.-Col. John Dyde of the militia, and the Thistle Club.[15] Members of these clubs frequently met the officers and men of the 71st Highlanders in matches and then treated them to dinner. The problem of entertaining a team made up of lieutenants, sergeants, corporals, and privates was solved by two separate dinner parties, one at Mack's for the non-commissioned officers and privates, who "spent the evening in great harmony together," and another at Sword's Hotel where officers were regaled by Dr. Mathieson, who recalled "his boyish days with the 71st."[16]

At St. Helen's Island where cricket matches were played by soldiers as early as 1838,[17] one officer commented that the "best nurses of cricket in our colonies are the army and navy."[18] Montreal had its own Cricket Club in the 1840s which played the garrison frequently, and matches between regimental teams drew civilian audiences.[19] The army's promotion of cricket and ball games as a means of keeping its rank and file out of taverns and brothels led to the building of several ball courts in the 1850s at a cost to the military chest of some £723.[20]

The sport of rowing on the St. Lawrence was initiated by non-commissioned officers of the 89th Regiment. In the summer of 1844 they purchased a ten-oared cutter, which they named *Sphynx* "in honour of their glorious career in Egypt." The *Gazette* applauded their efforts, remarking on 22 June 1844 that "it is singular there should be a total absence of taste for this innocent, healthy and truly national amusement." What began as an exer-

The Thistle Curling Club.

cise in 1844 was regarded by military authorities in 1847 as a duty. The commander of the forces announced that "in this country . . . of lakes and rivers, it appears expedient to exercise soldiers in rowing and the management of boats." His reasons were not altogether altruistic. The heavy expense of hiring boatsmen daily for the prison boat to St. Helen's and the "complaints which have reached him of the inconvenience generally experienced from the disorderly conduct, incivility and inefficiency of the Boatsmen presently employed on the public service" led the commander of the forces to withdraw the prohibition against employing soldiers as boatsmen and the civilian boatsmen were discharged.[21]

The art of fencing, although no longer a necessary prelude to a duel, was still one of the requisites of an officer and gentleman. The garrison has been acknowledged as one of the chief promoters of this sport.[22] There is little evidence of an active fencing group in Montreal until the late 1840s when an old soldier of the Swiss Guard, Monsieur Rosat, opened a salle d'armes on St. Jean Baptiste Street. In a fencing competition among Professor Rosat's pupils held 24 April 1849, Montrealer Augustus Heward competed with Captain Warden of the 19th Regiment for the gold medal. Heward, "distinguished for his skill in all manly games," was awarded the prize for getting the most hits, but Captain Warden was acknowledged as "being an equally skilful swordsman and wonderfully quick in his movements, and another trial might end differently."[23] The matches were described as "one of the best displays of the science of Fencing which we have ever seen out of Paris," and on 25 April the *Gazette* urged the "young gentlemen of the city to extend a little of their patronage to Professor Rosat." A second school of fencing was begun in 1850, and again it was the "Gentlemen of the Army" who were praised for bestowing their patronage on it. On 27 December 1850 the *Pilot* urged "our young men not to let slip the opportunity of becoming masters of the art."

In the area of duelling the officer corps of the garrison was a model of restraint compared with Montrealers in general and the lawyer corps in particular. Even duels among regular officers, duly reported in the press, sometimes turned out to be nothing "but a foolish story." Such was the case when the *Gazette* announced on 28 May 1840 that "it is our painful duty to report the fatal issue of an affair of honour between Lt.-Col. White [*sic*] of the 7th Hussars and Mr Grant, late of the 79th Regiment." In an unusual lapse of caution the *Gazette*, repeating details of the affair from a Toronto newspaper, admitted that "we are not in possession of the particulars, but it is understood that the Colonel fell from the fire of his opponent, and that the cause of the quarrel had reference to the conduct of Colonel White towards a young lady related to Mr. Grant."

Edward Hale quickly enlightened his wife at Sherbrooke as to the accuracy of the *Gazette* report. "You may have seen a foolish story about Grant and Col. White having had a duel on account of the conduct of the latter to Miss de Montenach. It is all my eye!"[24] The course of true love may not have been running smoothly between the commanding officer of the 7th Hussars and the granddaughter of the Baroness de Longueuil, but by 1842 Whyte had won the hand of Mary Anne de Montenach, whose mother was one of the Grants of the LeMoyne de Longueuil family.[25]

Much more accurate was the terse note in the *Transcript* of 24 May 1838 reporting that it was "our melancholy duty to state that a rencontre took place at the race course on Tuesday between Major [Henry John] Warde of the Royals and a Gentleman of this city . . . which proved fatal to the gallant Major." Warde was a popular officer who had led the grenadier company in the bayonet charge on the rebels at Saint-Charles. His antagonist was a former lieutenant of the Royal Montreal Cavalry, Robert Sweeny, the advocate son of the socially prominent potash inspector, Campbell Sweeny.[26] The duel, the most celebrated in Montreal's history,[27] originated in a case of mistaken identity. A bouquet from Major Warde, intended for a French-Canadian lady to whom he was directing his attention, was mistakenly delivered to Sweeny's wife, "an accomplished and attractive personage."[28] Sweeny, a somewhat hot-tempered cavalryman who could "hit a post at full gallop every time, so splendid a marksman was he,"[29] drove to the mess of the Royals to find Warde whom he accused of carrying on a clandestine correspondence with his wife. The result was a duel the next morning at the racecourse in Lachine near the Hadley homestead.[30] Capt. John Mayne of the Royals, who had acted a similar part a year earlier in a duel between Lieutenant Ormsby and Patriote Edouard Rodier,[31] was Major Warde's second, while Dr. Hurst of the Royals and Dr. A. H. David, a brother of Maj. Eleazar David of the Royal Montreal Cavalry, were in attendance.[32] In the first exchange Sweeny's bullet pierced Warde's arm and chest and he fell dead. The only witness other than the seconds and the medical men was a French-Canadian farmer who said to Sweeny, "Vous avez mal commencé votre journée."[33] Sweeny and his seconds fled to the United States while news of the fatal encounter shattered the "gay world" of Montreal society that had been enjoying its "balls, picnics and sleighing parties."[34]

A casual glance at the diaries of young officers[35] stationed in Montreal would lead to the conclusion drawn by a young American clerk who wrote plaintively to his sister at Schenectady that "Montreal can't boast of much amusements in winter . . . for the masses . . . but for the nobility, they 'go it,' in the way of parties and balls."[36] Capt. James Douglas, as son-in-law and aide-de-camp to Lord Cathcart in 1846–47, was much sought after by ambitious hostesses "who fill their residences with over a hundred guests who have to perch on stairs and landings like crows or bluejays on a ladder."[37] Not all local hostesses entertained in such a manner. Captain Douglas went to a "ball at Mrs Molson's, a very large house, but badly laid out."[38] The somewhat petulant young Royal Engineer officer, Arthur Freeling, when invited to an evening party by Mrs. George Moffatt, found Mrs. Moffatt "a vulgar but good-natured woman," while Moffatt was described as "a gentlemanlike-looking man."[39] Perhaps it was this propensity for peevishness that led to Freeling's writing on 25 December 1839, "Christmas Day with nothing to mark it." Such was not the case on New Year's Day when he, with other officers of the garrison, joined in the local custom of paying calls.[40] Freeling enjoyed the day "kept by everyone here, when visits are given and received; Ladies are in State and give you liqueurs and cake, the visiting lasting three days."[41]

There were scarcely enough days in the week to allow for the balls, evening parties, fêtes champêtres, musicals, tableaux vivants, and whist parties enjoyed by both officers and civilians. Officers of the 85th Regiment were hosts at a ball and supper at Rasco's Hotel "to their civil and military friends," the ballroom being decorated in military fashion with a portrait of the Queen, military heroes, and arms.[42] A fête champêtre was attended by Captain Douglas at "Mr. Desbarats [where] a tent was pitched in the garden which was illuminated and the night being very warm, it was a most agreeable place, . . . [and] stayed until three."[43] The sergeants of the 71st Highlanders sought permission to use the upper part of St. Ann's Market for a ball and were allowed to do so "on condition that arrangements be made with the Assurance Office with which the building is insured so that every precaution be taken."[44]

181

Like their civilian confreres, officers who found the Montreal summers something of a burden sought relief at the fashionable Caledonia Springs, situated a little west of the Ottawa River. Starting out by stage for Lachine, they could take the steamer *Oldfield* on the Ottawa River as far as Pointe Fortune where another stage took them to L'Orignal. Here the Caledonia omnibus awaited them for the last stage of their journey.[45] Advertised as a resort where "nothing will be left undone to restore the invalid or amuse the votaries of pleasure," Caledonia Springs would "furnish every comfort."[46] When Captain Douglas arrived, however, he found it a "dull place, nothing but a hut cut out of the forest, and the ground all swampy." He tried the waters of the springs "without much apparent benefit,"[47] an experience he had in common with Thomas D'Arcy McGee who some years later confessed he was at the Springs "drinking water with a strong savour of rotten eggs."[48] By the time that Captain Douglas had tried the baths, "got terribly bit by mosquitoes," played a bit of billiards and ten pins, he was ready to go on to Bytown and leave the "very stupid set staying in the house" behind.[49]

British officers thus enjoyed or endured the amenities of social life in Montreal, privately expressing their disappointments, pleasures, and opinions with a disarming frankness and, in their memoirs, providing a glimpse into Montreal life and personalities not found elsewhere. From those few Montrealers who recorded their memoirs, the garrison seldom received anything but uncritical praise. When the garrison left in 1870, it was with wistful nostalgia that Adele Clarke wrote, "With the departure of the Garrison, the character of Montreal society . . . entirely changed . . . and was replaced by another society which has gradually developed itself, but on totally different lines, not united as in the old days, but broken into numerous sets, who scarcely meet each other and are occupied with thoughts and avocations quite dissimilar."[50] That the memories of a young girl growing up in the Montreal of the 1830s and 1840s should be almost entirely intertwined with troop activities and personalities is an indication of the social importance of the garrison. That she should end her memoirs on a note of regret at the departure of the regulars from Montreal is a tribute to the men who formed that garrison.

Part

Financial Aspects of the Garrison

The peculiar inconvenience under which the
Province labors is the want of a metallic colonial
currency. The Banks meet this inconvenience by
a supply of notes, for in a commercial country
there must be some means of barter. No national
paper can keep pace with coin. It is only the
sign, not of riches, but of Credit. Paper money
may be dispensed with, coin cannot.
Commissary General Sir R. I. Routh to military
secretary, 4 December 1830

12. The Commissariat, Colonial Banking, and Currency

While magistrates and volunteer firemen saw the garrison as a source of help, sportsmen as competition, and clergymen saw it as a source of increasing congregations or of corruption, Montreal merchants focused their attention on the building at 53 Notre Dame Street—the commissariat. Even when the garrison consisted of only an understrength battalion of soldiers and military expenditure was so small as to be marginal to the economy of the city as a whole, the commissariat operations were never treated with indifference by Montreal businessmen. The merchants were not, however, guilty of the charge levelled at them by some colonial reformers in England who asserted with more boldness than truth that rebellion in Lower Canada was deliberately encouraged by Montreal merchants eager to profit from increased military spending.[1]

That the city did benefit financially from the garrison is without doubt. Troops needed a daily supply of food, fuel, and candles, and often more than a daily sufficiency of drink. Medical supplies for the soldiers and forage for horses had to be bought locally, water taxes paid, and buildings hired as additional barracks, regimental hospitals, and officers' quarters. How much city fathers saved by relying upon troops to suppress civil disturbances, rather than increasing the police force, can only be hinted at. The military chest received occasional reimbursement from the provincial government for the garrison's part in suppressing disorders, usually in the form of payment for barrack accommodations for the additional troops that were kept in the city at the request of the government.[2] Yet even then military authorities could not be certain of payment. When the Provincial Cavalry was ordered up from the frontier in the summer of 1849 to help suppress disturbances, the provincial government refused to pay the bill for officers' lodgings.[3]

In the Montreal of the early 1830s—a city of a population of under 30,000—even the expenditure of a single regiment, calculated at something less than £10,000, was not unwelcome. By the early 1840s Montreal's population had risen to about 40,000 while the garrison had trebled in size and more than trebled its expenditure.[4] The city had now become military headquarters of the Canadas and thus enjoyed the additional largess resulting from the move of army departments from Quebec City to Montreal. As late as 1849 Earl Grey, the secretary of state for war and the colonies, considered the expenditure of a single regiment of sufficient financial importance to Montreal to propose withdrawing one "as a punishment on Montreal for its misconduct" during the Rebellion Losses agitation.[5]

As far as the financial and commercial life of the city in the 1830s was concerned, perhaps of more importance than the actual size of the military outlay were the attempts of commissary officers to influence colonial monetary policy. The commissariat, as the civilian branch of the military establishment, handled not only the payment of regimental and staff services and the purchase of supplies for the army, but also took care of the financial commitments of the mother country to the colony—the payment of the governor general's salary, the expenses of the Indian Department, the navy, the ecclesiastical establishment, pensions to retired soldiers, remittances to half-pay officers, and ordnance services.[6]

When provincial affairs became so strained by the tactics of the Assembly in refusing to vote supplies that the administration was without the necessary funds to carry on the day-to-day business of the government, it was the military chest of the commissariat that provided the wherewithal to tide the province over until the appointed Special Council took over the functions of government. And in the midst of rebellion itself, it was to the military chest at the citadel in Quebec City that Montreal bankers hastily sent their specie deposits for safekeeping.

The commissary general was usually an officer of vast financial experience whose duties still partook something of the original character of commissary officers who were expected to combine purely financial functions with those of intelligence agents.[7] Certainly, the commissary general of the Canadas in the 1830s and 1840s was officially regarded as the "confidential officer of the Lords of the Treasury" whose position and duties "required that he should possess an intimate acquaintance with all matters pertaining to the currency of the country."[8] He was expected to make reports to the Treasury not only on colonial currency, but also on provincial banking institutions, the amount of specie circulating, and colonial legislation dealing with financial matters. The lengthy and very able reports of Sir Randolph Routh, the commissary general who served in Canada from 1827 to 1842,[9] provide some of the best summaries of the development and problems of colonial banking and currency.

It was largely through Sir Randolph Routh that the imperial government tried to put pressure on the local Legislature to have existing colonial currencies replaced by British sterling, partly in the interests of imperial commercial policy and partly in the hope of solving the chronic shortage of specie in the provinces. The circulation of British sterling from the military chest, "almost the only specie that finds its way into Upper Canada," as Henry John Boulton reported in 1825,[10] was hindered in Lower Canada because sterling was not recognized as legal currency and a provincial law set the rate of exchange of the British shilling at thirteen pennies local currency.[11] Local currency simply meant other imported specie such as American and Spanish coins or the old French coins,[12] as Canada did not mint its own coinage until 1858. Routh considered the real value of the British shilling to be fourteen pence local currency.[13] Thus the soldier using his daily pay in Montreal lost a penny on every shilling, a serious loss for the soldier whose pay was small enough as it was. Even more serious was the loss to the military chest whenever large expenditures had to be made.

In a lengthy report Routh explained why British specie did not circulate. Sterling could not be issued at all in payment for army provisions and supplies, he said, unless it could be immediately returned to the military chest and "exchanged at a premium for

Spanish and American coins, and in no instance has the object of the British Government as regards its circulation been carried into effect." Indeed, Routh pointed out, "more frequently, it [sterling] has not been paid away at all, but a traffic made of the name, and the commissariat checks have been collected and presented as so much British money, and a Bill granted as such for the total sum. Thus, therefore, a large negotiation may be carried on under the name of British money though there may be a very small sum in the chest, and even that never issued in payment."[14]

The British shilling suffered similar disadvantages in relation to the inflated value of the American dollar in the lower province. By provincial law the rate of the American dollar was set at four shillings and sixpence sterling. Routh pointed out to the Treasury that although "all acknowledged . . . this rate . . . to be incorrect . . . there is not the same concurrence of opinion in regard to the true value which should be given to it."[15] The commissariat could not avoid buying American and Spanish dollars at this inflated rate, as many of its creditors insisted on payment in this form of currency.

The myth of the circulation of British specie in Lower Canada by means of the military chest is nowhere more evident than in the payment for the building of the Rideau Canal, by far the largest negotiation of the commissariat in Canada in the early 1830s. In this transaction, estimated to cost the British taxpayer £800,000 on its completion, the contractors took drafts on the Bank of Montreal which they then exchanged at a premium for bank notes.[16] Routh explained to the lords of the Treasury that the "balances in the Military Chests in Lower Canada, including Bytown, average £150,000 to £200,000, but this sum does not circulate for specie; [because] of its scarcity it is bought up immediately for duties, Treasury Bills, or other commercial purposes. . . . As the question now stands, the end of the Commissariat Cash payments is to circulate [local] Bank Notes."[17] Even a decade later there was no apparent change in the attitude of contractors or merchants towards their method of receiving payment from the military chest. In such a small commissariat operation as that in connection with the detachment of regulars at Cornwall, the officer in charge reported his balance was in "Montreal Bank Notes, reserved . . . for the payment of his fresh meat contractor, who applied for payment in these notes, as more negotiable than those of Upper Canada."[18]

Difficulties for regimental paymasters were compounded in the 1830s because the paymasters were prevented by army regulations from exchanging the regimental pay into local dollars through a broker or bank, a negotiation that would have given some financial advantage to the military.[19] The prohibition against the soldier being paid in any form other than specie was prompted by several considerations, not the least of which was protection against forgery and against the failure of private banks whose paper money would thus be valueless.[20] Although bank failure was rare in the Canadas,[21] Routh was wary of such a possibility and sent to the Treasury an excerpt from a weekly New York newspaper which contained a list of detected forgeries and broken banks in North America.[22]

The provincial government tried, in 1830, to enact a currency law which would have brought the exchange rate of British specie more in line with its actual value. Undoubtedly such a law would have made the circulation of British specie in the lower province easier. The proposed law, however, ran into difficulties, the prime one being a lack of agreement among legislators as to the true value of the American dollar. The commissary general warned treasury officials that it was "an essential point to establish for unless it be justly ascertained, the British Silver and Gold Coins can never impartially compete with it in circulation."[23] To corroborate his opinion that the real value of the dollar was four shillings and twopence, rather than four shillings and sixpence, Routh sent to the Treasury a report of a committee of the United States Senate. This report frankly admitted that the estimate of the American dollar as "being worth 4/6 and the English Pound Sterling as $4.44 is wholly erroneous. . . . The Spanish dollar has not, for a century, been worth 4 shillings and sixpence. The American dollar never was."[24]

The Legislature failed to pass a currency bill in 1830 owing, Routh said, to the "disinclination to adopt Sterling as the currency of the country." Currency reform had to wait another decade before the sterling rate was accommodated to its true value. In the meantime the province and the commissariat continued to labour "under the peculiar inconvenience . . . of the want of a metallic Colonial currency."[25]

The procedure by which military financial operations were carried out in the 1830s and 1840s was relatively simple. The commander of the forces issued a written warrant to the commissary general authorizing him to negotiate bills of exchange drawn on the Treasury through a provincial bank.[26] Funds were provided by the local banks, usually in paper notes. This method of payment would not do for the soldiers who had to be paid in specie.[27] Nor would it do for payment to the habitants who fed the army and who had a "strong objection to Bank Notes."[28]

As early as 1812 the commissariat had experienced this "prejudice of the Canadians to all paper money."[29] By the 1830s the attitude of French-Canadian farmers had not changed. Their reluctance to take anything but coin in payment for goods, according to Routh, "is one of the causes which retains the depreciated old French coins in circulation. Even in the market place . . . a Canadian will dispose of his goods at a less price for silver, and always endeavours to change his banknotes before he leaves town." Routh wished to have the old French crowns removed from circulation as they were "over-valued" and the coin itself "so old, with no means of adding to it, that . . . it would be better to call it in altogether."[30]

The commissariat's method of buying specie was to advertise for a certain amount by public tender.[31] Banks, merchants, or brokers would then state the amount of specie they had for sale, the rate of premium or discount asked, and the value of the specie in British sterling. As early as 1830 Routh had suggested that the commissariat resume the practice of importing specie directly from England "which generally can be done on better terms than by negotiation in the Province," but his suggestion was not taken up. The scarcity and subsequent high price of specie remained a problem for both the province and the commissariat. For example, in 1848 when Commissary General William Filder advertised locally for specie, he found that the amount offered by public tender was "insufficient to meet the wants of the Public Service and the rates at which it has been tendered . . . unreasonable." He therefore received permission from the commander of the forces to send an officer of the commissariat to New York "for the purpose of negotiating Bills on Her Majesty's Treasury to the requisite extent."[32]

Faced as the commissariat was with a disadvantageous exchange rate on British sterling and forced to deal with bank drafts on the Bank of Montreal or to cope with a variety of specie such as Spanish and American dollars, gold eagles, depreciated French coins, and pistorines, its officers had an unenviable task. In 1832, for example, the quarterly survey of the military chest revealed a balance of £97,762,[33] which was divided into £4,900 British gold currency, £2,410 in British sterling and copper, £88,833 in American and Spanish silver dollars; £800 in bills of exchange, and £819 in provincial currency, likely French crowns or bank notes.

By its control of the military chest, the commissariat represented one of the three major financial operations in Montreal, at times equalling or exceeding the operations of both the Bank of Montreal and the provincial government. In the period from the rebellion to the early 1850s, the annual military expenditure ranged from £1,000,000 in 1839 to £419,000 for most of the 1840s, and it did not drop to £171,566 until 1854 when most troops left for the Crimea.[34] The provincial revenue in 1839 was only £284,209, and by 1842 it had risen to £365,605.[35] On the other hand, the Bank of Montreal's paid-up capital stock on 1 December 1837 was £378,741, and by 1 June 1840 it had increased to £483,869.[36]

Similarly, the specie deposit of the military chest in Montreal frequently surpassed that of the Bank of Montreal. In the early 1830s the specie deposit in the military chest, which by military regulations was supposed to contain only enough for two months' expenditure,[37] ranged from £57,388 to £129,419.[38] After the abnormal expenditure of the rebellion era when the Montreal chest might hold as much as £200,000 at any given time,[39] the specie holdings returned to a more normal pattern. On 30 March 1841 a survey on the chest showed a deposit of £122,605, and throughout the decade the specie deposits ranged from £80,722 to £11,233.[40] By comparison, the specie holdings of the Bank of Montreal on 1 June 1840 was £89,526.[41] Clearly, then, the size of the holdings in the military chest was of major financial importance to the merchants and bankers of Montreal, even if its specie deposits did not circulate.

For the bank that received most of the commissariat business, there were not only the profits to be made on the negotiation of the bills of exchange, but what was perhaps of more importance—the prestige and credit rating that came with being acknowledged secure enough to handle the large military business, a position almost tantamount to being a government bank.[42] The Bank of Montreal received the bulk of the military business because commissariat authorities regarded it as considerably safer than its major rival, the Bank of Upper Canada, since its circulation of notes was more in keeping with its paid-up capital stock.[43]

Reciprocally, its position as the banking institution preferred by the commissariat enhanced its reputation for stability.

In the early 1830s the Treasury proposed to transfer all the commissariat work to local banks, a move which the directors of the Bank of Montreal would hardly fail to welcome. Yet, much as they might relish undertaking the entire financial business of the military establishment, the directors did not receive uncritical praise from the commissary general. Far from acquiescing in the wisdom of the proposal, Commissary General Routh took seventeen pages to explain to the lords of the Treasury why he considered such a step impractical. He assured the lords of the Treasury that "there is but one Bank in the Lower Province, probably in both, that could reasonably attempt all the military financial business which is the Montreal Bank," yet even the Bank of Montreal, which Routh admitted "continues to stand almost without a rival establishment," would be of "doubtful ultimate advantage since it has become too necessary to the enterprize of the Province."[44]

Routh discounted the argument that the solidity of the Bank of Montreal was guaranteed by its being under the control of the local Legislature. He asserted, "I never could discover any practical control, and where their interests are concerned, my own impressions would lead me to reverse the argument"—that is, that the Legislature was under the control of the Bank of Montreal. As proof of this, Routh referred to the application of the bank to the Legislature for a renewal of its charter, an application which had something of a threat about it. According to Routh, the directors pointed out that the bank had "£600,000 in Debts in the Lower Province, and that if the Charter was not renewed, the Debts must be called in, which would occasion a provincial bankruptcy." Routh considered that "if . . . the prosperity of the colony rests upon the will or interest of the Montreal bank . . . it was clearly imprudent to absorb the whole current of military business in one private Bank."[45]

In objecting to the proposal from a financial point of view, Routh laid bare some of the practices and problems of local banking institutions. He pointed out that if the Treasury lodged a large sum of money in advance with any private banks for the payment of military disbursements, "they would become the real capitalists of the Bank, trading on the Public funds." He described the limited responsibility of the directors of the Bank of Montreal who "with little personal risk" could undertake great speculations. In addition, Routh warned that "private institutions may monopolize coin and not let it circulate. Banks keep up a deposit of coin . . . [and] if a sudden large demand for specie arises, the Banks are the most ready competitors, having the money at hand."[46] The accuracy of Routh's analysis of local banking practices became apparent in 1837 with the outbreak of disturbances. There was a run on specie because "common people are not satisfied to hold paper."[47] With the suspension of specie payments by the banks,[48] the premium on specie rose from 4 to 8 per cent. Yet, in ordinary business transactions, people suffered the 8 per cent loss rather than take paper money.[49]

From the military point of view, Routh believed that both the efficiency and the secrecy of troop movements would be jeopardized if the commissariat could not act independently of the banks. He saw the difficulties that would arise if troops had to be moved quickly to the border in some emergency or cantoned in the villages where the peasantry objected to payment in paper money. The proposal might work if the troops were stationary, but Routh insisted that a "body of Troops must possess a military Chest . . . [since] a distant or doubtful payment paralyzes the life and efficiency of every operation."[50]

The difficulties experienced by the commissariat because British sterling was not legal tender in the 1830s were somewhat obviated by a new currency act in 1841. Under this law the British sovereign became legal tender at the rate of twenty-four shillings and fourpence local currency.[51] The American dollar was valued at four shillings and twopence,[52] the rate which commissariat officers had been advocating throughout the thirties. Yet, despite this improvement in the legal status and exchange rate of British specie, the commissariat gave up the task of attempting to promote its circulation to the exclusion of other coinage. The use of Spanish and American silver dollars was too much a part of the financial system in Montreal, and by the early 1840s the commissariat finally acknowledged this by paying the troops in Spanish silver dollars.[53]

It was not until most of the British troops had been withdrawn for service in the Crimea that the Bank of Montreal received the entire financial business of the military establishment. In 1854 the Treasury agreed with Deputy Commissary General William Robinson that the "altered position of the Commissariat in Canada, arising from the reduction of the permanent military force," rendered it expedient to "discontinue the system of payments in specie from the Commissariat Chests and to transact all money operations through the Bank of Montreal."[54]

The economic importance of the British garrison to Montreal in the 1830s and 1840s lay as much in its influence on local currency policies and in the prestige it lent to the Bank of Montreal as it did in actual cash outlay for goods and services, though that outlay was far from marginal. The great increase in the size of the garrison following the years of civil disturbance and open rebellion meant a considerable augmentation in military spending—a development that lent some substance to the claims of colonial reformers. Yet no evidence has been found to justify their suggestion that rebellion was openly encouraged by Montreal merchants who hoped to profit from such turbulence. On the contrary, the postrebellion decade was one of economic instability for the city which felt acutely the effects of new imperial economic policies that opted for free trade. It may well be that the presence of the larger garrison in the 1840s and its concomitant increased spending helped tide the city over a depressed period.

13.
Army Pay and Purchases

The steady rise of wages and prices in Montreal during the late 1830s and the 1840s posed difficulties for the commissariat in its day-to-day spending and forced military personnel to exercise both caution and talent in their dealings with Montreal business and professional men. In transactions involving the military chest, commissariat officials showed great care and tenacity in getting the most for the military pound. Nor is there any evidence during this period of jobbery within the department, for Sir Randolph Routh's reputation was built on his ability to cleanse the commissariat of favouritism and any close association of commissary officers with local contractors.

From the rebellion period until 1845 the number of troops in the city never fell below 1,500,[1] roughly three regiments. As the yearly cost of a battalion of infantry had by 1841 risen to £26,415,[2] Montreal merchants garnered at least part of this yearly regimental outlay of some £79,000. From 1846 to 1853 the garrison was gradually reduced to about two regiments, with a corresponding reduction in military spending.

But Montreal did not benefit only from regimental expenditure. There were also commissariat purchases for the whole of Canada and the outlay for the headquarters' staff. Some fluctuation occurred from year to year in the size of the headquarters' staff and from the occasional change of military policy, such as the prohibition in 1845 against the use of military personnel as clerks and messengers.[3] Yet, on the whole, the headquarters' staff of some twenty-two regular officers, sixteen civilians, and eighteen noncommissioned officers and privates received an annual pay of about £13,419.[4]

The commander of the forces received a daily pay of £9. 9s. 6d., a yearly income of close to £3,550, which was about half the salary received by the governor general. The commandant of the Montreal station—usually a major-general—received £750 a year. The soldier's daily pay was one shilling, with an extra penny for beer, given out each morning after drill,[5] "a great improvement," as one officer noted, "over the old system of paying once a month when such scenes of riot and drunkenness prevailed that it was hard to find enough sober men to carry on the duties of the Regiment."[6]

From his daily pay a private usually received only three or four pennies to spend, for sixpence was deducted for his daily pound of beef and bread and a further three or four pennies came out for his messing. The latter amount was collected by the orderly corporal of the day who then went to the nearest and cheapest market to buy such items as coffee, sugar, milk, potatoes, and fresh vegetables to supplement the soldier's daily rations of beef and bread. Part of the soldier's pay also went to the army canteens at the Quebec Gate Barracks or St. Helen's Island to buy extra provisions or drink in the evening,[7] as the army provided only breakfast and a noonday meal. This arrangement of barrack canteens for the sale of bread, vegetables, and other food as well as drink was started in the hopes of keeping the men out of taverns. Some officers viewed the canteens as "drunkenness made easy for the men,"[8] but the canteens were gradually brought under stricter military supervision with the profits going to the men to assist in the maintenance of reading rooms and other comforts.

The Quebec Gate Barracks canteen was run by a Montrealer who paid £10 a year rent for a house used both as a dwelling and as a canteen. He paid a further amount each month for every ten noncommissioned officers and privates occupying the barracks during the year. This gave him "exclusive permission for the sale of Provisions, as well as Liquors of every description within the limits of the Barracks."[9] Canteen keepers were not always scrupulous about paying their rent and monthly fees to the commissariat. Upon a complaint being lodged with the commander of the forces that "Mr. Tilton was indebted . . . £270. 14s. sterling on account of the Canteen of which he was virtually tenant," military authorities tried to exact the money from him by withholding from his wife the money due to her for supplying bread to the troops, but the commissary general forbade this type of pressure.[10]

Officers who dined and wined at their own messes complained bitterly about the high cost of eating and drinking at the Montreal station where "the daily price of the officers' mess Dinner amounts to as much as it did in the West Indies" because although "in Canada provisions are cheap . . . [but] servants' wages are high, particularly cooks of even *ordinary* [*sic*] capacity . . . whereas in the West Indies provisions were high, but servants cheap."[11] One of the chief complaints of officers serving in Montreal was that they did not receive the annual Regent's allowance of £25 per company towards lessening the cost of the mess wine.[12] Regiments serving in England and Ireland and on some foreign stations received this bounty from the Crown to counter local high prices.

Lt.-Col. Charles Hay of the 19th Regiment, who was stationed in Montreal in 1849 and 1850, stated that "officers find themselves much straitened in circumstances because of the high prices and the high duties imposed on wines, liquors." He protested that "never since the Regiment has been abroad have the officers felt so severely the deprivation of the Regent's allowance as in Canada."[13] The colonial duty on wine was one shilling and sixpence per gallon, an import duty which Americans thought so extraordinary that they would not believe Lord Elgin when he told them that it was "actually the practice to charge with duties articles imported . . . for the use of troops maintained there."[14]

Import duties were also collected on military clothing and stores as well as on wines and "cordials for the officers' mess."[15] In fact the colonial government bore down so heavily on such imports that protests flew from commanding officers to the military secretary and from the military secretary to the provincial inspector general of revenue. In 1849, for instance, a lieutenant was "obliged to pay £6. 7s. 2d. duty on a shell jacket, 1 pair of boots, 1 fraze cap, and a sash and cross belt, exclusive of the Freight and price of the articles imported."[16] The military secretary complained to Francis Hincks, the provincial inspector general, of the "excessive impost levied on wines . . . military clothing and appointments." He added that the Regent's allowance "would not have been withheld from Troops serving in Canada but upon the reliance and conviction that the Provincial Government would secure the service, sent for its protection, from any such burdensome impost."[17] Hincks saw the justice of the military claims to exemption from such duties, and he prevailed upon the provincial government to remove the duty on wines. Commenting on this gesture, Lord Elgin, still smarting from the treatment he had received in Montreal in 1849 and not entirely convinced of the military's goodwill towards him, told Earl Grey, "It is gratifying to reflect that henceforth the Gentlemen of Her Majesty's Army will be able to drink confusion to the Governor-Genl. and his administration in untaxed liquor."[18]

Officers could avoid the high colonial duty on liquors and beer by patronizing local brewers and distillers. Both officers and soldiers did so, but on a moderate scale judging by the amount of ale, beer, and spirits imported annually into Montreal.[19] Still, officials at Molson's brewery referred approvingly to "the tramp of the famous British Regiments which became the Brewery's neighbours,"[20] and not without reason. Cashbooks at Molson's during the forties and fifties showed daily deliveries of beer and ale to the officers' and sergeants' messes of the 19th, 23rd, and 71st Regiments and to the officers' mess of the Royal Artillery.[21] Deliveries also went daily to individual officers and noncommissioned officers. To accommodate the popular officers of the 71st Regiment who were stationed at St. Johns, Molson's assumed the cost of cartage and toll charges.[22] The commander of the forces was not above drinking local beer; his account with Molson's for three months in the spring of 1849 ran to £39.[23] In an average year Molson's earned about £253 from its direct beer sales to military personnel and messes, not to mention an additional £128 from rent on a house used as a military hospital.[24]

For officers and soldiers there was no way to avoid the purchase of additional winter clothing from Montreal merchants. Officers had to buy at their own expense a "great coat with fur, cap and gloves of fur, and snow boots of a regimental pattern . . . which adds considerably to the expense of an officer's outfit."[25] For each soldier arriving in Canada, an allowance of £1. 10s. sterling was allotted for the purchase of winter clothing, and an additional five shillings a year for the upkeep of the clothing. Soldiers were to be provided with "1 pr. boots not exceeding 15s. currency, 1 Fur cap at 7s. 6d. and 1 pr. mitts 1s. 6d. . . . the boots to be made of Stout shoe hide, grain side out and unblacked, closed in with a tongue, stout double soles, length of leg 15 inches and wide enough to allow trousers inside and large enough to admit of 2 prs. of worsted socks being worn."[26] The soldier's winter cap was to be "wedge-shaped, 8 inches high and made of muskrat, with ear covers and turned down over the neck; the mitts the common mitts of the country." Army regulations stipulated that the cap was to last at least three years, the boots and mitts two years, "the articles to be kept in repair at the expense of the soldiers."[27]

By the early 1850s the sum of £1. 10s. was far from adequate because of the "great rise that has taken place in Canada, not only in the price of all articles of clothing . . . but still more in wages and labour. It is quite impossible to provide soldiers with the necessary articles of winter equipment [at £1. 10s.]. . . . The increased expense tends to throw the soldier heavily in debt upon his first arrival in Canada and [causes] discouragement. . . which, added to the nearness of the frontier, induces desertion."[28]

Whenever possible military supplies were bought in England. Only those items such as fresh food, wood, medical supplies, and forage that were too bulky or too perishable to survive ocean transport were purchased in the colony. When a commissariat voucher indicated purchases in Montreal of local stationery, the secretary at war sharply reprimanded the commander of the forces and prohibited any further such purchases. Sir Richard Jackson, by way of explanation, replied that "a great portion of the stationery sent from England during the last two years was of a very inferior description, some of it so bad, indeed, that I was compelled to order many articles to be purchased here."[29]

Montreal merchants competed eagerly for military tenders calling for supplies of fresh beef "of the best quality . . . equal proportions of Fore and Hind Quarters . . . none of the Suet withdrawn" to be delivered daily to the troops, and for daily forage for the horses of the Royal Artillery and of officers of the general staff to the amount of "10 lbs. of oats, 12 lbs. of hay and 8 lbs. of straw, all to be of the best quality, the oats and hay to be of the growth of the year 1840." Tenders for 7,750 barrels of 196 pounds each of flour, "the whole to be warranted to keep sweet and sound for six months after delivery," were eagerly sought, as were tenders for firewood and hospital supplies.[30]

At least 2,750 cords of wood were needed each year at the Quebec Gate Barracks and St. Helen's Island.[31] As wood became more expensive because of the depletion of the supply in the Montreal district, the military began experimenting with the use

199

of coal for heating the barracks. By 1845 the 1,145 soldiers in barracks were warmed by 622 cords of wood costing £590. 18s., supplemented by 9,951 bushels of coal at a cost of £428. 19s.[32] To fill the palliasses used as mattresses by soldiers some 20,000 bundles of twelve pounds each of "good oaten straw, free from weeds," were needed each year.[33] Tenders were also called for 2,500 birch brooms,[34] required each year to keep the barracks swept. Contracts for whitewashing the barracks ran as high as £970. 17s.[35]

The transport of troops within Canada was a lucrative business for which Montreal firms keenly competed and often Molson's steamers, plying between Montreal, Sorel, and Quebec City, came out ahead. Some idea of the cost of transporting troops is indicated in the movement of the 19th Regiment from Kingston to Montreal. This regiment of 35 officers, 629 men, 38 women, and 136 children, together with their baggage, was transported by steamer at a cost of £472. 5s.[36] D. Torrance and Company of Montreal offered to transport troops from Montreal to Halifax at the rate of eighteen dollars for officers and ten dollars for each soldier.[37] Samuel Perry offered the same service on the schooner *Florence* and guaranteed the troops "good and wholesome provisions during the voyage such as is usually provided for a ship's crew, consisting of salt pork and beef, with potatoes, biscuits or soft bread, together with tea or coffee, sugar, the officers to be provided with proper cabin fare, bedding and liquors." His rate was nineteen dollars for officers and ten dollars for each soldier. Another competitor for troop transport proposed being paid only half the fare at the beginning of the voyage, "the other half to be paid at Halifax, providing that the officer in charge signs a certificate that the Master did furnish good and wholesome rations."[38]

The purchase and sale of army horses were negotiated through the commissariat, the regulated price of a horse being £31.[39] When two cavalry regiments were ordered to Canada in 1838, officers were sent out in advance to buy horses.[40] The success of their local purchases was indicated by the appearance of the 7th Hussars on parade at the Champ de Mars. It was remarked that "nothing can look better . . . considering that upwards of half of the horses have been bought since coming to this country."[41]

Horses were required chiefly for the Royal Artillery and the Provincial Cavalry. Artillery officers preferred to buy their horses in the Eastern Townships rather than in Montreal,[42] while officers of the Provincial Cavalry more often went to the United States to get horses, perhaps because of a wider choice at a lower price. It may have been this preference for American-bred horses that led the provincial government to levy a 20 per cent duty on imported horses, a measure which the officers of the Provincial Cavalry protested vigorously against.[43]

Montreal auctioneers managed the sale of redundant military horses and bitterly complained if the army business was taken out of their hands. Norman Bethune, lieutenant-colonel of the 1st Battalion of the Montreal Volunteer Militia raised in 1837, was Queen's auctioneer, a post given him by Lord Dalhousie in 1824.[44] When the commissary general advised Bethune in 1843 that "the practice of holding . . . sales of army horses in the Public streets or Market Place is not calculated to . . . ensure such prices as shall be most advantageous to the Public," Bethune replied that he and his predecessor had always sold horses "at the head of New Market . . . but he was willing to change to any other locality which the commissary general pointed out."[45] Shortly afterwards Bethune was annoyed to see an advertisement by auctioneer John Jones of "19 Horses belonging to the Royal Artillery to be sold in consequence of a reduction" at Tattersall's, the horse market, the horses being described as "handsome carriage horses, well adapted for family use." Bethune protested to the military secretary of the governor general and pointed out that he "had the sales of all Government property in the city . . . and outposts of the Districts, and frequently the performance of the duty has been attended with pecuniary loss . . . by reason of the trifling proceeds of the sales." He complained that "if the Queen's Auctioneer is only to have the petty sales of Government property, his commission would not be worth holding."[46]

The army's dealings with the Montreal Water Works were no more cordial than they were with the Queen's auctioneer.[47] Although the men who headed the Water Works might have been dinner companions and comrades-in-arms of regular officers in times of rebellion and civil strife, their financial affairs in reference to the military were scrutinized with care by the officers of the commissariat. The military's quarrel with the Montreal Water Works dated from 1817. In that year the company had bought a lot of land near the summit of Citadel Hill from the military. There a reservoir for supplying the city with water had been built "at great expense." Peter McGill, one of the directors of the Water Works, along with Moses Judah Hays protested to the commander of the forces, Sir Richard Jackson, that the levelling of Citadel Hill shortly afterwards by the military caused the newly built reservoir to leak so that another reservoir had to be built. The company took legal action in 1839 against the Crown and asked "damages of £433 with interest."[48]

The case went before the Court of King's Bench and, like good tacticians, military authorities decided on a counterattack. They instituted legal proceedings against the company for £491. 5s. 8d. plus interest at 6 per cent from 28 December 1819 for nonpayment of two-thirds of the purchase price of the land.[49] The case dragged on from 1839 until 1843 when the city corporation bought the Water Works and a settlement was worked out.[50]

In spite of the legal squabbles, troops could not exist without water. Military authorities entered into an agreement with the Water Works in 1837 for "fixing . . . pipes into the Barracks to supply water . . . at a cost of £30 a year for 450 men or 1s. 4d. per year for each soldier in Barracks." By 1844, with the rise of prices, the commissariat agreed to increase the rate of payment to two shillings per soldier a year after the company had refused to accept one shilling and fourpence as payment because it was insufficient. The Treasury Board agreed that the "sum of 2 shillings per man . . . is not more than a fair and reasonable compensation for the supply of water to the troops in Barracks at Montreal."[51]

Professional Montrealers such as notaries and lawyers benefited from the military chest. Although he had to wait until 1845 for the settlement of his account, Charles Richard Ogden, the attorney general of rebellion days, received £440. 7s. for services to the military from 1837 to 1841 "after the account had undergone a very careful examination in the office of the Military Secretary."[52] Lewis Thomas Drummond, the attorney general during the trials of the soldiers charged in connection with the Gavazzi riot, received £100 for attending the general court-martial and "other works" for fifteen days.[53] As all military contracts for purchases of supplies and for work had to be notarized, the military notary business was heavy. Until 1840 Louis Guy, father of the French-Canadian loyalist officer who had undertaken to mobilize the Montreal volunteers in 1837, received much of the notary work from military authorities.[54] During the forties and fifties it was shared, among others, by T. Doucet, H. Griffin, Joseph Belle, and J. H. Jobin.[55]

When it came to dealing with Montreal landlords, commissariat officials showed surprising pertinacity. Montreal was a garrison city without any accommodations whatever for officers,[56] and even its accommodations for troops—a former nunnery and an old jail—left something to be desired. Commissariat officers became experienced in bargaining with local proprietors for houses and buildings suitable for temporary barracks. For instance, when Deputy Quartermaster-General Sir Charles Gore took it upon himself to rent a house on St. Lewis Street as an office, he was severely rebuked by the commander of the forces, who informed him that "in consequence of your previously engaging the house at £70 currency per annum, no room had been left for action on the part of the Commissariat in the settlement of the terms . . . [and] that the House might have been obtained at a lower rent if the negotiation had not been taken out of the hands of the Commissariat." Gore was told that the commissariat was instructed to pay only £43, "the balance [to] be borne by yourself until the circumstance be made known to the Secretary at War . . . for a decision."[57]

In renting Montreal properties, the commissariat faced the problems of inflation over the period from 1840 to 1855 when prices "of all the necessities of life . . . attained double the price demanded of them in 1840."[58] In 1837 a regimental mess could be hired at £65 a year, but in 1841 the amount paid for hiring officers' quarters was about £1,328 a year.[59] By 1849 the rent paid to Montrealers for buildings hired as barracks, offices, and stores amounted to £2,403. 13s. 9d. sterling a year, while an additional sum of £3,213 sterling was paid to various regimental and staff officers as lodging money. Thus Montreal landlords received a total of some £5,616 yearly from military personnel.[60] This amount included £250 paid to Baron Grant of Longueuil for the rent of the Water Street Barracks, but the commissariat demanded and received reimbursement from the provincial government for this sum because the barracks was used for a regiment retained in Montreal as an aid to civil power.[61]

Other Montrealers enjoyed the largess of the commissariat. Sir James Stuart's property on St. Mary's Street was leased as officers' quarters at a rental of £600 a year. George Gregory and J. Tobin leased buildings as officers' quarters and messes at a yearly rental of £250. John Donegani received £150 for a building used as an ordnance storehouse, and George-Etienne Cartier received £140 a year for a building used as the Royal Artillery hospital.[62] In 1852, after two great fires of that year destroyed some 1,400 houses, the scarcity of living accommodations put the rental of houses at such a premium that the ordnance had to apply for increased rates of lodging allowances for officers.[63]

In 1845, under pressure of the Oregon crisis, military authorities determined to solve the problem of poor barracks accommodations for soldiers and the lack of quarters for officers. A new cantonment was to be built on part of the Logan farm between Papineau Road and Amherst Street. The estimated purchase price of the property was £10,000.[64] Moses Judah Hays was hired as an "agent of property" to prepare an estimate of what the Quebec Gate Barracks "including the Barrack and Ordnance offices, stabling, commissariat stores, fuel yard, Military Hospital" would sell for. Hays considered that the property would "realize sixty thousand pounds currency [about $300,000][65] . . . as this property has been much enhanced in value since the Corporation has purchased the adjoining property . . . as well as . . . the Montreal Water Works property . . . for the creation of a New Market."[66]

The local Ordnance Board considered that the sale of the Quebec Gate Barracks would more than compensate for the building of a new cantonment,[67] but when it became known that the military was interested in purchasing seventy acres of the Logan farm as well as some adjoining property, the price of land soared. The original sum of £10,000 laid down by the Treasury for the purchase had to be increased by an additional £21,444.[68] By the spring of 1846 most of the land had been bought from Sir William Logan and twelve other Montrealers.[69] Lord Cathcart, as soon as he had assumed the mantle of commander of the forces, began to put pressure on the Board of Ordnance in England to begin construction of the new military quarters. In October of 1845 he wrote "of the deficiency of quarters for officers . . . especially at Montreal . . . by which individuals suffer not only very considerable inconvenience and hardship, but the efficiency of the service is thereby frequently prejudiced by the distance officers, in many cases, are necessarily separated from their men, and such extra expense occasioned to the Public by the amount expended in lodging money."[70]

By 1846, with the signing of the Oregon treaty, the threat of war passed and enthusiasm in England for a new cantonment in Montreal waned. With the arrival of Lord Elgin as governor general and his eagerness to implement the policy of reducing colonial garrisons, troops remained quartered at the old Quebec Gate Barracks and St. Helen's until more serious work in the Crimea removed most of the regulars from Montreal.

With the departure of the troops for the Crimea, Montreal was without a British garrison for the first time in almost a hundred years. Merchants were among the first to feel their absence, and with the return of a regiment in 1856 Thomas Molson lost no time in sending to the commanding officer "186 cases of ale and porter with his compliments to make them welcome."[71]

Within five years the garrison would mushroom once more to some 3,400 men in the wake of the crisis created by the *Trent* incident in 1861 when an American captain seized two Confederate agents who were on board the British mail packet, the *Trent*. For a few weeks war loomed imminently near with Canada as the likely battlefield. The *Trent* affair was soon settled amicably for neither country wanted war, particularly not the United States which was engaged in the fratricidal Civil War. It was not until the Civil War drew to a close in 1865 that Canada began to experience new threats from the south, this time the work of Fenians, who launched border raids in 1866 and 1870. In all these incidents, Montreal and the province were caught up in tensions that represented imperial interests and conflicts. Yet for local merchants the greatly enlarged garrison of the 1860s, like that of the 1840s, brought them out of the commercial slump of the late 1850s. One of the merchants, Hamilton Ferns, who became chairman of the Board of Assessors in Montreal, had no doubt about the part played financially by the garrison. Recalling the Montreal of the 1860s, he declared, "Montreal has many reasons to remember gratefully the days when the Imperial troops formed part of our civic life. The money put into circulation by the Imperial Government at that time not only brought relief from the stringency which was crippling commerce and labor, but laid the foundations of the financial and commercial prosperity which has made Montreal one of the richest cities per capita on the continent."[72]

Ferns's enthusiasm for the military may have led him to overstate the case, but his eulogy underlines the financial importance of the garrison. What he failed to emphasize was a less obvious aspect of the financial role of the garrison—that in their everyday business transactions and in their efforts to cope with the problems posed by the rise of wages and prices, military authorities have left records that provide a fruitful source for the economic history of Montreal, a legacy that may prove to be one of the most lasting and valuable contributions of the garrison to the city.

14. Epilogue

In the years from 1832 to 1854 the British garrison in Montreal evolved from a small station commanded by a major or colonel into the major military establishment of the Canadas, its officers and men immersed in the cultural, economic, and political life of the city. In its most important role—that of aiding the civil power in times of internal disturbances—the garrison often found itself acting as a somewhat reluctant policeman, keeping antagonistic colonials from each other's throats and thereby reducing personal injury and destruction of property.

When civil turmoil erupted into open rebellion in 1837 and 1838, the military hierarchy tried, with some success, to steer an impartial course. It emphasized the loyalist, rather than the British, character of the coalition of Montrealers who rallied to aid the regulars in suppressing rebellion. The man chosen by the military command to mobilize the Montreal volunteers was a French-Canadian loyalist and the advance troops in the attack on Saint-Eustache were largely French-Canadian loyalists from Saint-Eustache. Yet, if the loyalist coalition included Montrealers of all backgrounds, whether French, British, American, Irish, Jewish, Indian, Protestant, Catholic, Constitutionalist, or reformer, the hard core of the loyalists emerged from the British, or

206

Constitutional, party that advocated the assimilation of French culture and institutions into the British system.[1]

As the imperial government in the postrebellion period approved the idea of voluntary assimilation of the French to British institutions, the garrison found itself in the somewhat anomalous position of adjusting to the new imperial policy while trying to solve one of its most serious postrebellion problems—that of disentangling itself from its close association with the loyalist coalition. The association had been demanded by the exigencies of the rebellion period, but it could not be maintained indefinitely if the imperial garrison was to fulfil its function of providing protection for all law-abiding subjects, including the disaffected elements who by the 1840s were returning to conventional politics under the leadership of Louis-Hippolyte La Fontaine.

Former Patriotes were not the only ones to merge with La Fontaine's moderate liberal party; so, too, were elements within the Irish community which was coming under the spell of the genial and ambitious Lewis Thomas Drummond. It was this political realignment that was breaking up the loyalist coalition of rebellion days and that eventually paved the way for the garrison to extricate itself from its close identity with the remnant of the coalition—the more militant of the British party. Yet, initially, the garrison's task of resuming an impartial role was not easy. Officers and soldiers had been glad enough to have the aid of the Montreal volunteers and the moral support of the loyal population of the Montreal district during the rebellion period when, at critical moments, it was far from certain to what degree the rural population was disaffected.

The ties between the garrison and the British party were still strong enough in 1844 for the commander of the forces and several of his senior officers to vote in the provincial elections in favour of the governor, Lord Metcalfe, and the conservatives under William Draper. Though the conservative press praised the military's political participation and justified the voting as acts of private individuals, liberal reformers denounced it. The military took the hint. As the decade wore on, officers avoided direct political action but watched with concern the new signs of tension within the English-language community. They were all the more relieved at the evident desire of the French community of Montreal to avoid physical force no matter how provoking or insulting the militants of the British party became.

With the English community showing increasing signs of turmoil and the French community assuming a neutral stance, the military hierarchy took care to cultivate friendly relations with both the Roman Catholic hierarchy and French-Canadian society. Thus in 1849, when the government, headed by a French Canadian and supported by many former rebels, found itself forced to call upon British regulars to quell civil disorders, it did so with some misgivings but not entirely with repugnance. Before the disturbances were suppressed, British soldiers were protecting former rebels against avowed British loyalists.

Yet, liberal reformers in 1849 still thought in terms of the garrison being a preserve of the British party, while the new civil governor, Lord Elgin, felt very much an outsider in comparison with the senior military staff. Many of these had been in the colony ten or fifteen years and knew the country and political personalities intimately. It is not surprising that Elgin urged the Colonial Office to use its influence to have such officers recalled and claimed, with some justice, that "they have become identified with all manner of local parties and prejudices."[2]

In the troubled spring of 1849 the military hierarchy, aware of Elgin's attitude, trod warily, trying to keep its distance from the political turmoil over the Rebellion Losses Bill and yet exercising great caution in its dealings with the La Fontaine administration. Working through the garrison liaison police officer, Capt. Charles Wetherall, they cooperated with La Fontaine in raising, equipping, and training a new provincial mounted police, especially since they had put pressure on La Fontaine to dismiss the hastily raised armed force that the government had authorized after the burning of Parliament House. But this new mounted force, dubbed derisively by the British party as the "Elgin Guard," proved abortive, too, and within a year it was disbanded probably because of its partisan image. In helping La Fontaine to raise this force, however, the officers of the garrison established links with the liberal reformers who, under La Fontaine, finally broke through the closed circle that had tied the garrison to the British party since rebellion days. This new rapport between the military and the liberal reformers was an indication to Montrealers that the garrison was an imperial institution that was above local politics and tensions, and that all segments of the populace had equal rights to its protection and support.

The military's contribution to the development of a regular police force, though somewhat less direct, was nevertheless significant. After the first rebellion it was largely the military that instigated measures to bring about an enlarged and well-organized city force under the superintendency of the loyalist Pierre-Edouard Leclère. A policy of retrenchment, inaugurated in 1840 by the new governor general, Charles Poulett Thomson, cut the police force in half and greatly reduced its budget.

When the city was incorporated once more in 1840, municipal fathers were understandably reluctant to increase the police budget when there was an available source of security nearby at the Quebec Gate Barracks. Thus riot control remained largely the responsibility of the garrison throughout the forties and early fifties. From the ranks of the military came the three most important police officers of the forties—William Ermatinger, Charles Wetherall, and Thomas Wily. In suppressing election disturbances and the riots accompanying the passage of the Rebellion Losses Bill, these former military men together with the regulars of the garrison set the tone for the discipline of the police force and imposed standards of impartiality not usually found in other rapidly growing North American municipalities. It was Chief of Police Wily's fear that the carefully developed spirit of impartiality which he had nurtured in the city police would be impaired if the force had to be integrated with the provincial police force, and this fear led to Wily's premature resignation as police chief. For its part the city corporation resisted the urgings of the military and of its own Police Committee for an armed police. It was not until the fall of 1849 that the city finally agreed to arm the police, but this was to be done only in cases of extreme emergency. The policy showed colonial authority resisting imperial pressure to Americanize its police and maintaining, instead, the imperial model of an unarmed police.

The Gavazzi riot of 1853 not only shattered the cordial relationship that had always existed between the garrison and the British party in Montreal, but it also showed the extent to which changing military policies and practices over the first half of the nineteenth century were reflected in Montreal. In 1832 the troops engaged in aid of civil power at an election riot maintained perfect discipline under far more severe conditions than those the troops faced in 1853. But in the intervening years regulations covering troop action at riots had been modified. While troops in 1844 could push against an angry crowd with the butts of their muskets or fire blanks in an attempt to frighten or disperse a crowd, by 1853 soldiers were warned not to let a mob close in on them and only live bullets were used. Moreover, the legal precedent set in the Six Mile Bridge affair in Ireland the previous year meant that soldiers could fire in self-defence without a command from their officers—a novel situation in which the rank and file assumed responsibility for firing into riotous crowds.

Coming just before the Crimean War resulted in the withdrawal of almost the entire garrison from the city, the Gavazzi riot of 1853 meant that the garrison's long stay in the city ended abruptly on a somewhat sad and sour note. Yet the tragedy and the garrison's temporary withdrawal emphasized to Montrealers that in a city as racially and religiously diverse as Montreal its inhabitants must forego their increasing tendency to violence and assume responsibility for their own internal order.

The unpopularity suffered by the soldiers in performing duties in connection with the maintenance of internal order was balanced to some extent by the warm esteem with which they were regarded for their part in fighting fires. Troops provided armed guards to protect property from looters. They blew up buildings to prevent the spread of fires, and when the city water supply failed, Royal Engineers were able to improvise temporary supplies from the St. Lawrence River. In the two worst fires that Montreal experienced in the nineteenth century, soldiers and officers worked with local firemen and townsmen until they dropped from exhaustion.

If the garrison's role as an aid to civil power in the years from 1832 to 1854 was somewhat uneven, its impact as a social institution and an economic boon was less in doubt. In these years the size of the garrison never fell below 400 and at times reached 3,190. In sheer weight of numbers, then, the soldiers and highly sophisticated officer corps of the postrebellion garrison represented the heaviest link of the imperial centre with the colony. The economic importance of the garrison was indicated by the fact that the military chest in Montreal at times equalled or surpassed the holdings of the Bank of Montreal and even of the provincial Treasury. And much of the money expended from the military chest found its way into the coffers of Montreal merchants and the vaults of Montreal banks. Moreover, the combination of high tariffs on garrison imports and an unfavourable rate of exchange for British currency illustrated the colonials' propensity for taking advantage of their British defenders.

Both officers and men looked to the city to supply their social needs. Although the decade of the forties saw a gradual improvement in barrack accommodations and facilities for the ordinary soldier—schools, libraries, savings banks, canteens, bowling alleys, and ball courts—these activities were confined to the barracks. For the soldier who wanted to get away from the cantonment on his off-hours, his choice was the grogshop, the brothel, or sharing in the amusements, worship, sports, and clubs of Montrealers. In some cases such as snowshoeing, bowling, and lacrosse, the soldiers absorbed indigenous pastimes. Curling and rowing they initiated.

Charges that the garrison represented a corrupting influence on the city, particularly with regard to drinking and prostitution, were made and admitted by the military. What was less frequently acknowledged by colonials was that the corrupting influences were not entirely one-sided. Senior officers sent young officers back to England to get them away from what they considered bad influences in the city, and the effort to improve the quality of barrack life for the ordinary soldier was a means of keeping him away from local centres of corruption.

If a garrison mentality existed, it was obvious neither to Montrealers nor to the men who composed the garrison. The military command was quick to acknowledge the services of Montrealers upon whom they depended when the limited numbers of available regulars raised doubts about the outcome of armed insurrection. When riots got beyond the control of the military, there was mutual interdependence between the garrison and those townsmen willing to help preserve peace. Similarly, the regulars welcomed the aid of the Provincial Cavalry not only in suppressing riots in the city, but also in acting as a border guard to prevent desertion, a service of vital importance to the regulars and one which they themselves could not perform.

Although Montrealers seldom doubted their ability to provide for their own internal order, amusement, economy, and cultural life if need be, they readily acknowledged the contribution of the garrison. They welcomed the largess of the military chest, the theatricals of the Garrison Amateurs, the steeplechases and cricket matches, and the services of the troops in fighting fires and quelling riots.

Within the upper eschelons of society, the military wined, dined, wooed, and wed Montrealers of both French and English backgrounds. Indeed, so interrelated by marriage were leading French, British, and military families by the 1830s and 1840s that the advent of the most bitter political tension, tinged as it was by racial tension, sprang often from the families of mixed backgrounds, the Nelsons, Bouchettes, Vigers, Lapailleurs, Macdonells, and Côtés. Yet, if family connections occasionally exacerbated tension in times of crisis, they also acted as an olive branch when tempers cooled. It was soldiers of the 1st Provincial Regiment who rowed the English wife of an insurgent across Missisquoi Bay to a rendezvous with her husband in exile at Highgate, Vermont, in 1839. And when Robert Shore Milnes Bouchette was wounded and imprisoned while leading an insurgent foray over the border in 1837, his mother appealed on his behalf to the Queen's mother, the Duchess of Kent, who was a personal friend of the family. By the sixties many of the rebels of 1837–38, such as Bouchette, Cartier, and Taché, were among the most loyal and devoted servants of the Crown.

Part of their conversion from rebel to loyal subject was due to the attitude of some British officers of the Montreal garrison who made efforts to assuage the bitterness of rebellion days. British regulars were the first to acknowledge the mettle of the rural insurgents. At Saint-Denis Crown forces had been repulsed by habitants. At Saint-Charles the regulars won only after an hour-long siege with field pieces and a bayonet charge by one of Britain's finest regiments, the 1st Royal Scots. At Saint-Eustache the Patriotes withstood for four hours the advance of overwhelming numbers of British troops. It is not surprising that a British officer singled out French-Canadian gentlemen as men with exceptional military aptitude.[3]

Other British officers urged that colonials from both the French and English communities be encouraged to enter the army as officers, and in the postrebellion period many did. While it was possible for colonials to purchase or compete for the commissioned ranks in the army, they could not gain entry into the noncommissioned ranks. Even the relaxed imperial policy of 1841 that allowed discharged soldiers to reenlist in the Royal Canadian Rifles forbade the enlistment of any settler.[4] It was not until the Indian Mutiny that the prohibition against enlisting settlers into the army was removed. With the raising of the 100th Prince of Wales's Royal Canadian Regiment in 1858, native-born Canadians, as well as settlers, were allowed to be recruited for general service in the British army.[5] The British government's decision to raise a single Canadian regiment ostensibly was to give the imperial power auxiliary troops composed, for the first time, of enlisted trans-Atlantic colonials. The real aim was to establish a new link between the two countries at a time when Canada's political links with Britain were being weakened or broken. Maj.-Gen. George Wetherall, adjutant general at Horse Guards, was candid about it. "The object of raising a Regiment in Canada," he wrote, "is not so much the need for men, for we enlist in England faster than we can dispose of them, but as a connecting link between the two countries."[6]

Wetherall had been one of the very popular senior staff officers in Montreal whom Lord Elgin had regarded as far too much embroiled in local affairs. Undoubtedly Wetherall was one of the officers who believed firmly that the two countries should continue to be linked, particularly by military ties—if not by having the imperial army in Canada, then by having colonial troops in Britain. The commander of the forces, Sir William Eyre, agreed that the raising of a regiment in Canada would "give an opening to the sons of leading families and connect still more clearly the Mother Country with the colony, gratifying the public mind with the idea of aiding the Mother Country and sharing in its glory."[7] Among the officers commissioned in the new Canadian regiment were C. H. Carrière, H. T. Duchesnay, L. A. Casault, and L. C. A. de Bellefeuille, an indication of the success of the British military's gestures towards French Canada in the previous decade. Their entry into the 100th Regiment also indicated the increasingly friendly relations between the French and British communities in Montreal as they approached the decade of the 1860s when invasion from the south once more appeared imminent. This growing amity reflected too the entente cordiale between England and France as they emerged for the first time in modern history as allies rather than as enemies in a war.

By arousing and maintaining the interest of Montrealers in army activities and personalities abroad, the garrison thus linked the townsmen with a wider world overseas. Not only did Canadians join the 100th Prince of Wales's Royal Canadian Regiment for service abroad, but in the next decade French Canadians privately raised the Papal Zouaves to aid their spiritual leader in Rome. By 1885 Caughnawaga Indian Warriors, renowned for their skill as boatsmen, volunteered to serve on the Nile and, at the turn of the century, Canadians of British origin stampeded to the call for volunteers for the Boer War. As Wetherall had predicted, when other imperial links weakened, those forged and nurtured by the military establishment would create new ones.

Appendix

Commanders of the Forces in Canada, 1831–1855

1831–35 Lt.-Gen. Lord Aylmer, Matthew, 1775–1850; entered army as an ensign in the 49th Foot; served throughout the Napoleonic Wars; named one of the first Knights Commander of the Bath in 1815, and in 1836 was gazetted Knight Grand Cross of the Bath; succeeded to the barony in 1825 upon the death of his father. He served as governor-in-chief and commander of the forces in the Canadas from February 1831 until August 1835. Like previous commanders of the forces who also served as governors-in-chief, Lord Aylmer was resident in Quebec City which was, therefore, headquarters of the British army in the Canadas.

1835–39 Lt.-Gen. Sir John Colborne, first Baron Seaton, 1778–1863; only son of Samuel Colborne of Lyndhurst, Hampshire; entered army as an ensign in 20th Lancashire Fusiliers, 1794, winning every step of promotion without purchase; served with distinction in the Peninsula and at Waterloo where he commanded the 52nd Oxfordshire Light Infantry in a charge and rout of the Imperial Guard; promoted to major-general and awarded a gold cross and three clasps and made one of the first Knights Commander of the Bath. In 1821 Colborne became governor of Guernsey where he was instrumental in promoting the restoration of Elizabeth College. In 1828 he was appointed lieutenant-governor of Upper Canada and on 18 September 1835 was named commander of the forces in the Canadas. In February 1836 he fixed his headquarters at Montreal which remained headquarters of the British army in the Canadas until the withdrawal of imperial troops in 1870. Colborne acted as administrator of government of Lower Canada in the spring of 1838 upon the departure of Lord Gosford and again in the fall of 1838 when Lord Durham returned to England. Colborne was appointed governor general of the Canadas 22 January 1839, a post he held until November 1839. From 1855 to 1860 he was commander of the forces in Ireland and was made a field marshal in 1860. His two elder sons, Francis and James, who served as his aides-de-camp during the 1837–38 Rebellions, became generals in the British army.

1839–45 Lt.-Gen. Sir Richard Downes Jackson, 1778–1845; entered army as an ensign in 1794; served in Ireland during the Rebellion of 1798; served with distinction in the Peninsula; commanded the northern military district in England in the early 1830s during the anti-Poor Law agitation and opening phase of Chartism; succeeded Colborne as commander of the forces in November 1839; was administrator of government from the time of the death of Lord Sydenham until the arrival of Sir Charles Bagot; died suddenly at Montreal 9 June 1845.

1845–47 Lt.-Gen. Earl Cathcart, Charles Murray, 1783–1859; entered army as a cornet in 1799; served in the Walcheren expedition and greatly distinguished himself in Peninsula and at Waterloo; promoted major-general in 1830; from 1837 to 1842 he was commander of the forces in Scotland; made lieutenant-general in 1841; and succeeded to title of second Earl and eleventh Baron Cathcart in 1843. On the death of Sir Richard Jackson, Earl Cathcart was named commander of the forces in Canada 15 June 1845. He served as administrator of government when Lord Charles Metcalfe returned to England in the fall of 1845 and was appointed governor general in January 1846, a post he held until January 1847. He remained commander of the forces until May 1847. His younger brother Sir George Cathcart served in Montreal as colonel of the 1st King's Dragoon Guards during the 1838 Rebellion.

1847–49 Lt.-Gen. Sir Benjamin D'Urban, 1777–1849; entered army as a cornet in 1793 in 2nd Dragoon Guards; served in the West Indies, Ireland, and the Peninsula. Like Sir John Colborne, he was one of the first Knights Commander of the Bath. He was promoted to major-general in 1818; served as governor at Antigua, British Guiana, and the Cape of Good Hope. He succeeded Earl Cathcart as commander of the forces in Canada in 1847. He died suddenly in Montreal 25 May 1849, a month after the burning of Parliament House.

1849–55 Lt.-Gen. Sir William Rowan, 1789–1874; eighth son of Robert Rowan of County Antrim, Ireland; entered army as an ensign in 52nd Oxfordshire Light Infantry in which his uncle, Charles Rowan, and two elder brothers, Charles (later Sir Charles, first commissioner of the London Metropolitan Police) and Robert, also served. Rowan served throughout the Peninsular War and at Waterloo under Sir John Colborne and took part in the charge of the 52nd against the Imperial Guard. He was later in Paris with the army of occupation under Wellington. In 1823 Rowan was posted to New Brunswick with his regiment, and in 1830 went on half pay. In 1832 he joined Sir John Colborne in Upper Canada to serve as his military and civil secretary until 1839 when Colborne returned to England. He was promoted to major-general in 1848 and returned to Canada to assume command at Kingston. Upon the sudden death of Sir Benjamin D'Urban, he was appointed commander of the forces in Canada.

Appendix

Regiments Serving in Montreal, 1832–1855 (Compiled from troop returns dated 1 January of each year, WO17/1536–59)

Year	No. of Troops	Regiment	Year	No. of Troops	Regiment
1832	75	Royal Artillery	1836	70	Royal Artillery
	401	15th		385	32nd
	476	Total*		455	Total
1833	96	Royal Artillery	1837	65	Royal Artillery
	349	15th		444	32nd
	165	24th		509	Total
	162	79th			
	772	Total	1838	122	Royal Artillery
1834	74	Royal Artillery		487	1st
	424	24th		464	24th
	498	Total		468	32nd
1835	75	Royal Artillery		499	83rd
	401	24th		2,040	Total
	476	Total			

*Total troops in garrison, exclusive of headquarters' staff and of those miscellaneous soldiers on detached duty.

Year	No. of Troops	Regiment	Year	No. of Troops	Regiment
1839	455	Royal Artillery	1845	177	Royal Artillery
	205	7th Hussars		83	52nd
	785	Grenadier Guards		599	89th
	595	1st		559	93rd
	2,040	Total		1,418	Total
1840	207	Royal Artillery	1846	176	Royal Artillery
	252	7th Hussars		110	46th
	867	Grenadier Guards		551	52nd
	598	1st		556	93rd
	470	24th		1,393	Total
	2,394	Total			
			1847	177	Royal Artillery
1841	185	Royal Artillery		539	52nd
	238	7th Hussars		80	71st
	623	23rd		634	Royal Canadian Rifles
	142	67th			
	639	73rd		1,430	Total
	630	85th			
	2,457	Total	1848	172	Royal Artillery
				574	23rd
1842	177	Royal Artillery		60	71st
	177	7th Hussars		570	77th
	540	23rd		1,376	Total
	674	74th			
	629	85th	1849	188	Royal Artillery
	828	Royal Canadian Rifles		580	19th
				582	23rd
	3,025	Total		72	71st
1843	188	Royal Artillery		1,422	Total
	29	1st King's Dragoon Guards	1850	195	Royal Artillery
	649	43rd		544	19th
	644	71st		534	23rd
	597	73rd		81	71st
	2,107	Total		1,354	Total
1844	177	Royal Artillery	1851	201	Royal Artillery
	648	43rd		995	20th
	122	74th		1,196	Total
	647	89th	1852	183	Royal Artillery
	1,594	Total		986	20th
				1,169	Total

Year	No. of Troops	Regiment	Year	No. of Troops	Regiment
1853	174	Royal Artillery	1855	22	Royal Artillery
	990	20th		57	16th
	1,164	Total		194	Royal Canadian Rifles
1854	101	Royal Artillery		273	Total
	611	26th			
	712	Total			

Appendix C

Officers Commanding the Montreal Garrison, 1832–1855
(Compiled from WO17/1536–59)

1832 Lt.-Col. A. F. Macintosh, 15th Regt.
1833 Maj. McDougall, 79th Regt., Jan.–May
        Maj. Hughes, 24th Regt., June–Aug.
        Lt.-Col. F. S. Tidy, 24th Regt., Sept.–Dec.
1834 Lt.-Col. F. S. Tidy, 24th Regt., Jan.–Dec.
1835 Lt.-Col. F. S. Tidy, 24th Regt., Jan.–May
        Maj. Hughes, 24th Regt., June
        Maj. Wingfield, 32nd Regt., July–Dec.
1836 Maj. Wingfield, 32nd Regt., Jan.–Dec.
1837 Maj. Wingfield, 32nd Regt., Jan.–July
        Lt.-Col. G. A. Wetherall, 1st Regt., Aug.–Oct.
        Lt.-Col. John Maitland, 32nd Regt., Nov.–Dec.
1838 Lt.-Col. John Maitland, 32nd Regt., Jan.
        Lt.-Col. G. A. Wetherall, 1st Regt., Feb.–Dec.
1839 Lt.-Col. G. A. Wetherall, 1st Regt., Jan.–May
        Maj.-Gen. John Clitherow, June–Dec.
1840 Maj.-Gen. John Clitherow, Jan.–Dec.
1841 Maj.-Gen. John Clitherow, Jan.–July
        Lt.-Col. Maunsell, 85th Regt., Aug.–Oct.
        Lt.-Col. Elliott, Royal Canadian Rifle Regt., Nov.–Dec.
1842 Lt.-Col. Elliott, Royal Canadian Rifle Regt., Jan.–May
        Maj.-Gen. Sir James A. Hope, June–Dec.
1843 Maj.-Gen. Sir James A. Hope, Jan.–May

Lt.-Col. England, 71st Regt., June–Aug.
Lt.-Col. Furlong, 43rd Regt., Sept.–Dec.

1844 Lt.-Col. Furlong, 43rd Regt., Jan.–May
Lt.-Col. Spark, 93rd Regt., June–July
Lt.-Col. Bouverie, 89th Regt., Aug.–Dec.

1845 Lt.-Col. Bouverie, 89th Regt., Jan.–Feb.
Maj. Smyth, 93rd Regt., Mar.–May
Maj. French, 52nd Regt., June
Lt.-Col. Spark, 93rd Regt., July–Nov.
Maj.-Gen. Sir James A. Hope, Dec.

1846 Maj.-Gen. Sir James A. Hope, Jan.–Dec.

1847 Maj.-Gen. Sir James A. Hope, Jan.–Feb.
Col. Campbell, R.A., Mar.–Apr.
Maj.-Gen. Charles Gore, May–Dec.

1848 Maj.-Gen. Charles Gore, Jan.–Dec.

1849 Maj.-Gen. Charles Gore, Jan.–July
Lt.-Col. Charles Hay, 19th Regt., Aug.–Dec.

1850 Lt.-Col. Charles Hay, 19th Regt., Jan.–Apr.
Lt.-Col. Crutchley, 23rd Regt., May
Lt.-Col. Horn, 20th Regt., June–Dec.

1851 Lt.-Col. Horn, 20th Regt., Jan.–Dec.

1852 Lt.-Col. Horn, 20th Regt., Jan.–June
Maj. Hugh Crofton, 20th Regt., July–Sept.
Lt.-Col. Horn, 20th Regt., Oct.–Dec.

1853 Lt.-Col. Horn, 20th Regt., Jan.–June
Lt.-Col. A. T. Hemphill, 26th Regt., July–Dec.

1854 Lt.-Col. A. T. Hemphill, 26th Regt., Jan.–July
Lt.-Col. Grubbe, 66th Regt., Aug.–Sept.
Maj. Hill, Royal Canadian Rifle Regt., Oct.–Dec.

1855 Maj. Hill, Royal Canadian Rifle Regt., Jan.
Maj. Holmes, Royal Canadian Rifle Regt., Feb.–Aug.
Capt. Hamilton, Royal Canadian Rifle Regt., Sept.–Oct.
Capt. Grange, Royal Canadian Rifle Regt., Nov.–Dec.

Appendix D

General Orders, Quebec, 26 May 1837 (RG8/C316/162–63)

The Lieutenant General Commanding directs that the following Regulations shall be strictly observed in this Command with regard to the employment of the Troops in aid of the Civil Power.

1. No application for Military assistance is to be complied with, unless accompanied by a written Requisition from a Magistrate distinctly specifying the Service on which it is intended to employ the Troops and that the ordinary Civil Force is insufficient either to maintain the peace or to overcome any manifestly illegal and forcible resistance to the due execution of the Laws.

2. All Parties employed in aid of the Civil Power are if practicable to be commanded by a Commissioned Officer and must be constantly accompanied by a Magistrate and act under his orders only.

3. As soon as the Service is completed, the Officer Commanding at the Station will transmit to the Military Secretary a detailed report on the subject with a Copy of the Requisition, in order that the Lieutenant General may be enabled to judge whether the circumstances of the case have been such as to justify the employment of the Troops.

(signed) John Eden
D.A.G.

Appendix  E

Order of Precedency in the Colonies (De Salaberry papers, MG24/G45, VIII, 1899)

Whereas some doubts may arise with regard to the Rank of Precedency to be observed between the Commanders in Chief, Generals, and other Officers of our Forces in America: the Governors, Lieut. Governors, and Presidents of Councils of our Several Colonies;—In order to fix the same, and to prevent all Disputes, we do hereby declare that it is our Will and Pleasure that the following Rule be observed in America—Vizt.

1st.   The Commander in Chief of our Forces by Commd. under our Great Seal of Great Britain.

2.   Captain General, and Governors in Chief of our Provinces & our Colonies when in their respective Governments as appointed by Commissn. under our Great Seal of Great Britain.

3.   General Officers on the Staff.

4.   Captain General and Governors of our Provinces & Colonies when out of their respective Governments.

5.   Lieut. Governors & Presidents of Councils when Commndr. in Chief of our Provinces and Colonies in their respective Governments.

6.   Colonels.

7.   Lieut. Governors and Presidents of Councils when Commander in Chief of Provinces & Colonies out of their respective Governments.

8.   Lieut. Govrs. of Proprietary Governmts. when in their respective Governmts.

9.   Lieut. Govrs. of our Provinces & Colonies not being Commanders in Chief of their respective Governments.

10. All Field Officers under the Rank of Colonels.
11. Lieut. Govrs. of Proprietary Governmts. out of their respective Governmts.

Rules of Precedency composed & adjusted from the several Acts & Statutes in England for the Settlement of the Precedency of Men & Women in America:

Governor of the Province	his Wife
Lieutenant governor	his Wife
President of the Council	his Wife
Membrs. of Her Majesty's Council	their Wives
Speaker of the Council & H. of Assembly	his Wife
Chief Justice	his Wife
Treasurer	his Wife
Associate Judges	their Wives
Baronets	their Wives
Her Majesty's Att. Gen.	his Wife
Judge of the Admiralty	his Wife
Secretary of the Province	his Wife
Membrs. of the House of Assembly	their Wives
Mayor	his Wife
Aldermen	their Wives
Members of Corporation	their Wives

The Members of the Assembly, Crown Officers, etc. of any particular Province, have no other rank out of that Province than what belongs to them in their private capacities as men.

The widow of a late Governor has not any Precedency as such. A Governor of a Province, or his Wife, coming into another Province, have not in that Province where they visit any Precedency above their rank in Private Life.

(signed by Edmonston, herald to Her Majesty)

Appendix

Excerpt from Coroner Joseph Jones's Charge to the Jury at the
Inquest into the Deaths that Occurred during the Gavazzi Riot,
9 June 1853 (*Transcript*, 12 July 1853)

With reference to the casualties from the firing of the troops, it must be
borne in mind as a settled rule of law, that soldiers are merely armed
citizens, and may, like other citizens, interfere to suppress an affray or
riot; and if resisted are justified in killing the resister; and like other citizens they are subject to the law and its punishments, for the manner in
which they may conduct themselves upon such occasions. In case of any
sudden riot or disturbance, any of Her Majesty's subjects, without the
presence of a peace officer of any description, may arm themselves, and of
course may use any ordinary means of force to suppress such riot and
disturbance. And what Her Majesty's subjects may do, they also ought to
do, for the suppression of public tumult, when any exigency may require
that such means be resorted to. Whatever any other class of Her Majesty's subjects may allowably do in this particular, the military may un-
questionably do also. By the common law, every description of peace
officers may, and ought to do, not only all that in him lies, towards the
suppression of riots, but may and ought to command all other persons to
assist therein. However, it is by all means advisable to procure a justice
of the peace to attend, and for the military to act under his immediate
orders, when such attendance and sanction of such orders can be obtained, as it not only prevents any disposition to unnecessary violence on
the part of those who act in repelling the tumult, but induces also from
the known authority of such magistrates, a more ready submission on

the part of the rioters, to the measures used for that purpose; but still in cases of great and sudden emergency, the military, as well as all other individuals, may act without their presence, or without the presence of any other peace officer, whatever. But in these and all similar cases the necessity for the killing must be evident, and the law, in this respect, is positive and distinct. In case of a riot, or a rebellious assembly, officers and others, in endeavouring to disperse the mob, are justified in killing them both by common law, and under the riot act, if the riot cannot be otherwise suppressed, and it is laid down that private persons may justify killing dangerous rioters, *when they cannot otherwise suppress them, or defend themselves from them,* inasmuch as any person seems to be authorized by law, to arm himself for such purpose. Upon this portion of the enquiry, it has been admitted that the military force was called out upon the requisition of the civil authority, the Mayor of the city, under his immediate orders.—You will determine whether the public peace was sufficiently disturbed, by a subsisting riot, to justify the application for a military force, whether any civil means at the disposal and command of the Mayor had been previously exhausted by him: whether notice of the employment of military force had been given by the usual proclamation for silence, as required by the statute, and the reading of the riot act by the Mayor in the presence of the people; whether reasonable time was allowed to elapse for the people to disperse; or whether circumstances of extreme necessity compelled him to bring the military into immediate collision with the people.

You will find upon these circumstances, bearing in mind that Mr. Wilson as Mayor would not be justified in transferring his civil authority to the military until it became necessary, nor before any disorder was sought to be quelled by the legal precaution of making the proclamation, which is intended to intimidate rioters, and to separate the innocent from the guilty, by giving due notice to all the thoughtless people who, without any malevolence, are mixed with the multitude to separate from the ill-meaning; and moreover, Mr. Wilson was under double ties, for besides the general obligations of duty and humanity as a magistrate, a particular confidence was reposed in him as Mayor of the city, which, at the peril of his life, he was bound to account for and sustain.

To justify a resource to this extreme necessity a riot must exist, and to constitute a riot, three or more persons must be unlawfully assembled together; and to constitute this crime, it is not necessary that personal violence should have been committed; it is sufficient that there is some circumstance, either of actual force or violence, or at least of an apparent tendency thereto, naturally apt to strike terror into the people, or even into *one* of Her Majesty's subjects, as the show of firearms, threatening menaces, or turbulent speeches; nor is it necessary to constitute a riot that the riot act should be read: before the proclamation can be read a riot must exist, and the effect of the proclamation will not change the character of the meeting, but will make those guilty of felony who do not disperse within an hour after the proclamation is read.

You will then find under what circumstances the military did fire and whether under the sanction of civil or military authority. It will be scarcely necessary to state that the firing without command and not for self-defence would entail the charge of murder, that the firing even by command would be equally criminal if no apparent or justifiable necessity for the Act existed, and in that case the Commanding Officer is equally implicated with his men. That the firing without such necessity, even under a mistake of the command proceeding from the officer would not relieve the soldier firing, from a similar charge, and that the firing by command, whilst it might relieve the soldiers if some necessity did in fact exist, would attach that criminality upon the commanding officer unless it be shewn that such necessity was real and apparent, no order from any magistrate whatever can justify the homicides caused by the firing of the troops without necessity. Had the Mayor ordered the officer to fire upon the people when there was no cause for so doing, such an order might subject the Mayor to the penal consequences which attend murder, but could not acquit the officer who might order the fire, who was not bound to obey such illegal order, and who, therefore, would have acted at his peril.

N otes

Unless otherwise indicated, all original sources cited are at the Public Archives of Canada and all newspapers quoted were published in Montreal.

CHAPTER ONE
1. Ernest J. Chambers, *The Canadian militia*, 9–10; Louise Dechêne, "La Croissance de Montréal au 18ème siècle," *Revue d'histoire de l'Amérique française*, 27, no. 2 (Sept. 1973), 163–79.
2. *Returns to addresses of the Senate and House of Commons relative to the withdrawal of the troops from the Dominion; and on the defence of the country*, 1871; Charles P. Stacey, *Canada and the British army, 1846–1871*, 241.
3. For various discussions of Montreal's military position, see Col. W. Holloway, commanding officer, Royal Engineers, to inspector general of fortifications, 22 Apr. 1847 (McCord Museum, McCord papers); Maj. George Talbot to Hon. Robert Bruce, 28 Nov. 1849 and 9 Jan. 1850 (Record Group [henceforth cited as RG] 8/C1305/86–87 and 129); Sir William Eyre to Sir Edmund Head, 12 Dec. 1856 (Eyre papers, Manuscript Group [henceforth cited as MG] 24/F38); Maj. T. L. Gallway, Royal Engineers, Notes on Montreal as a military position, 7 Jan. 1862 (RG8/C1671); Hereward Senior, "Military Montreal," *Bulletin of the Organization of Military Museums of Canada*, 3 (1974), 1–15.
4. Colborne to secretary of state for war, 18 May 1836, and Colborne to Lord Hill, 21 Nov. 1836 (RG8/C1277/99, 136).
5. Susanna Moody, *Roughing it in the bush*, 6.

6. Public Archives of Canada (henceforth cited as PAC), Atlas 350, Military property, Montreal, 1868, plan no. 1.
7. *Gazette*, 2 May 1840.
8. John McGregor, *British America*, II, 312–13.
9. John Richardson, *Eight years in Canada*, 74.
10. *Gazette*, 2 May 1844; *Starke's almanac*, 1844, 26.
11. Wily memoirs, MG29/F46/59–60, 69.

CHAPTER TWO
1. F. Ouellet, *Le Bas-Canada, 1791–1840*, 348–51; Helen Taft Manning, *The revolt of French Canada, 1800–1835*, 346–54.
2. W. Nelson to A. A. Bruneau, 28 Oct. 1905 (Nelson papers, MG24/B34/2).
3. Petition of Bull to Colborne, 20 June 1833 (Upper Canada Sundries, RG5/A1).
4. Bull to Lord Kenyon, 10 Nov. 1832 (Great Britain, *Fourth report from the select committee appointed to enquire into the origin, nature, extent and tendency of the Orange Institutions in Great Britain and the colonies*, appendix to the report, no. 23/200).
5. Troop returns, 1 May 1832, War Office (henceforth cited as WO) 17/1536.
6. Matthew Hayes to editor, *The Constitution*, Toronto, 16 Aug. 1836 (Public Archives Ontario, Mackenzie-Lindsey papers, clipping 2311).
7. MG11/Q201/II/477.
8. MG11/Q202/I/120.
9. MG11/Q202/I/99–100.
10. Ibid.
11. MG11/Q201/II/460.
12. MG11/Q202/I/24; MG11/Q201/II/497.
13. MG11/Q202/I/150.
14. Testimony of Temple (MG11/Q202/I/71); RG8/C316/139–42.
15. Testimony of Holmes (MG11/Q201/II/496).
16. MG11/Q202/I/71.
17. MG11/Q202/I/52.
18. For Mondelet, see MG11/Q202/I/49; for Rodier, see Montreal Military and Maritime Museum, 1832 riot; Affidavit of Alex McMillan, 29 May 1832 (MG11/Q202/I).
19. MG11/Q202/I/195.
20. MG11/Q201/II/497–98.
21. RG8/C316/140–41; see also Dr. William Caldwell's testimony (MG11/Q202/II/33).
22. Deposition of Macintosh, 1 June 1832 (MG11/Q202/I/101).
23. Ibid.
24. John Jones's testimony (MG11/Q202/I/52); Macintosh's testimony, 26 May and 1 June 1832 (MG11/Q202/I/66 and 103).
25. MG11/Q202/I/33.
26. MG11/Q202/I/17.
27. MG11/Q202/I/104.
28. Ibid.

29. MG11/Q202/I/11–12, 16.
30. Ibid.; see also Tavernier's statement, Montreal Military and Maritime Museum, 1832 riot.
31. Aylmer to Goderich, 7 June 1832 (MG11/Q202/I/198).
32. Amédée Papineau, *Journal d'un Fils de la Liberté*, I, 20.
33. Mondelet's testimony (MG11/Q202/I/49).
34. Papineau, *Journal*, I, 19–20.
35. Papineau to his wife, 6 Dec. 1832 (Papineau papers, MG24/B2/2/1610–13).
36. Papineau to John Neilson, 6 June 1832, cited in Manning, *Revolt of French Canada*, 380.
37. MG11/Q202/I/55–56; MG11/Q203/I/108.
38. Macintosh to military secretary, 29 May 1832 (RG8/C316/84–85).
39. RG8/C316/81–82.
40. Ogden to Lt.-Col. Craig, 12 June 1832 (MG11/Q202/I/8, 55–56).
41. RG8/C316/85.
42. Aylmer to Goderich, 16 June 1832, private (MG11/Q202/I/21).
43. Aylmer to Goderich, 9 Oct. 1832 (MG11/Q203/I/150).
44. *Constitution*, Toronto, 23 Aug. 1836 (Public Archives Ontario, Mackenzie-Lindsey papers, clipping 2311).
45. MG11/Q203/I/149; Bull to Lord Kenyon, 10 Nov. 1832 (Great Britain, *Fourth report from select committee*, appendix to report, no. 23/200).
46. François-Xavier Garneau, *History of Canada from the time of its discovery till the union year 1840–41*, III, 324; Manning, in *Revolt of French Canada*, 344, refers to the incident as the "Massacre of Montreal."

CHAPTER THREE

1. Jean Turmel, *Police de Montréal, historique du service*, I, 35.
2. RG8/C316/162.
3. Wetherall to Eden, 19 July 1837 (Colborne papers, MG24/A40/2340–41).
4. Colborne to Gosford, 24 Oct. 1837 (RG8/C1272/21).
5. Walcott to Ogden, 4 Nov. 1837 (RG7/G15D/I/221, Letterbook of the law officers of the Crown).
6. Colborne to Gosford, 11 Nov. 1837 (RG8/C1272/27).
7. Colborne to Gosford, 31 Oct. 1837 (RG8/C1272/23); Goldie to commissary general, 12 Dec. 1837 (RG8/C1271/81).
8. Memorial of John Shay, late lieutenant, Queen's Light Dragoons, to Duke of Wellington, 8 May 1849 (RG8/C803/24).
9. Col. William Rowan to T. A. Young, 10 Apr. 1838, same to same, 5 May 1838 (Young papers, MG24/B4/VIII/549, 565).
10. An ordinance to provide for an efficient system of police in the cities of Montreal and Quebec, 28 June 1838, in *Gazette*, 3 July 1838.
11. Ibid.
12. *Journal of the Special Council*, Apr. to June 1840, appendix 4, see under Pay and contingencies of the police; Morrogh to Young, 28 June 1838 (Young papers, MG24/B4/VIII/592); Leclère to C. N. Montizambert, 1 Feb. 1840 (MG24/B49); Jean-Louis Roy, "Pierre-

Edouard Leclère," in *Dictionary of Canadian Biography* (henceforth cited as *DCB*), IX, 459–60.

13. For the size of the new force, see Newton Bosworth, *Hochelaga depicta*, 180–81; for the police force before 1837, see *Rules and regulations of the police force for the city and suburbs of Montreal*, 1821; J. C. Lamothe, *Histoire de la corporation de la cité de Montréal depuis son origine jusqu'à nos jours*, 111–13; William H. Atherton, *Montreal, 1535–1914*, II, 419–20; E.-Z. Massicotte, "Les tribunaux de police à Montréal," *Le bulletin des recherches historiques*, 26, no. 5 (1920), 182; Turmel, *Police de Montréal*, I.

14. Gérard Filteau, *Histoire des Patriotes*, III, 57.

15. Comeau retained his job until 1844; he subsequently secured a post with the Hudson's Bay Company (*Gazette*, 30 Apr. 1844). For the expense of the force, see *Journal of the Special Council*, Apr. to June 1840, app. 4, showing the pay and contingencies of the police for the year ending 31 Oct. 1839.

16. *Herald*, 29 June 1838, reprinted in *L'Ami du Peuple*, 4 juillet 1838.

17. E. B. O'Callaghan to Thomas Falconer, 24 June 1838, see also same to same, 9 Sept. 1838 (MG24/B31/I/39, 46).

18. *L'Ami du Peuple*, 4 juillet 1838; see also *Appendix to the Journal*, Legislative Assembly, 1843, no. 2, III, app. AA, see Returns of appointments in Lower Canada from 1791 to the Union.

19. Ibid., see Abstract of warrants, pay, and contingencies for rural police for the district of Montreal, 31 Oct. 1839; William Coffin, commissioner of police, to military secretary, 15 July 1840 (RG8/C76).

20. Ibid.

21. Proposals for the establishment of a rural police, registry offices, courts of requests (Colborne papers, MG24/A40/8327).

22. MG24/A40/8237.

23. For O'Callaghan, see Chapman papers, MG24/B31/I/37–44; see also *Transcript*, 18 June 1840.

24. Colborne to Lord Fitzroy Somerset, 22 Dec. 1837 (RG8/C1272/58).

25. MG24/A40/8103–8.

26. Cathcart to Dixon, 29 Mar. 1838 (MG24/A40/4204–10).

27. Ibid.

28. Leclère to Montizambert, 1 Feb. 1840 (MG24/B49).

29. Chief Secretary T. W. Murdock to Daly and Campbell, 7 Mar. 1840 (MG24/B4/IX/924).

30. *Journal of the Special Council*, Apr. to June 1840, 21, 45, and 78, Ordinance to provide for an efficient police in the cities of Quebec and Montreal; Lamothe, *Histoire de la corporation*, 113; James Starke, *Compilation of the by-laws and police regulations in force in the city of Montreal*, 1842; for the best work on the Montreal police force in the nineteenth century, see Turmel, *Police de Montréal*, I, 26–68.

31. *Appendix to the Journal*, Legislative Assembly, 1841, no. 1, I, app. Z; ibid., 1843, no. 2, III, app. KK, see Annual expenses of the corporation of the city of Montreal; *Montreal directory*, 1842–43, 240.

32. Edward Hale to his wife, 4 June 1840 (McCord Museum, Hale pa-

pers); *Gazette*, 6 June 1840; *Transcript*, 9 June 1840; *Appendix to the Journal*, Legislative Assembly, 1843, no. 2, III, app. V, see Appointment of Leclère as police magistrate at Saint-Hyacinthe.

33. *Appendix to the Journal*, Legislative Assembly, 1843, no. 2, III, app. V.
34. William F. Coffin, commissioner of police, to Daly, 1 Aug. 1841 (*Appendix to the Journal*, Legislative Assembly, 1841, no. 1, I, app. Z); for a more elaborate description of the reduction, see Coffin to civil secretary, 23 Nov. 1840 (ibid., 1850, no. 1, A–Z, IX, app. X, no. 4).
35. *Journal of the Special Council*, Apr. to June 1840, app. 6, Expenditure accounts; Edward Hale to his wife, 4 June 1840 (McCord Museum, Hale papers).
36. Jean-Paul Bernard, "Thomas Bouthillier," in *DCB*, IX, 73–74.
37. Bouthillier to Gugy, 26 July 1840, in B. C. A. Gugy, *Some incidents related by credible witnesses in the life of a provincial*, 14.
38. *Gazette*, 18 July 1840.
39. Memorial of Charles Wetherall to Duke of Wellington, 11 Apr. 1846 (RG8/C802/86); see also *Appendix to the Journal*, Legislative Assembly, 1843, no. 2, III, app. T, Beauharnois riots.
40. For appointments as rural magistrates, see *Gazette*, 18 July 1840; for Juchereau-Duchesnay, see ibid., 4 June 1840; for Coleman, see Wily memoirs, MG29/F46/154.
41. *Transcript*, 13 Mar. and 23 Apr. 1841.
42. Memorial of Driscoll to Jackson (RG8/C710/272); general orders, 14 Dec. 1837 (RG8/C1192/24); for a hostile description of Driscoll, see E. B. O'Callaghan to Falconer (Chapman papers, MG24/B31/I/29–32).
43. For Ermatinger's appointment, see *Appendix to the Journal*, Legislative Assembly, 1843, no. 2, III, app. V, dated 16 Feb. 1842; on Ermatinger, see Aylmer to D. R. McCord, 17 July 1901 (McCord Museum, McCord papers); Elinor Senior, "Frederick William Ermatinger," in *DCB*, IX, 242–43. Ermatinger's mother was referred to among her white contemporaries and relatives as an Indian princess; among her Indian relatives and people, she held the rank of a daughter of a head chief.
44. Lt.-Col. Robert Lovelace, "The Montreal active volunteer force," 1864 (McCord Museum, McCord papers).
45. For the composition of the force, see *Montreal directory*, 1842–43, 240; for wages, see *Transcript*, 28 Mar. 1843.
46. Wily memoirs, MG29/F46/1, 108, 128.
47. *Gazette*, 13 July 1844; *Transcript*, 7 June 1849.
48. Maitland diary, entry 2 Mar. 1846 (MG24/I78).
49. John Spurr, "Sir Charles Stephen Gore," in *DCB*, IX, 327–29.
50. Château Ramezay Archives, Alfred Sandham, "Montreal illustrated," XVI, 125.
51. Department of National Defence Library, "Montreal garrison, pt. II," troop dispositions, 1840, 1842–43.
52. WO17/1545, troop returns for Jan. 1841; WO17/1548, troop returns for June 1844.

53. General orders, 30 Apr. 1840, RG 8/C801/490; general orders, 24 Sept. 1840, RG8/C1194/226; *Transcript*, 16 May 1840, *Gazette*, 23 May 1840.
54. Lt.-Gen. W. Rowan to Col. R. Airey, Horse Guards, 13 May 1853 (WO1/567).
55. For a description of the regulations of the formation of the Royal Canadian Rifles, see general orders, 28 Sept. 1840, RG8/C1194C; for a discussion on the origin of the Royal Canadian Rifles, see Great Britain, *Hansard*, 3rd ser., 56 (1841), 1361–62; for a discussion of the Royal Canadian Rifles and desertion, see John Richardson, *Eight years in Canada*, 82; general orders, 11 Sept. 1841, RG8/C1194A/44; McCord Museum, McCord papers, Orderly book, Queen's Light Dragoons, general orders dated 4 Mar. 1841; G. Tylden, "The Royal Canadian Rifle Regiment, 1840–1870," *Journal of the Society for Army Historical Research*, 34 (June 1956).
56. Jackson to Treasury, 7 May 1842 (RG8/C1279).
57. *Transcript*, 20 Mar. 1841; McCord Museum, McCord papers, Orderly book, Queen's Light Dragoons, general orders, 4 Mar. 1841.
58. *Transcript*, 25 Aug. 1838.
59. Only one instance of an immigrant being permitted to enlist in Canada as a recruit has been found in the course of this study; see Petition of Edward Gray of Detroit, a native of Ireland, 12 Aug. 1846, praying to be enlisted as a recruit (RG8/C35/257). For examples of Montrealers entering the service as commissioned officers by purchase or examination, see RG8/C26/29; C1278/218; C1282/328; C1304/457; C1305/248; C1311/379, 492, 497; C1313/416, 472, 479; C1320/99.
60. Jackson to secretary of war, 18 Feb. 1842 (RG8/C1279/88); general orders, 20 Sept. 1841, RG8/C1194A/46.
61. *Transcript*, 20 Mar. 1841.
62. Department of National Defence Library, "Montreal garrison, pt. II," troop dispositions for 1841 and 1843.

CHAPTER FOUR
1. John McGregor, *British America*, II, 312–13.
2. Henry Christmas, *The emigrant churchman in Canada by a pioneer in the wilderness*, I, 49.
3. Fanny Kemble to Charles Mathews, cited in Murray D. Edwards, *A stage in our past*, 12.
4. Susanna Moodie, *Roughing it in the bush*, xviii.
5. Maj. T. E. Campbell to Lt.-Gen. William Eyre, 18 Dec. 1856 (Eyre papers, MG24/F38).
6. See Appendix E.
7. Ibid.
8. Ibid.
9. *DCB*, x, 444.
10. Campbell to Eyre, 18 Dec. 1856 (Eyre papers, MG24/F38).
11. *Gazette*, 29 Oct. 1839; for later levées where the same procedure was followed, see *L'Ami du Peuple*, 14 juillet 1838; *Morning Courier*, 12 Feb. 1841.

12. Jacques Monet, *The last cannon shot*, 113.
13. Many had resigned, either voluntarily or under compulsion, during the rebellions, and although Colborne had declared these resignations noneffective, the militia officer corps was still in a state of some confusion; see list of officers who resigned their commissions, Nov. 1837 (RG4/A1/390/II/237).
14. Edward Hale to his wife, 10 May 1840 (McCord Museum, Hale papers).
15. Bellingham memoirs, MG24/B25/II/135.
16. Benjamin G. Sack, *History of the Jews in Canada from the earliest beginnings to the present day*, I, 129, 138.
17. David family genealogy, privately held.
18. For David's acceptance into military circles, see Lower Canada commissions, 1846–63, entry dated 12 Oct. 1852 (RG9/1C7/I); for the marriage of his daughters, see Christ Church Cathedral Archives, Montreal, Register 1853–65, entry dated 4 Apr. 1861; Register 1866–76, entry dated 30 Apr. 1866 and entry p. 327.
19. Christ Church Cathedral Archives, Montreal, Register 1831–32, entry dated 6 Sept. 1832; C. O. Ermatinger to David Ross McCord, 9 Apr. 1917 (McCord Museum, McCord papers, Genealogies folder, no. 9889).
20. Stewart Derbishire's report to Lord Durham on Lower Canada, 1838, in *Canadian Historical Review*, 18, no. 1 (Mar. 1937), 57.
21. Bellingham memoirs, MG24/B25/II/141.
22. McGregor, *British America*, II, 275.
23. Wily memoirs, MG29/F46/154.
24. Laurent-Olivier David, *Biographies et portraits*, 290; Wolfred Nelson, *Wolfred Nelson et son temps*, 12–13.
25. *DCB*, x, 219.
26. John Douglas Borthwick, *History and biographical gazetteer of Montreal to the year 1892*, 481.
27. *DCB*, IX, 485.
28. Bellingham memoirs, MG24/B25/II/275.
29. For Whyte, see *Gazette*, 8 Oct. 1842; for Campbell, see John Fennings Taylor, *Portraits of British Americans*, II, 216.
30. *DCB*, x, 18.
31. G. C. Moore Smith, *Life of John Colborne*, 268–69.
32. For Charles Wetherall, see Petition of Capt. C. Wetherall, 11 Apr. 1846 (RG8/C802/86); for Lysons, see Sir Daniel Lysons, *Early reminiscences*, 24; for Wily, see Wily memoirs, MG29/F46/63–64; for Denny, see Denny to Lord Monck, 16 Dec. 1861 (MG24/F33); for Taylor, see Lysons, *Early reminiscences*, 145; for Lovelace, see Borthwick, *Gazetteer of Montreal*, 513; for Girard, see Notice addressed to officers of the army lately arrived in this city, in *Transcript*, 7 July 1838.
33. Amédée Papineau, *Journal d'un Fils de la Liberté*, I, 15–17.
34. For Chamberlin and Lowe, see Chamberlin papers, MG24/B19/II/7; for Bellingham, see Bellingham memoirs, MG24/B25/II/98.
35. Laurent-Olivier David, *Mes contemporains*, 153–54.
36. For McCord, see McCord Museum, McCord papers, Genealogies

folder; for Aylwin, see *Transcript*, 15 Oct. 1853; Borthwick, *Gazetteer of Montreal*, 192.

37. For Molson, see *Gazette*, 2 Mar. 1844; for Bagg, see MG11/Q202/ I/195; for Weir, see William Weir, *Sixty years in Canada*, 19.
38. Nelson to Sophia Nelson, 24 Mar. 1838 (Nelson papers, MG24/B34/ II/20–22).
39. Sophia Nelson Brosnan to L.-O. David, 21 Mar. 1906, and Walter Nelson to A. A. Bruneau, 28 Oct. 1905 (ibid.).
40. Moore Smith, *John Colborne*, 268–69.
41. W. C. H. Wood, *The storied province of Quebec*, I, 212.
42. De Salaberry papers, MG24/G45.
43. Bellingham memoirs, MG24/B25/II/140.
44. Salaberry to his father, n.d. (MG24/G45/I/479).
45. Memorial of Guy to Lord Dalhousie, 15 Oct. 1825 (RG8/C799/54– 55).
46. Charles de Salaberry to military secretary, 15 Oct. 1825 (RG8/ C799/56).
47. Capt. T. L. Goldie to Guy, 23 Nov. 1837 (RG8/C1271/18–19).
48. Same to same, 16 Nov. 1837 (RG8/C1271/11).
49. Goldie to Lt.-Col. Henry Dyer, 2 Dec. 1837 (RG8/C1271/45).
50. Lysons, *Early reminiscences*, 67.
51. Ibid., 81.
52. RG8/C1717/77; see also Ogden autograph book, MG24/C19/70.
53. Gugy to Christie, n.d. (Robert Christie, *A history of the late province of Lower Canada*, V, 27–28).
54. Louis Philippe Turcotte, *Le Canada sous l'union, 1841–67*, 216–17; Jacques Monet, *The last cannon shot*, 3.
55. Nelson to editor of *La Minerve*, 21 août 1848 (Christie, *History of the late province*, IV, 535); E. B. O'Callaghan to Thomas Falconer, 24 June 1838 (Chapman papers, MG24/B31/I/37–44).
56. Wily memoirs, MG29/F46/138; Lady Colborne to her mother, 18 Dec. 1837 (Moore Smith, *John Colborne*, 291); William Kingsford, *The history of Canada*, X, 69; Capt. J. O. Kemp to Colborne, 7 Dec. 1837 (Christie, *History of the late province*, IV, 485–87).
57. Wily memoirs, MG29/F46/138.
58. Wood, *Storied province of Quebec*, I, 212; Monet, *Last cannon shot*, 398.
59. David, *Biographies et portraits*, 276–77.
60. Wolfred Nelson to Christie, 1851 (Christie, *History of the late province*, IV, 516).
61. T. Bland Strange, *Gunner Jingo's jubilee*, 25.
62. Lysons, *Early reminiscences*, 65.
63. Laurent-Olivier David, *Les Patriotes de 1837–38*, 76–77.
64. Lysons, *Early reminiscences*, 65, 66.
65. David, *Les Patriotes de 1837–38*, 78.
66. Grey's journal, entry dated 15 Aug. 1838 (William G. Ormsby, *Crisis in the Canadas, 1838–9*, 104–5).
67. *The Albion*, New York, 5 Jan. 1839.
68. *Transcript*, 27 Apr. 1844.

69. Joly's journal, 20 Aug. 1857 (Hampden Burnham, *Canadians in the imperial naval and military service abroad*, 202–3).
70. MG24/F64; Château Ramezay, The Elgin period: The late Hon. Mrs. Robert Bruce—interesting memoirs, in Alfred Sandham, "Montreal illustrated," III, 140.
71. *The Albion*, New York, 2 Dec. 1848.
72. Wily memoirs, MG29/F46/133–35.
73. Return of troops employed on the expedition to Saint-Eustache, 13 Dec. 1837 (MG11/Q239/11/342).
74. Girod's journal, *Public Archives Report* (1923), 371.
75. RG4/A1/390/II/237.
76. *Transcript*, 16 May 1840.
77. George Cathcart to his brother, Earl Cathcart, 8 Apr. 1845 (Cathcart papers).

CHAPTER FIVE
1. WO, *Manual of military law*, 217, 216.
2. Ibid., 216–33; for a discussion of the application of the Riot Act, see *Gazette*, 23 Apr. 1844.
3. For a discussion of this problem, see Appendix F.
4. *Transcript*, 4 and 28 Mar. 1843.
5. *Transcript*, 4 Mar. 1843.
6. Ibid.
7. Ibid. and 28 Mar. 1843.
8. Dominick Daly to Col. Ermatinger, 25 Mar. 1843, in *Appendix to the Journal*, Legislative Assembly, 1843, no. 2, III, app. T; Elinor Senior, "Frederick William Ermatinger," in *DCB*, IX, 242–43.
9. *Gazette*, 23 May 1844. Details of the Beauharnois Canal riot are from "An Enquiry into disturbances on the line of the Beauharnois Canal during the summer of 1843," in *Appendix to the Journal*, Legislative Assembly, 1843, no. 2, III, app. T.
10. Laviolette's deposition, 27 June 1843 (*Gazette*, 23 May 1844).
11. Ibid.
12. *Appendix to the Journal*, Legislative Assembly, 1843, no. 2, III, app. T; *Times*, 19 July 1843.
13. Cathcart to Jones, 28 June 1843 (McCord Museum, McCord papers, Queen's Light Dragoons, box 1).
14. *DCB*, IX, 396–97.
15. For the by-election campaign, see *Gazette*, 27 Feb. 1844, 29 Feb. 1844, and 9 Mar. 1844; Francis Hincks, *Reminiscences of his public life*, 30; Arthur H. Freeling diary, entry 16 Apr. 1844 (MG24/F72).
16. *Gazette*, 29 Feb. 1844.
17. *Gazette*, 23 Mar. 1844.
18. *Gazette*, 27 Feb. 1844.
19. *Gazette*, 9 Apr. 1844.
20. *Gazette*, 21 Mar. 1844.
21. *Gazette*, 13 Apr. 1844.
22. Ibid.
23. RG8/C316/162–63.

24. Wetherall to Lt.-Col. Furlong, 15 Apr. 1844 (RG8/C317/129–31).
25. F. C. Mather, *Public order in the age of the Chartists*, 153–54.
26. *Gazette*, 15 Oct. 1839.
27. *Gazette*, 18 Apr. 1844, 4 May 1844.
28. *Gazette*, 18 Apr. 1844; testimony of Brush at inquest, *Gazette*, 23 Apr. 1844.
29. Wetherall to magistrates of Montreal, 17 Apr. 1844 (RG8/C316/251–53).
30. *Gazette*, 30 Apr. 1844.
31. For the testimony of Brush at inquest, see *Gazette*, 23 Apr. 1844; for the testimony of Dyer at inquest, see *Gazette*, 25 April, 1844; for the testimony of Macdonald, see *Pilot*, 26 Apr. 1844.
32. Testimony of D'Arcy, *Gazette*, 25 Apr. 1844.
33. Testimony of Comeau, *Gazette*, 23 Apr. 1844.
34. Ibid.
35. Testimony of Louis Lavigne, *Gazette*, 25 Apr. 1844.
36. *Gazette*, 18 Apr. 1844.
37. Deposition of Champeau, *Gazette*, 25 Apr. 1844.
38. Drs. Wolfred Nelson, Pierre Beaubien; Holmes and L. F. Tavernier; see their testimony at the inquest, *Gazette*, 23 and 25 Apr. 1844.
39. *Gazette*, 27 Apr., 4 May 1844; *La Minerve*, 29 Apr. 1844.
40. D'Arcy to Lt.-Col. Bouverie, officer commanding 89th Rgt., 30 Apr. 1844 (RG8/C316/256–57).
41. A. Buchanan to Capt. Brook Taylor, 6 May 1844 (RG8/C316/280–82).
42. *La Minerve*, 8 Aug. 1844.
43. *Gazette*, 30 Apr. 1844.
44. *Statesman*, Brockville, 1 May 1844.
45. Hereward Senior, *Orangeism in Ireland and Britain, 1795–1836*, app. B, 302–3 and 271.
46. Testimony of D'Arcy, *Gazette*, 25 Apr. 1844.
47. Testimony of Brush, *Gazette*, 23 Apr. 1844.
48. Statement of Cartier at inquest, ibid.
49. Ibid.
50. *La Minerve*, 2 May 1844.
51. *Gazette*, 28 Oct. 1844.
52. RG8/C316/308.
53. Circular from Wetherall to major-generals commanding Canada East and West, 28 Sept. 1844 (RG8/C317/123–26).
54. *Gazette*, 23 Oct. 1844.
55. *Gazette*, 22 Oct. 1844.
56. Protest of defeated candidates Drummond and Beaubien, *Gazette*, 30 Oct. 1844.
57. *Gazette*, 24 Oct. 1844.
58. *Gazette*, 22 Oct. 1844; 31 Oct. 1844, reprinted from *Pilot*.
59. Instructions to police magistrates and general orders to police and returning officers from Coffin, commissioner of police, 18 Feb. 1841 (*Appendix to the Journal*, Legislative Assembly, 1850, no. 1, IX, app. X, no. 5).

60. Ibid.
61. *Gazette*, 23 Oct. 1844.
62. Arthur H. Freeling diary, entry dated 22 Oct. 1844 (MG24/F72); *Gazette*, 24 Oct. 1844.
63. *Gazette*, 2 Nov. 1844.
64. *Gazette*, 24 and 25 Oct. 1844.
65. *Gazette*, 25 and 31 Oct. 1844.
66. Sir Richard Bonnycastle, *Canada as it was, is, and may be*, I, x.
67. Protest of Drummond and Beaubien, *Gazette*, 30 Oct. 1844.
68. John Young to Jackson, 26 Oct. 1844 (RG8/C316/7). For Metcalfe, see J. M. Higginson, civil secretary to the governor general, to Capt. Brook Taylor (RG8/C316/323–24). Jackson to troops, 6 Nov. 1844 (RG8/C1194B/273). For the Duke of Wellington, see Lord Fitzroy Somerset to Jackson, 3 Dec. 1844 (RG8/C1194B/297; see also C316/337–39). For the Queen, see Lord Fitzroy Somerset to Jackson, 19 Dec. 1844 (RG8/C316/345).
69. *Gazette*, 2 Nov. 1844, see reprint from *Montreal register*.
70. Bourret to Jackson, 5 Nov. 1844 (RG8/C316/330); for the petition, see RG8/C316/333.
71. RG8/C316/340.
72. Wetherall to military secretary, 31 Dec. 1844 (RG8/C316/342–43); see also *Transcript*, 3 and 5 Dec. 1844.
73. Major Davis, field officer of the week, to Colonel Campbell, 2 Mar. 1847 (RG8/C317/95).
74. Maitland diary, entry dated 2 Mar. 1846 (MG24/I78).
75. Elgin to Grey, 18 May 1848 (*Elgin-Grey papers*, edited by Sir Arthur Doughty, I, 166–67).
76. Gore to D'Urban, 1 Jan. 1848 (RG8/C1275/23).
77. Hartley to Gore, 8 Jan. 1848 (RG8/C317/135–36).
78. Jones to military headquarters, 12 Feb. 1848 (RG8/C802/176); Maj. Vesey Kirkland to Hon. R. Bruce, 30 Dec. 1848 (WO1/565).
79. Egerton to Macdonald, 11 Jan. 1848 (RG8/C317/137–43).
80. *Pilot*, 14 Jan. 1848.
81. Egerton to Macdonald, 11 Jan. 1848 (RG8/C317/137–38).
82. RG8/C317/139.
83. RG8/C317/141.
84. RG8/C317/141–42.
85. RG8/C1275/30.
86. RG8/C1275/31.
87. D'Urban to Earl Grey, 1 Mar. 1849 (WO1/560).
88. RG8/C1275/30.
89. *Pilot*, 29 July 1848.
90. Maj. Robert Sanders, commanding 19th Rgt., to asst. adj. gen., 1 Aug. 1848 (RG8/C860/32).
91. Gore to military secretary, 1 Aug. 1848 (RG8/C860/34).
92. Sanders to asst. adj. gen., 1 Aug. 1848 (RG8/C860/32).
93. D'Urban to Earl Grey, 1 Mar. 1849 (WO1/560); D'Urban to Jones, confidential, 8 Jan. 1849 (McCord Museum, McCord papers, Queen's Light Dragoons box); *The Albion*, New York, 2 Sept. 1848.

CHAPTER SIX

1. For one of the most balanced accounts of the Rebellion Losses Bill agitation, see Sir Francis Hincks, *Reminiscences of his public life*, 188–200.
2. *Journal of the Special Council*, Apr. to June 1840, app. 6.
3. Ibid.
4. First report of the commission to enquire into the losses occasioned by the troubles during the years 1837 and 1838, and into the damages arising therefrom, by Commissioners Joseph Dionne, P. H. Moore, Jacques Viger, John Simpson, and J. U. Beaudry (*Appendix to the Journal*, Legislative Assembly, 1846, no. 2, v, app. X).
5. John Fraser, *Canadian pen and ink sketches*, 105.
6. RG4/B37/507. For details of the following claims, see *Appendix to the Journal*, Legislative Assembly, 1846, no. 2, v, app. X.
7. Solicitor General Drummond to P. H. Moore, 7 May 1851 (RG4/B37/V/498).
8. *Gazette*, 16 Dec. 1837; Ogden, Report on the late unhappy rebellion in this province, 31 May 1838 (Colborne papers, MG24/A40/8198); Gosford to Glenelg, 28 Dec. 1837 (MG11/Q239/II); O'Callaghan to Falconer, 9 Sept. 1838 (Chapman papers, MG24/B31/I/57).
9. *Spectator*, London, quoted in the *Transcript*, 1 May 1849.
10. Bellingham memoirs, MG24/B25/II/138.
11. Quoted in *Transcript*, 1 May 1849.
12. Joshua Chamberlin to his cousin Almira Chamberlin, 9 July 1849 (Chamberlin papers, MG24/B19/IV).
13. Rev. W. R. Seaver to his wife, 25–28 Apr. 1849, in "The Montreal riot of 1849," edited by Josephine Foster, *Canadian Historical Review*, 32, no. 1 (Mar. 1951), 64.
14. *Gazette*, 20 Apr. 1849.
15. Laurent-Olivier David, *Les Patriotes de 1837–38*, 274.
16. Elgin to Grey, 1 Mar. 1849, cited in Hincks, *Reminiscences*, 190.
17. Robert Christie, *A history of the late province of Lower Canada*, IV, 481, see footnote.
18. J. Joseph to Campbell, 1 Aug. 1849 (RG8/C80/33); Wetherall to Talbot, 27 Aug. 1849 (ibid.).
19. WO17/1553, monthly troop returns dated 1 Jan. 1849.
20. Kirkland to Bruce, 30 Dec. 1848 (WO1/565); Wetherall to Jones, 9 Jan. 1849 (McCord Museum, McCord papers, Queen's Light Dragoons box); Elgin to Grey, 21 May 1849 (WO1/560); Wetherall's memo on the Provincial Cavalry, n.d. (WO1/565).
21. Kirkland to Bruce, 30 Dec. 1848 (WO1/565).
22. Elgin to Grey, 29 Jan. 1849, private (*Elgin-Grey papers, 1846–52*, I, 290).
23. WO17/1553, monthly troop returns dated 1 Jan. 1849.
24. Denny to Hay, commandant, Montreal garrison, 17 Apr. 1849 (RG8/C317/252).
25. Hincks, *Reminiscences*, 194.
26. Report of Ermatinger on the burning of the Parliament Building, 10 May 1849 (RG4/B25/I); Debates, Legislative Assembly, in *Pilot*, 27 Apr. 1849, see MacNab's speech; Elgin to Grey, 30 Apr. 1849, in

Transcript, 7 June 1849; Seaver to his wife, 25–28 Apr. 1849, in "The Montreal riot of 1849," 61–65.

27. *Pilot*, 27 Apr. 1849. For eyewitness accounts of the trouble, see Henry Rose to William Manson, 7 May 1849 (MG24/B56); Capt. F. A. Grant to his father, 1 May 1849 (MG24/A53); Sir James Alexander, *Passages in the life of a soldier*, I, 3–13; Catherine Blake, "The riots of 1849 in Montreal," *Canadian Historical Review*, 15, no. 3 (Sept. 1934), 284–88; Seaver to his wife, 25–28 Apr. 1849, in "The Montreal riot of 1849," 61–65.
28. Report of Ermatinger, 10 May 1849 (RG4/B25/I).
29. *Pilot*, 27 Apr. 1849; *Gazette*, 27 Apr. 1849.
30. *Pilot*, 27 Apr. 1849.
31. Report of Ermatinger to government, 10 May 1849 (RG4/B25/I).
32. Report of Gore to military secretary, 26 Apr. 1849 (RG8/C1275/45–47).
33. The library alone was estimated at a value of £40,000, see Grant to his father, 1 May 1849 (MG24/A53). Rev. W. R. Seaver put the value of the library at £100,000 and the entire loss of the Parliament Building at £300,000, see Seaver to his wife, 25–28 Apr. 1849, in "The Montreal riot of 1849," 63.
34. Report of Ermatinger to government, 10 May 1849 (RG4/B25/I); MacNab's speech in the Legislative Assembly, see *Pilot*, 7 Apr. 1849. For criticism of the military, see Rose to Manson, 7 May 1849 (MG24/B56); *Transcript*, 3 May 1849.
35. Gore to Kirkland, 26 Apr. 1849 (RG8/C1275/45–47).
36. For sketches of these men, see Château Ramezay, Alfred Sandham, "Montreal illustrated," III, 124; see also Alexander, *Passages*, I, 14; William H. Atherton, *Montreal, 1535–1914*, III, 666; for the attack on Mackenzie's press, see letter of Mackenzie in *Niagara Mail*, 27 June 1849 (Public Archives Ontario, Mackenzie-Lindsey papers, clipping no. 5528).
37. *Gazette*, 27 Apr. 1849.
38. Report of Ermatinger to government, 10 May 1849 (RG4/B25/I).
39. Sir Richard Bonnycastle, *Canada as it was, is, and may be*, II, 272.
40. Rose to Manson, 7 May 1849 (MG24/B56).
41. Bonnycastle, *Canada as it was*, II, 273; see also Alexander, *Passages*, I, 14.
42. Gore to Monteith, 29 Apr. 1849 (RG8/C1275/47).
43. Report of Ermatinger to government, 10 May 1849 (RG4/B25/I); see also Seaver to his wife, 26 Apr. 1849, "The Montreal riot of 1849," 63.
44. Report of the committee of the Executive Council, 27 Apr. 1849 (RG1/E1/vol. 72/67).
45. *Pilot*, 30 Apr. 1849.
46. Arms issued from ordnance, 27 Apr. 1849 (RG8/C80/26); Kirkland to ordnance storekeeper, 27 Apr. 1849 (RG8/C1304/290); *Pilot*, 30 Apr. 1849.
47. Grant to his father, 1 May 1849 (MG24/A53).
48. Alexander, *Passages*, I, 21; *Gazette*, 30 Apr. 1849; *Transcript*, 3 May 1849.

49. Report of Ermatinger to government, 10 May 1849 (RG4/B25/I).
50. Grant to his father, 1 May 1849 (MG24/A53).
51. Elgin to Grey, 27 Aug. 1849, encl. clipping from *Pilot* (*Elgin-Grey papers*, II, 460); *Transcript*, 3 May 1849; Taché to government, 30 May 1849 (RG4/B25/I).
52. Remark attributed to Sir Benjamin D'Urban, commander of the forces, in *Transcript*, 3 May 1849; see also Grant to his father, 1 May 1849 (MG24/A53).
53. Blake, "The riots of 1849 in Montreal," 287. For Moffatt, see *Transcript*, 1 May 1849.
54. Elgin to Grey, 27 Aug. 1849, encl. clipping from *Pilot* (*Elgin-Grey papers*, II, 460).
55. *Pilot*, 30 Apr. 1849; see also Col. W. D'Urban to Jones, 27 Apr. 1849 (McCord Museum, McCord papers, Queen's Light Dragoons box, Orderly book, 66).
56. Lt.-Gen. B. D'Urban to Harvey, 11 May 1849 (RG8/C1304/304).
57. *Pilot*, 30 Apr. 1849.
58. Jones to Wetherall, 31 Jan. 1859 (McCord Museum, McCord papers, Queen's Light Dragoons box).
59. Instructions for troops having occasion to act against an insurgent mob in streets, or elsewhere, and also for officers commanding in detached quarters, issued by Wetherall, reprinted 5 May 1849 (McCord Museum, McCord papers, Queen's Light Dragoons box).
60. Garrison order no. 2, 30 Apr. 1849 (McCord Museum, McCord papers, Queen's Light Dragoons box).
61. Grant to his father, 1 May 1849 (MG24/A53); Bonnycastle, *Canada as it was*, II, 275; *Transcript*, 1 May 1849.
62. *Gazette*, 2 May 1849.
63. Bonnycastle, *Canada as it was*, II, 275.
64. *Gazette*, 2 May 1849. Rose to Manson, 7 May 1849 (MG24/B56).
65. Grant to his father, 1 May 1849 (MG24/A53).
66. *Gazette*, 11 Sept. 1849.
67. Lt.-Col. W. D'Urban to Jones, 22 June 1849 (McCord Museum, McCord papers, Queen's Light Dragoons box, no. M12228, 77).
68. Elgin to Grey, 16 July 1849 (*Elgin-Grey papers*, I, 407). Grey to Elgin, 12 Sept. 1849 (ibid., II, 451).
69. Capt. Wetherall to government, 2 May 1849 (RG1/E1/vol. 72/89); Elgin to Grey, 20 Aug. 1849 (*Elgin-Grey papers*, II, 450); *Punch in Canada*, 30 June 1849, 96.
70. *Gazette*, 28 May, 9 July 1849.
71. Grey to Elgin, 1 June 1849 (*Elgin-Grey papers*, I, 356).
72. Kirkland to Charles Wetherall, 30 Apr. 1849 (RG8/C1304/292); Leslie to Kirkland, 17 May 1849 (RG8/C80/14).
73. Capt. Wetherall to military secretary, 10 May 1849 (RG8/C80/12–13); see also RG8/C1304/303.
74. Kirkland to Wetherall, 19 May 1849 (RG8/C1304/311–12).
75. Elgin to Grey, 20 Aug. 1849 (*Elgin-Grey papers*, II, 449).
76. Kirkland to Leslie, 23 May 1849 (RG8/C1304/316–18).
77. McCord to Kirkland, 1 June 1849 (RG8/C317/208).
78. Wetherall to Leslie, 21 May 1849 (RG8/C80/15).

79. Leslie to Kirkland, 22 May 1849 (RG8/C80/18).
80. Wetherall to Leslie, 21 May 1849 (RG8/C80/15–16).
81. *Punch in Canada*, 30 June 1849, 95; Wily to J. P. Sexton, city clerk, 5 June 1849 (*Gazette*, 8 June 1849).
82. *Punch in Canada*, 30 June 1849, 96.
83. Alexander, *Passages*, I, 25. Château Ramezay, clipping in Sandham, "Montreal illustrated," III, 106.
84. Memo on hiring the Water Street Barracks (WO1/560/180).
85. Report of the board of officers assembled to report on the Water Street Barracks, 8 Mar. 1849 (WO1/560).
86. WO1/560/213.
87. Grey to Elgin, 20 June 1849 (WO1/560/224); Grey to Rowan, 20 June 1849 (RG8/C860/69).
88. Kirkland to Bruce, 27 June 1849 (RG8/C1304/351).
89. Rowan to Earl Grey, 31 Oct. 1849 (WO1/560/251).
90. Delisle to Drummond, 20 Aug. 1849 (RG4/B25).
91. Wetherall to Gosford, 6 Nov. 1837 (MG11/Q239/II/372); *Gazette*, 25 June 1840, 27 Feb. 1844, 15 and 22 Aug. 1849; *Montreal pocket almanac*, 1849, 98; annual returns of militia, 1849 (RG9/IC2/IV); *Witness*, 20 Aug. 1849.
92. *Pilot*, 18 Aug. 1849.
93. Requisition for troops from Wetherall, McCord, and Ermatinger, 14 Aug. 1849 (RG8/C616/239).
94. Statement of Coroner Coursol at inquest, *Gazette*, 23 Aug. 1849; see also La Fontaine's testimony, *Pilot*, 21 Aug. 1849.
95. Testimony of C. Wetherall, *Pilot*, 25 Aug. 1849.
96. Testimony of La Fontaine, *Pilot*, 21 Aug. 1849 and 23 Aug. 1849.
97. Elgin to Grey, 2 Dec. 1849 (*Elgin-Grey papers*, II, 552).
98. Testimony of Taché, *Pilot*, 23 Aug. 1849.
99. Ibid.; see also testimony of Lubin Leblanc, *Gazette*, 24 Aug. 1849.
100. Statement of Coursol at inquest, *Gazette*, 23 Aug. 1849.
101. Testimony of Taché and La Fontaine at inquest, *Pilot*, 23 Aug. 1849.
102. Testimony of C. Wetherall, *Pilot*, 25 Aug. 1849.
103. Capt. J. Rooke to field officer of the day, 17 Aug. 1849 (RG8/C616/257–59); Hay to Rooke, 17 Aug. 1849 (RG8/C616/259).
104. For the disturbance, see *Pilot*, 18 Aug. 1849; Hay to military secretary, 16 Aug. 1849 (RG8/C616/250–53); Colley to Macdonald, 16 Aug. 1849 (RG8/C616/242–45).
105. McCord's testimony at inquest, *Pilot*, 25 Aug. 1849; letter to editor signed Justice, *Pilot*, 18 Aug. 1849.
106. For an account of the events, see James Mason's testimony at inquest, *Pilot*, 25 Aug. 1849; *Prescott Telegraph*, 22 Aug. 1849; La Fontaine's testimony, *Pilot*, 23 Aug. 1849; Lubin Leblanc's testimony, *Gazette*, 24 Aug. 1849; C. Wetherall's testimony, *Pilot*, 21 Aug. 1849; *Pilot*, 18 Aug. 1849.
107. C. Wetherall's testimony, *Pilot*, 21 Aug. 1849.
108. McCord's testimony, *Pilot*, 25 Aug. 1849.
109. *Gazette*, 16, 23, 24, Aug. 1849; *Pilot*, 23 Aug. 1849.
110. C. Wetherall's testimony, *Pilot*, 25 Aug. 1849.
111. *Pilot*, 25 Aug. 1849.

112. *Pilot*, 21 Aug. 1849.
113. Elgin to Grey, 20 Aug. 1849 (*Elgin-Grey papers*, II, 449). *Gazette*, 17 Aug. 1849.
114. C. Wetherall to Leslie, 18 Aug. 1849 (RG4/B25/I). Elgin to Grey, 20 and 27 Aug. 1849 (*Elgin-Grey papers*, II, 449, 453).
115. On the number of military guards used, see Hay to Macdonald, 18 Aug. 1849 (RG8/C616/284), and Magistrates McCord and Ermatinger to military authorities, 19 Aug. 1849 (RG8/C616/289).
116. *Pilot*, 21 Aug. 1849.
117. Hamilton to field officer of the day, 20 Aug. 1849 (RG8/C616/290).
118. Alexander, *Passages*, I, 20.
119. *Pilot*, 21 Aug. 1849.
120. Capt. H. G. Anderson to field officer of the week, 20 Aug. 1849 (RG8/C616/291); Macdonald to military secretary, 21 Aug. 1849 (RG8/C616).
121. *Pilot*, 25 Aug. 1849.
122. Taché's testimony, *Pilot*, 23 Aug. 1849.
123. For troop involvement, see Château Ramezay, Sandham, "Montreal illustrated," III, 138; *DCB*, IX, 174–78. For mounted police involvement, see *Gazette*, 16 Aug. 1849. For La Fontaine's denial, see his testimony, *Pilot*, 23 Aug. 1849; see also Sheriff William F. Coffin to Leslie, 15 Aug. 1849 (RG4/B25/I).
124. Elgin to Grey, 3 Sept. 1849 (*Elgin-Grey papers*, II, 465); Sexton to Leslie, 22 Aug. 1849 (RG4/B25/I); Macdonald to military secretary, 25 Aug. 1849 (RG8/C616/300).
125. Military Secretary George Talbot to Bruce, 25 Aug. 1849 (RG8/C1304/425).
126. Drummond to Bruce (*Gazette*, 16 Sept. 1849).
127. *Gazette*, 22 Aug. 1849.
128. Talbot to Bruce, 25 Aug. 1849 (RG8/C1304/425).
129. For lists of officers dismissed, see *Pilot*, 11 and 29 Dec. 1849; see also RG4/B29/V and VI; and RG4/B37/IV.
130. Elgin to Grey, 20 Nov. 1849, and Grey to Elgin, 20 Dec. 1849 (WO1/560); Elgin to Grey, confidential, 9 Feb. 1850 (*Elgin-Grey papers*, IV, 1501); same to same, private, 11 Feb. 1850 (ibid., II, 593–94, encl. no. 1).
131. Rowan to Brown, adjutant general, Horse Guards, 8 Mar. 1851, and Report of R. Rollo, 12 June 1857 (Eyre papers, MG24/F38).
132. Ermatinger and R. B. Johnson to Talbot, 10 Oct. 1850 (RG8/C80/79).

CHAPTER SEVEN
1. For what is probably the most balanced account of the Gavazzi riot, see Sir James E. Alexander, *Passages in the life of a soldier*, I, 161–95.
2. Ibid.; *Gazette*, 10 June 1853.
3. Ermatinger's testimony at inquest, *Transcript*, 20 June 1853.
4. For accounts of the Gavazzi riot in Quebec, see *Gazette*, 9 June 1853; Mayor Tessier to commandant, Quebec garrison, requesting troops,

6 and 7 June 1853 (RG8/C318/369, 371); Alexander, *Passages*, I, 168–69.

5. John Douglas Borthwick, *History and biographical gazetteer of Montreal to the year 1892*, 129.

6. For a description of these riots, see RG8/C318/197–209.

7. For measures undertaken by Wilson and his administration to preserve peace during the provincial election of December 1851, see *Gazette*, 1, 3, 14, 15 Dec. 1851.

8. W. Ermatinger's testimony, *Transcript*, 20 June 1853.

9. For a description of the Water Police, see *Evening Pilot*, 17 and 19 Jan. 1859.

10. W. Ermatinger's testimony, *Transcript*, 20 June 1853; see also testimony of High Constable Benjamin DeLisle, *Gazette*, 4 July 1853.

11. Wilson's testimony, *Transcript*, 21 June 1853.

12. Alexander, *Passages*, I, 91, 93–94, 97.

13. Ibid., 92, 171–72.

14. Lt.-Col. George Hogarth's testimony, *Transcript*, 20 June 1853.

15. *Transcript*, 4 and 9 June 1853; see also general order no. 1, dated 1 June 1853 (RG8/C1194E/598).

16. Alexander, *Passages*, I, 192–93.

17. Wilson's testimony, *Transcript*, 21 June 1853.

18. W. Ermatinger's testimony, *Transcript*, 20 June 1853.

19. J. Sadlier to editor, *Transcript*, 2 July 1853; see also *Gazette*, 9 June 1853.

20. Wilson's testimony, *Transcript*, 21 June 1853.

21. Alexander, *Passages*, I, 173.

22. Ibid., 179; Rowan to Col. Airey, military secretary, Horse Guards, 10 June 1853 (RG8/C1282/163–64); testimony of Constable Jean-Baptiste Simard, *Gazette*, 1 July 1853; testimony of Sgt. R. Wylie Hutchinson, *Gazette*, 9 July 1853; testimony of Constable François Monette, *Gazette*, 4 July 1853; testimony of William Palmer, *Transcript*, 21 June 1853.

23. Wilson's testimony, *Transcript*, 21 June 1853.

24. Cameron's testimony, ibid.

25. Alexander, *Passages*, I, 177.

26. Wilson's testimony, *Transcript*, 21 June 1853; W. Ermatinger's testimony, *Transcript*, 20 June 1853.

27. Testimony of Hutchinson, *Gazette*, 9 July 1853.

28. Testimony of C. O. Ermatinger, *Transcript*, 21 June 1853; testimony of Dr. R. MacDonnell, *Transcript*, 20 June 1853; testimony of Chief Constable Patrick Brien, *Gazette*, 22 June 1853.

29. Testimony of C. O. Ermatinger, *Transcript*, 21 June 1853.

30. Testimony of W. Ermatinger, *Transcript*, 20 June 1853.

31. Testimony of C. O. Ermatinger, *Transcript*, 21 June 1853.

32. *Orange Lily*, Bytown, 10 June 1854.

33. Testimony of Medill, *Gazette*, 12 July 1853; statement of MacCrae at inquest, *Gazette*, 11 July 1853; *Transcript*, 14 June 1853.

34. Testimony of Hutchinson, *Gazette*, 9 July 1853.

35. Testimony of Simard, *Gazette*, 1 July 1853; testimony of Renaud, *Gazette*, 5 July 1853.

36. Cameron's testimony, *Transcript*, 21 June 1853.
37. See majority report of jury at coroners' inquest, *Transcript*, 12 July 1853.
38. Cameron's testimony, *Transcript*, 21 June 1853; W. Ermatinger's testimony, *Transcript*, 20 June 1853.
39. Testimony of David G. Sloane, *Transcript*, 21 June 1853.
40. Testimony of Quarterley, *Transcript*, 21 June 1853.
41. Ibid.; Alexander, *Passages*, I, 192.
42. WO, *Manual of military law*, 200, footnote; see also Alexander, *Passages*, I, 192.
43. Wilson's testimony, *Transcript*, 21 June 1853; Hogarth's testimony, *Transcript*, 20 June 1853.
44. WO, *Manual of military law*, 224.
45. Wilson's testimony, *Transcript*, 21 June 1853.
46. Quarterley's testimony, ibid.
47. See testimony of Ptes. James Macullock, John Dougherty, John Cousie, and Sgts. James H. Goodfellow and John Conner, in *Transcript*, 24, 27, 28 June 1853.
48. Hogarth's testimony, *Transcript*, 20 June 1853; Cameron's testimony, *Transcript*, 21 June 1853.
49. Ibid.; W. Ermatinger's testimony, *Transcript*, 20 June 1853.
50. Macdonald's testimony, *Transcript*, 29 June 1853; Alexander's testimony, *Transcript*, 23 June 1853.
51. Macdonald's testimony, *Transcript*, 29 June 1853.
52. Routh's testimony, *Transcript*, 20 June 1853.
53. Alexander's testimony, *Transcript*, 23 June 1853; Macdonald's testimony, *Transcript*, 29 June 1853.
54. Coursol's testimony, *Transcript*, 23 June 1853.
55. Alexander's testimony, ibid.
56. *Gazette*, 11 June 1853; *Transcript*, 20 June 1853; see also special returns of coroners' jury, in *Transcript*, 12 July 1853. As the summer wore on, others died of their wounds; see *Transcript*, 4 Nov. 1853, which states that fourteen were known to have been slain and that at least six others were believed to have died of wounds received 9 June.
57. Since the dismissal of the Provincial Cavalry in 1850, Capt. Walter Jones had resumed medical practice in the city.
58. Rowan to Col. Airey, Horse Guards, 10 June 1853 (RG8/C1282/163–64).
59. F. W. Torrance to Rowan, 11 June 1853 (RG8/C318/389–90); Griffin to Torrance, 11 June 1853 (RG8/C318/391); see also RG8/C1307/242; *Gazette*, 11 June 1853.
60. *Gazette*, 11 June 1853.
61. *Gazette*, 15 June 1853.
62. Sexton to Bruce, 9 July 1853 (RG7/G20/vol. 55/no. 5909); RG8/C80/110–11; the increase in pay did not bring a policeman's wage up to the level of a common day labourer. In 1853 the wage for a labourer was from four shillings and fivepence to five shillings a day; see *Gazette*, 14 June 1853; J. C. Lamothe, *Histoire de la corporation de la cité de Montréal*, 114.

63. Ordnance memo, 15 July 1853 (RG8/C80/110–11).

64. Alexander, *Passages*, I, 193.

65. *Transcript*, 8 July 1853, see report of the proceedings of the corporation. *Gazette*, 11 June 1853.

66. Alfred Sandham, *Ville-Marie*, 125.

67. *Transcript*, 21, 23, and 25 July 1853.

68. Both the *Transcript* and *Gazette* published the proceedings of the coroners' inquest; see issues between 20 June and 12 July 1853.

69. *Transcript*, 29 June 1853.

70. Macdonald's testimony, *Transcript*, 29 June 1853.

71. Quarterley's testimony, 21 June 1853; James Bailie's testimony, 20 June 1853; testimony of Pte. John Cousie, 24 June 1853; John Dougherty and W. Wylie, 28 June 1853; and Sgt. James H. Goodfellow, 27 June 1853, all in *Transcript*.

72. Ptes. Thomas Briggs and John Dougherty, 28 June 1853; Pte. John Cousie, 24 June 1853; James Macullock, 27 June 1853; see also testimony of bystander Daniel Deane, 8 July 1853, all in *Transcript*.

73. See Parker's testimony, *Transcript*, 8 July 1853.

74. Cameron's testimony, *Transcript*, 21 June 1853.

75. Macdonald's testimony, *Transcript*, 29 June 1853; Hogarth's testimony, *Transcript*, 20 June 1853.

76. Cameron's testimony, *Transcript*, 21 June 1853.

77. Routh's testimony, *Transcript*, 20 June 1853; Hogarth's testimony, ibid.

78. *Transcript*, 29 June 1853.

79. Confidential instructions for troops having occasion to act against an insurgent mob in streets, or elsewhere; and also for officers commanding in detached quarters, no. 15, 5 May 1849 (McCord Museum, McCord papers, Queen's Light Dragoons box).

80. *Transcript*, 12 July 1853.

81. Ibid.

82. Rowan to Col. Airey, Horse Guards, 18 July 1853 (RG8/C1282/176); *Transcript*, 21 July 1853; Rowan to Airey, 18 July 1853 (RG8/C1282/176).

83. *Transcript*, 27 Oct. 1853.

84. Lt.-Col. D. G. Tullock to Hon. R. Bruce, 21 Sept. 1853 (RG7/G20/vol. 55/no. 5949, and no. 5968, dated 4 Nov. 1853); Bruce to Rowan, 10 Oct. 1853 (RG8/C80/116).

85. *Orange Lily*, Bytown, 10 June 1854.

86. Ibid.

87. *Evening Pilot*, 17 and 19 January 1859.

88. Capt. F. Griffin to Attorney General Drummond, 15 Nov. 1853 (RG8/C318/386).

89. *Transcript*, 19 Nov. 1853.

90. *Transcript*, 24 Nov. 1853; RG8/C318/400.

91. See coroners' charge to jury, *Transcript*, 12 July 1853.

92. *Transcript*, 24 Nov. 1853.

93. Ibid.

94. Ibid.

95. *Transcript*, 1 Nov. 1853, 24 and 27 Oct. 1853.

96. *Transcript*, 3 Nov. 1853.
97. RG8/C318/400.
98. *Transcript*, 29 Nov. 1853.
99. This is suggested by later historians; see William H. Atherton, *Montreal, 1535–1914*, II, 171; Kathleen Jenkins, *Montreal*, 349–50.
100. General order no. 5, dated 10 Mar. 1854, cited in *Transcript*, 25 Mar. 1854; general order no. 6, 10 Mar. 1854 (ibid.).
101. Article from *Herald*, reprinted in *Transcript*, 25 Mar. 1854.
102. *Transcript*, 30 Mar. and 19 Oct. 1854.
103. Alexander, *Passages*, I, 193–94.
104. RG8/C880/53, and C881/20, 21, 25.
105. RG8/C881/52.
106. Newcastle to Rowan, 18 Aug. 1854 (Eyre papers, MG24/F38); troop returns dated 1 Jan. 1855 (WO17/1559) showed 278 officers and men at the Montreal station.

CHAPTER EIGHT

1. James Starke, *Compilation of the by-laws and police regulations in force in the city of Montreal*, 1842, 35–59.
2. *Gazette*, 11 May 1841.
3. *Starke's pocket almanac*, 1843, 98.
4. *Montreal directory*, 1849–50, 345.
5. Annual militia returns, RG9/IC6/I/15–29; see also II, 1846, returns for Montreal Fire Battalion; for general references to this Fire Battalion, see William H. Atherton, *Montreal, 1535–1914*, II, 401; Ernest J. Chambers, *The Canadian militia*, 63; Charles P. Stacey, *Canada and the British army, 1846–1871*, 96, see footnote; George F. Stanley, *Canada's soldiers*, 211; C. F. Hamilton, "Defence, 1812–1912," in *Canada and its provinces*, VII, 395.
6. Gugy to Christie, n.d. (Robert Christie, *A history of the late province of Lower Canada*, V, 27).
7. Annual militia returns, 1846, RG9/IC6/II, see Montreal Fire Battalion; Chambers, *The Canadian militia*, 63.
8. Annual militia returns, 1849, RG9/IC2/IV, see Montreal Fire Battalion returns dated 10 July 1849.
9. *Pilot*, 27 Apr. 1849; see also Sir Allan MacNab's speech in the Legislative Assembly, *Gazette*, 27 Apr. 1849.
10. Alfred Perry, John Orr, and Robert Cooke, see chapter 6; see also militia returns, 10 July 1849 (RG9/IC2/IV).
11. Testimony of Constable Sandeleines, *Transcript* and *Gazette*, 11 July 1853.
12. For a description of these stoves, see Sarah Lovell, *Reminiscences of seventy years*, 26.
13. RG8/C316/392.
14. General orders, 14 Oct. 1845 (RG8/C1194B/448).
15. J. M. Higginson to Capt. G. Talbot, 11 Oct. 1845 (RG8/C316/399).
16. Maj.-Gen. Charles Gore to Capt. Vesey Kirkland, 20 Apr. 1848 (RG8/C317/186).

17. Lt.-Gen. Sir Benjamin D'Urban to Earl Grey, 1 Mar. 1849 (WO1/560).
18. Montreal commandant to Kirkland, 3 Mar. 1848 (RG8/C317/172).
19. Major Granville to Town Major Colin Macdonald, 26 Apr. 1848 (RG8/C317/183–84).
20. Gore to Kirkland, 30 Apr. 1848 (RG8/C317/186–91).
21. Ibid.
22. Chester to Macdonald, 28 Apr. 1848 (RG8/C317/185).
23. Gore to Kirkland, 30 Apr. 1848 (RG8/C317/188–89).
24. Same to same, 27 Nov. 1848 (RG8/C317/198).
25. See report of fire, 20 Dec. 1848 (RG8/C1275/40).
26. Report of prison governor, 20 Dec. 1848 (ibid.).
27. Gore to Major G. Talbot, 29 Dec. 1848 (RG8/C1275/41).
28. Report of inquiry into prison fire, 31 Dec. 1848 (RG8/C1275/42).
29. See Fletcher's account of the fire (Montreal Military and Maritime Museum, "Old Montreal" scrapbook, clipping dated 24 Apr. 1889).
30. Gore to Kirkland, 26 Apr. 1849 (RG8/C1275/45–47).
31. Fletcher's account of the fire (Montreal Military and Maritime Museum, "Old Montreal" scrapbook, clipping dated 24 Apr. 1889).
32. *Transcript*, 3 May 1849.
33. Gore to Kirkland, 26 Apr. 1849 (RG8/C1275/45–47); Rev. W. F. Seaver to his wife, 26 Apr. 1849 ("The Montreal riot of 1849," edited by Josephine Foster, *Canadian Historical Review*, 32, no. 1 [Mar. 1951], 63).
34. Town Major Colin Macdonald's report on fire, 23 Aug. 1850 (RG8/C318/161).
35. This is the figure used by Lt.-Gen. W. Rowan in his report to Lord Fitzroy Somerset, 30 July 1852 (RG8/C318/318). Sir James Alexander says 1,160 buildings were destroyed and 12,000 left homeless; see *Passages in the life of a soldier*, I, 106. Alfred Sandham, in *Ville-Marie*, 131–33, says 30 houses were burned on 6 June and 1,100 on 8 July.
36. Beaudry to commandant, 6 June 1852 (RG8/C318/284).
37. Captain MacKenzie to Macdonald, 6 June 1852 (RG8/C318/282).
38. Maj. Hugh Crofton's report on the fire, 10 July 1852 (RG8/C318/301–5); Alexander, *Passages*, I, 107.
39. Capt. T. L. Gallway's report to the commanding officer, Royal Engineers (RG8/C318/309).
40. Maj. J. W. Mitchell's report to acting deputy adj. gen., 9 July 1852 (RG8/C318/299–300).
41. Alexander, *Passages*, I, 110–11.
42. Ibid., 109.
43. Crofton's report, 10 July 1852 (RG8/C318/301–5).
44. A rumour persisted that the second outbreak of fire was the work of a soldier who wished to vent his spite on Moses Judah Hays, the owner of the Hays Theatre on Dalhousie Square, whom the soldier believed had wronged him. There is no evidence for this rumour which is repeated in Franklin Graham, *Histrionic Montreal*, 100.
45. Gallway's report to commanding officer, Royal Engineers (RG8/C318/309).

46. Mitchell's report on the fire, 9 July 1852 (RG8/C318/299–300).
47. Alexander, *Passages*, I, 109.
48. Crofton's report on the fire, 10 July 1852 (RG8/C318/303).
49. Sandham, *Ville-Marie*, 133; Alexander, *Passages*, I, 106.
50. Lord Elgin to military secretary, 15 July 1852 (RG8/C318/315); Alfred Sandham, *Ville-Marie*, 132; A. Leblond de Brumath, *Histoire populaire de Montréal*, 385.
51. Somerset to Rowan, 30 July 1852 (RG8/C318/318); Crofton's report on fire, 10 July 1852 (RG8/C318/301–5); report on the fire, 19 Aug. 1852 (RG8/C318/325–27).

CHAPTER NINE

1. Newton Bosworth, *Hochelaga depicta*, 212.
2. Robert L. Jones, *History of agriculture in Ontario, 1613–1880*, 23–24; E.-Z. Massicotte, *Nos athlètes canadiens-français*, 13.
3. John Richardson, *Eight years in Canada*, 78; William Hutton to editor of *British Farmers Magazine*, Apr. 1835, cited in Edwin C. Guillet, *Early life in Upper Canada*, 298.
4. WO1/560, 213; in 1841 Molson's sold 12 per cent overproof whiskey at 2s. 3d. per gallon (Molson Archives, see Mabel Good's notes, II, 1).
5. Sir William Eyre to Bower St. Clair, 18 Apr. 1857 (Eyre papers).
6. General order no. 1, 24 July 1857 (ibid.).
7. General order no. 1, 30 Oct. 1840 (RG8/C1194/279).
8. Alexander, *Passages*, I, 97, 105; Monet, *The last cannon shot*, 282–83; see also chapter 7.
9. Confidential instructions to the commander of the forces, 15 May 1857 (Eyre papers).
10. Edward Hale to his wife, 10 May 1840 (McCord Museum, Hale papers).
11. Deputy Adj. J. W. Forster to Sir William Eyre (Eyre papers, see PRO 30/46/19/145).
12. *Standing orders of the 23rd Regiment or Royal Welsh Fusiliers*, 1 Jan. 1841, 52.
13. Private report on desertion by Lt.-Gen. William Rowan to General Brown, adjutant general, Horse Guards, 1 Mar. 1851 (Eyre papers).
14. Anon., *Ramble, a visitor to Montreal in 1816*.
15. *Montreal pocket almanac*, 1844, 26.
16. *Gazette*, 15 June 1844.
17. *Gazette*, 29 Oct. 1849.
18. Richardson, *Eight years in Canada*, 181–82.
19. Private report on desertion by Rowan to Brown, 1 Mar. 1851 (Eyre papers).
20. Sir John Colborne to Maj.-Gen. Lord Fitzroy Somerset, 11 May 1837 (RG8/C1277/188).
21. Report on the Quebec Gate Barracks, 21 Aug. 1856 (Eyre papers).
22. RG8/C860/122.
23. A. Gun, ordnance storekeeper, report on Quebec Gate Barracks, 21 Aug. 1856 (Eyre papers).
24. RG8/C35/185.
25. Richardson, *Eight years in Canada*, 77.

26. RG8/C1194B/431; general orders, 6 May 1845 (RG8/C1194B/378–79).
27. Proceedings of a board of inquiry . . . into school rooms, 19 Sept. 1853 (RG8/C880/23).
28. RG8/C1285/52.
29. General orders, 19 June 1857 (RG8/C36/I/105).
30. Eyre papers, MG24/F38, see PRO 30/46/16/131.
31. Paedar MacSuibhne, *Paul Cullen and his contemporaries with their letters from 1820–1902*, II, 236.
32. General orders, 26 Feb. 1845 (RG8/C1194B/325).
33. Frank Adams, *History of Christ Church Cathedral*, 20–21; John I. Cooper, *The blessed communion*, 2–4.
34. Robert Campbell, *A history of the Scotch Presbyterian Church*, 23–27.
35. Capt. Brook Taylor, military secretary, to bishop of Montreal, 25 Nov. 1844 (RG8/C1300/358–59); same to same, 5 Dec. 1844 (RG8/C1300/371–72).
36. Anglican Archives, Canon A. R. Kelley papers, see "History of St. Stephen's Church, 1822–1947," compiled by George Merchant, and "Biography of Reverend B. B. Stevens," compiled by Canon Sydenham B. Lindsay, 5.
37. Ibid., see especially George Durnford to Rev. R. Y. Overing, 26 Jan. 1916.
38. Anglican Archives, Charles Abrahall, "History of the Diocese of Montreal, 1850–1908," I, 81; see also Edward Hale to his wife, 4 June 1840 (McCord Museum, Hale papers).
39. Sarah Lovell, *Reminiscences of seventy years*, 12.
40. Anglican Archives, Canon E. E. Dawson papers, see "History of St. Edward's Church."
41. Capt. Brook Taylor to bishop of Montreal, 5 Dec. 1844 (RG8/C1300/371–72); general order no. 4, 10 Sept. 1842 (RG8/C1194A).
42. General orders, 25 May 1847 (RG8/C1194C/223–24); see also RG8/C880/44.
43. Sir Richard Jackson to secretary of war, 26 Sept. 1842 (RG8/C1279).
44. Jackson to secretary of war, 10 June 1842 (ibid.).
45. Campbell, *Scotch Presbyterian Church*, 214, 397.
46. RG8/C1312/21.
47. *Montreal pocket almanac*, 1844, 26.
48. Léon Pouliot, *Mgr. Bourget et son temps*, II, 10.
49. For Major-General Clitherow, see *Transcript*, 14 Aug. 1838. For the visits to the Sisters of the Congregation of Notre Dame, see Col. Charles Grey's journal, 3 July 1838 (William G. Ormsby, *Crisis in the Canadas, 1838–9*, 64). For regimental bands at Roman Catholic services, see *Transcript*, 29 June 1843.
50. Maitland diary, entries dated 29 Jan. and 20 July 1846 (MG24/I78).
51. For a discussion, see Richardson, *Eight years in Canada*, 59.
52. Grey's journal, 20 May 1838 (Ormsby, *Crisis in the Canadas*, 19).
53. Léon Pouliot, *La réaction catholique de Montréal, 1840–41*, 8.
54. Ibid., 12.
55. Christ Church Archives, Register of births, marriages, and deaths,

1866–96, 296, see clipping of obituary of Dean Bethune.
56. For Robertson, see Anglican Archives, Abrahall, "History of the Diocese of Montreal," I, 41; for his appointment as chaplain, see general orders, 1 Apr. 1842 (RG8/C1194A/131).
57. Taylor to bishop of Montreal, 5 Dec. 1855 (RG8/C1300/371–72).
58. Taylor to bishop of Montreal, 25 Nov. 1844 (RG8/C1300/358–59).
59. Ibid.
60. Printed notice of Church Society of the Diocese of Quebec, 7 July 1842, encl. in letter of William Dawes, secretary, to Edward Hale, 12 July 1842 (McCord Museum, Hale papers).
61. Christ Church Archives, Register of births, marriages, and deaths, 1866–96, 296, see obituary of Dean Bethune.
62. For a description of Dr. Barry, see Bellingham memoirs (MG24/B25/II/169).
63. Eyre to dean of Montreal, 24 Jan. 1859 (Eyre papers).
64. Eyre to military secretary, Horse Guards, 21 Feb. 1859, and Eyre to dean of Montreal, 25 Feb. 1859 (Eyre papers).
65. Sir Daniel Lysons, *Early reminiscences*, 82.
66. Bosworth, *Hochelaga depicta*, 232.
67. *DCB*, VI, 249.
68. Sir James Alexander, *Passages*, I, 23–24.
69. *Gazette*, 28 May 1849.
70. Alexander, *Passages*, I, 25.
71. Château Ramezay, Sandham, "Montreal illustrated," III, 106.

CHAPTER TEN
1. Sir John Colborne to Colonel Foster, commanding at Toronto, 10 Oct. 1837 (RG8/C1272/10–11); Sir Edmund Head to secretary of state, 7 Aug. 1855 (Eyre papers, MG24/F38).
2. General orders, 19 Aug. 1843 (RG8/C1194B/47).
3. General order no. 2, 27 Nov. 1844 (RG8/C1194B/281).
4. *Gazette*, 28 Nov. 1845.
5. Secretary Joseph Smith Lee's annual report, 1845, to the Shakspeare Club, in *Annual report of the club for the year 1845*, 5–6.
6. *Gazette*, 18 June 1845.
7. General orders, 18 Mar. 1846 (RG8/C1194C/39).
8. Troop returns, 1840, WO17/1544.
9. *Transcript*, 26 May 1840.
10. *Gazette*, 18 June 1840; for descriptions of other field days, see general order no. 1, 22 May 1841 (RG8/C1194), 23 May 1842 (RG8/C1194A/153); *Transcript*, 14 June 1843; *Gazette*, 25 May and 18 June 1844.
11. *Transcript*, 19 May 1838; Col. Charles Grey's journal, 16 May 1838 (William G. Ormsby, *Crisis in the Canadas, 1838–9*, 18).
12. Grey to his father, 2 July 1838 (Ormsby, *Crisis in the Canadas*, 18).
13. Prieur, *Notes of a convict of 1838*, 31.
14. Wily memoirs (MG29/F46/168).
15. Address dated 21 Apr. 1842 (MG24/F33).
16. Grey's journal, 2 July 1838 (Ormsby, *Crisis in the Canadas*, 64).

17. *Transcript*, 7 Aug. 1838.
18. Grey's journal, 3 July 1838 (Ormsby, *Crisis in the Canadas*, 64).
19. *Gazette*, 16 Sept. 1849, *Transcript*, 29 June 1843.
20. For the events on St. George's Day see, *Transcript*, 27 Apr. 1843; for St. Andrew's Day, see *Transcript*, 1 Dec. 1849; for the firemen's picnic, see *Gazette*, 13 Aug. 1849.
21. Adele Clarke, *Old Montreal*, 39–40.
22. The term "muffin" was defined by Sir Desmond O'Callaghan in his *Guns, gunners, and others*, 21, when describing "the real Canada, mark you, Quebec, Montreal, and Kingston ... the land of the 'muffins,' a term which we found when we got there was on no account used. It had originated, we were told, 'Oh! long, long ago,' when it was said (and quite untruly) that girls used to drive about in sleighs with soldier admirers and without a chaperone. But now there was no such thing! ... When we drove damsels in sleighs to the driving meets we always took a chaperone and I well remember the run on a cheery old lady who was stone deaf." I am indebted to Professor Richard Preston for introducing me to the subject of muffins.
23. Sir Daniel Lysons, *Early reminiscences*, 63.
24. Sarah Lovell, *Reminiscences of seventy years*, 12; petition to Sir Richard Jackson, 4 Nov. 1843 (RG8/C76).
25. See his advertisement in *Transcript*, 11 Mar. 1841.
26. *Gazette*, 15 June 1849.
27. Maitland diary, entry dated 13 Nov. 1846 (MG24/I78).
28. Lysons, *Early reminiscences*, 145.
29. P. 11.
30. Derek Clifford, *Collecting English watercolours*, see section entitled "Drawing masters at military academies." I wish to acknowledge my indebtedness to Professor Richard Glover for drawing my attention to the importance of this aspect of the contribution of the garrison.
31. See System of marks for quarterly examinations of candidates for direct commission (RG8/C158/78).
32. Lysons, *Early reminiscences*, 104, 146, 160, and 192.
33. For a copy of this map, see Colborne papers, MG24/A40/8227.
34. Lysons, *Early reminiscences*, 119.
35. Dubois, pp. 168 and 192; Schull, between pp. 114 and 115.
36. For Bainbrigge, see Bell, *Painters in a new land*, 12, 83, 87, 94; for Cockburn, see ibid., 11–12, 74, 80, 82–83.
37. Henry Warre, *Sketches in North America and the Oregon territory*.
38. For Warre, see Bell, *Painters in a new land*, 85–86; for Ainslie, see ibid., 98.
39. William H. Atherton, *Montreal, 1535–1914*, II, 132.
40. Franklin Graham, *Histrionic Montreal*, 68.
41. Ibid., 77; Clarke, *Old Montreal*, 34; *Gazette*, 18 June 1840.
42. *Albion*, New York, 18 Nov. 1848; for a somewhat more flattering account of the Garrison Amateurs, see a letter to the editor signed One who was there, *Morning Courier*, 8 Feb. 1841.
43. Edgar A. Collard, *Call back yesterday*, 111.

44. Château Ramezay, printed notice of Charles Dickens playing at the Theatre Royal, document no. 2219.

45. Graham, *Histrionic Montreal*, 83–85; Patricia Conroy, "History of the theatre in Montreal," 131; McGill University, Mott papers, no. 32.

46. McGill University, see Account of the Shakspeare Dramatic and Literary Club in a letter to the editor, *Star*, 15 Mar. 1902, in frontispiece of *The Shakspeare Club*.

47. Wily memoirs, MG29/G46/194–96.

48. Secretary's report for 1846 in *The Shakspeare Club*, 9.

49. Kingsford enlisted as a young lad in the 1st Dragoon Guards and came to Canada in 1837 where he served until 1841. Upon obtaining a discharge, he took up engineering and began writing his *History of Canada* at the age of sixty-five; *Canada and its provinces*, XII, 499.

50. See Henry Morgan's account of the Shakspeare Dramatic and Literary Club, in frontispiece of *The Shakspeare Club*; see also list of members, 25 May 1847, ibid., 1–3; *Annual report of Shakspeare Club*, 1846, 5.

51. See program of literary exercises for winter 1846, ibid., 10–11.

52. Graham, *Histrionic Montreal*, 97.

53. Wily memoirs, MG29/F46/195.

54. J. McCord, corresponding secretary of Natural History Society, to Sir John Colborne, 21 Aug. 1837 (RG8/C76).

55. *Gazette*, 28 Apr. 1840.

56. *Gazette*, 22 June 1853.

57. John H. Graham, *Outlines of the history of freemasonry in the province of Quebec*, 37 and 177.

58. Sir George Bell, *Soldier's glory*, 186.

59. Prieur, *Notes of a convict of 1838*, 35.

60. *Report of the state trials held before a general court-martial, 1838–39*, I, 293; II, 141, 530.

61. Bell, *Soldier's glory*, 141–42; Sir Garnet Wolseley, *The story of a soldier's life*, I, 81.

62. Graham, *Outlines of freemasonry*, 177.

63. *Starke's Montreal pocket almanac*, 1851, 102.

64. George Moffatt to J. S. McCord, 8 Feb. 1845, and Memorial of the masters of the city of Montreal, 4 Feb. 1845 (McCord Museum, McCord papers, miscellaneous Masonic papers, no. 12468).

CHAPTER ELEVEN

1. *Gazette*, 12 Mar. 1844; *Montreal street directory*, 1844–45, 297.

2. *Gazette*, 4 July 1840.

3. *Gazette*, 12 Mar. 1844.

4. Maitland diary, entries dated 18 and 19 Aug. 1846 (MG24/I78).

5. See, for example, Jones to Hon. J. Lindsay, 3 June 1842 (RG8/C1330/II); *Starke's Montreal pocket almanac*, 1851, 98.

6. *Transcript*, 17 Oct. 1840; Arthur Freeling diary, entry dated 15 Oct. 1840 (MG24/F72).

7. *Gazette*, 19 and 21 May 1841; Capt. Walter Jones of the Queen's

Light Dragoons, one of the earlier masters of the Montreal Hunt, died of wrist injuries sustained when he fell on the judges' platform while attending the annual steeplechase in his capacity as steward; see obituary, *Transcript*, 29 Oct. 1864; see also Cooper, *Montreal Hunt*, 30 and 38.

8. Adele Clarke, *Old Montreal*, 32.
9. Maitland diary, entries dated 14 Jan., 4 Feb., 4 Mar. 1846.
10. Lysons, *Early reminiscences*, 103.
11. Clarke, *Old Montreal*, 34, 35.
12. Maitland diary, entries dated 8, 10, 12, 17 Jan. 1846.
13. Hugh W. Becket, *Montreal Snow Shoe Club*, 75.
14. Kathleen Jenkins, *Montreal*, 408.
15. According to Robert Campbell, the first curling club in Montreal was founded in 1807; see his *History of the Scotch Presbyterian Church*, 157. A third club, the Caledonia Curling Club, was formed in 1849 by George H. Gillespie; see *Gazette*, 28 Jan. 1853; *Transcript*, 26 Nov. 1844.
16. *Gazette*, 16 Feb. 1841.
17. Col. Charles Grey's journal, 10 Aug. 1838 (William G. Ormsby, *Crisis in the Canadas, 1838–9*, 96).
18. Francis Duncan, *Our garrisons in the west*, 168–69.
19. Maitland diary, entries dated 10 and 15 Sept. 1846; Freeling diary, 3 Sept. 1844.
20. Col. Ord, R. E., to Lt.-Gen. William Eyre, 3 Mar. 1859 (Eyre papers, MG24/F38).
21. General orders, 10 Aug. 1847 (RG8/C1194C/295).
22. E.-Z. Massicotte, "L'escrime et les maîtres d'armes à Montréal," *Le bulletin des recherches historiques*, 29, no. 9 (Sept. 1923), 260.
23. *Gazette*, 25 Apr. 1849.
24. Edward Hale to his wife, 30 May 1840 (McCord Museum, Hale papers).
25. *Gazette*, 7 and 8 Oct. 1842.
26. For a description of the Sweeny family, see *Centenary of the Montreal Board of Trade, 1822–1922*, 15; Campbell, *Scotch Presbyterian Church*, 425–26.
27. For accounts of the Warde-Sweeny duel, see Bellingham memoirs, MG24/B25/II/134; John Fraser, *Canadian pen and ink sketches*, 5; Grey's journal (Ormsby, *Crisis in the Canadas*, 21); McCord Museum, McCord papers, Queen's Light Dragoons box, see undated account of the Warde-Sweeny duel; Clarke, *Old Montreal*, 33; John Douglas Borthwick, *History and biographical gazetteer of Montreal to the year 1892*, 178; Campbell, *Scotch Presbyterian Church*, 425–26; A. W. Patrick Buchanan, *The bench and bar of Lower Canada down to 1850*, 134.
28. Bellingham memoirs, MG24/B25/II/134.
29. Borthwick, *Gazetteer of Montreal*, 178.
30. Fraser, *Canadian pen and ink sketches*, 5.
31. Lysons, *Early reminiscences*, 65–66; see chapter 4.
32. McCord Museum, McCord papers, Queen's Light Dragoons box, see undated account of Warde-Sweeny duel.

33. Borthwick, *Gazetteer of Montreal*, 178.
34. Bellingham memoirs, MG24/B25/II/134.
35. Freeling diary; Maitland diary.
36. J. M. Moyster to his sister, 15 Jan. 1857 (MG24/I87).
37. Thomas Storrow Brown, *Montreal fifty years ago*, 24.
38. Maitland diary, entry dated 15 Jan. 1846.
39. Freeling diary, entry dated 11 Dec. 1839.
40. Sarah Lovell, *Reminiscences of seventy years*, 26; Maitland diary, entry dated 1 Jan. 1846.
41. Freeling diary, entry dated 1 Jan. 1840.
42. *Gazette*, 16 Feb. 1841.
43. Maitland diary, entry dated 12 Aug. 1846.
44. *Transcript*, 19 Jan. 1843.
45. Maitland diary, entry dated 30 June 1846.
46. *Gazette*, 14 May 1844.
47. Maitland diary, entry dated 1 July 1846.
48. McGee to Moylan, 28 Aug. 1866 (Moylan papers, MG29/G29).
49. Maitland diary, entries dated 5–11 July 1846.
50. Clarke, *Old Montreal*, 47.

CHAPTER TWELVE
1. For various appraisals, see *The Times*, 7 Mar. 1851; Henry John Boulton to R. J. W. Horton, 15 Dec. 1825, cited in Edith Firth, *Town of York, 1815–34*, 52; C. F. Hamilton, "Defence, 1812–1912," in *Canada and its provinces*, VII, 392; J. H. Ferns, *Military Montreal in the sixties*, 4; Charles P. Stacey, *Canada and the British army, 1846–1871*, 44–48; Paul Knaplund, "E. G. Wakefield on the colonial garrisons, 1851," *Canadian Historical Review*, 5, no. 3 (Sept. 1924), 231; Merrill Denison, *The barley and the stream*, 153; Merrill Denison, *Canada's first bank*, II, 10.
2. Lt.-Gen. W. Rowan to ——, 21 Nov. 1849 (RG8/C860/122); Lt.-Col. J. D'Urban to Major Talbot, 14 Aug. 1850 (RG8/C318/153); warrant dated 29 Feb. 1848 (RG8/C317/171).
3. Col. R. Bruce to Major Talbot, 19 Dec. 1849 (RG8/C803/87).
4. For the population of Montreal in the 1830s, see *Gazette*, 2 May 1840, which gives the figure of 27,297. In the 1830s regimental services for one regiment of about 600 men per year cost about £7,750 (RG8/C1276/214, 239, and 291, and C1277/77). For the population of Montreal in the 1840s, see *Montreal pocket almanac*, 1844, 26, which gives the figure of 40,290 for 1842. For the cost of regimental services in the early forties, see RG8/C1279, warrants dated 18 Aug., 26 Nov. 1841, 19 Mar., 9 July, 2 Sept., 23 Nov. 1842.
5. Grey to Elgin, 1 June 1849 (*Elgin-Grey papers, 1846–52*, I, 356).
6. For colonial financial commitments, see Edward B. De Fonblanque, *Treatise on the administration and organization of the British army*, 147–48. For the payment of the governor general's salary, see Major D. Hall to Commissary General Sir Randolph Routh, 2 Jan. 1840 (RG8/C1330/I). See also estimate of probable expenditure of the commissariat in Canada for three months, 1 Apr. 1848 (RG8/C154/33).

7. "The commissariat and the Treasury," *United Service Journal*, 3 (1850), 41. The commissary general's comparable military rank was brigadier general and his daily pay between three and four pounds (De Fonblanque, *Administration and organization of the British army*, 152 and 443).

8. Sir Richard Jackson to the secretary of war, 28 Oct. 1842 (RG8/C1279).

9. See article on the commissariat in *United Service Journal*, 3 (1850), 40–57; see also lords of the Treasury to commander of the forces, 4 July 1842 (RG8/C1279). For the reports of Routh, see especially those dated 26 Sept. 1828, 4 Dec. 1830, 17 May 1831 (RG8/C79/107–13, 121–38).

10. Henry John Boulton to R. J. W. Horton, 15 Dec. 1825, cited in Firth, *Town of York*, 52.

11. Routh's memorandum on currency to the lords of the Treasury, 26 Sept. 1828 (RG8/C79/107–8).

12. The value of these various coins in relation to British sterling was computed by means of a device called "Halifax currency" which, although called "currency," was not represented by coins; it was simply a paper calculation. For a discussion of Halifax currency, see G. N. Tucker, *The Canadian commercial revolution, 1845–51*, 52; Sir Robert Chalmers, *A history of currency in the British colonies*, chaps. 1 and 15; for a discussion of provincial currency as it applied to Upper Canada, see T. W. Acheson, "The nature and structure of York commerce in the 1820's," in *Historical essays on Upper Canada*, 185.

13. Routh's memorandum on currency, 26 Sept. 1828 (RG8/C79/107–8).

14. Ibid.

15. Routh to Captain Airey, 4 Dec. 1830 (RG8/C79/109).

16. Routh to Airey, 4 Dec. 1830 (RG8/C79/110); for a case of counterfeit money being found in the Montreal military chest, see RG8/C154/14–16. For the cost of the Rideau Canal, see Tucker, *Canadian commercial revolution*, 24.

17. Routh to Airey, 4 Dec. 1830 (RG8/C79/110–13).

18. Routh to Sir Charles O'Donnell, 26 Sept. 1840 (RG8/C343); for a discussion of the Bank of Upper Canada, see Acheson, "The nature and structure of York commerce," 187–89.

19. Routh's memorandum on currency, 26 Sept. 1828 (RG8/C79/107–8). The prohibition against payment in other than specie continued throughout the forties; see Sir Richard Jackson to secretary of war, 12 Sept. 1843 (RG8/C1279).

20. As a protection against forgery, see Routh to Hon. James Stewart, 17 May 1831 (RG8/C79/128; see also C154/14–16); as a protection against bank failure, see general order no. 1, 2 July 1842 (RG8/C1194A/185, see circular no. 900 from War Office dated 10 May 1842); Sir Richard Jackson to secretary of war, 12 Sept. 1843 (RG8/C1279); general orders, 19 Aug. 1843 (RG8/C1194B/47).

21. The failure of the Kingston bank in 1820 was an exception; see Gerald Craig, *Upper Canada*, 162.

22. Routh to Stewart, 17 May 1831 (RG8/C79/121).
23. Routh to Airey, 4 Dec. 1830 (RG8/C79/109); see also C79/116 for the enclosure "Extract from a report of the committee of the United States Senate on the expediency of establishing a uniform national currency."
24. Routh to Airey, 4 Dec. 1830 (RG8/C79/116).
25. Ibid., 109–10.
26. See examples of such warrants in RG8/C1276/196; C1278/76, 221, 228; C1279/58, 80, 90; C1298C/193.
27. Sir Richard Jackson to secretary of war, 12 Sept. 1843 (RG8/C1279); see also general orders, 19 Aug. 1843 (RG8/C1194B/47).
28. Routh to Stewart, 17 May 1831 (RG8/C79/121).
29. Commissary General W. H. Robinson to J. C. Herries, 17 Mar. 1815, cited in Glenn Steppler, "Logistics of the War of 1812–14," 102.
30. Routh to Stewart, 17 May 1831 (RG8/C79/121); Routh to Airey, 4 Dec. 1830 (RG8/C79/110). The French crowns were valued at five shillings and sixpence local currency in 1844 (*Gazette*, 9 May 1844).
31. See government notice in *Gazette*, 14 Sept. 1842; De Fonblanque, *Administration and organization of the British army*, 231.
32. Routh to Airey, 4 Dec. 1830 (RG8/C79/109–10); Commissary General W. Filder to Lt.-Gen. Sir Benjamin D'Urban, 8 and 9 Sept. 1848 (RG8/C154/47).
33. For various surveys on the military chest, see RG8/C343/9, 100, 120, 135, 151, 195, 210, 224, 236, 249, 262, 278, and 286; see also C153/236.
34. For the 1839 figure of £1,000,000, see warrants issued to the commissary general for bills of exchange on the lords of the Treasury dated 19 Oct., 2 Nov., 4 Dec. 1838 and 8 Jan. 1839 (RG8/C1278; see also 76, 221, and 228); Stacey, *Canada and the British army*, 18. The £419,000 figure is compiled from the estimates for expenditures by the commissariat in Canada for three months, 1 Apr. 1848 (RG8/C154/33), as follows: supplies £20,000, army services £44,000, ordnance £32,000, commissary £8,500, military prison at St. Helen's £300, for a total of £104,800, which computed for twelve months would average £419,200. For the 1854 figure of £171,566, see commissariat estimates for the army, 1854 (RG8/C158/16). The figure for 1854 was £161,668; see Report of the cost of several colonies of the Empire at the expense of the British Exchequer, 1853–54 (*British parliamentary papers, bills, reports, estimates, 1859*, xvii, sess. 1).
35. The £284,209 figure is computed as follows: £166,678. 15s. 8d., the revenue for Lower Canada for the year ending 10 Oct. 1839 (Château Ramezay, *Public accounts and statements for 1839 and estimates of civil expenditure for 1840*), and £117,530. 19s. 10d., the revenue for Upper Canada for 1839 (*Appendix to the Journal*, Legislative Assembly, 1841, i, app. no. 1, app. B). For the 1842 figure of £365,605, see statement of revenue and expenditure for 1842 (*Appendix to the Journal*, Legislative Assembly, 1843, iii, no. 1, app. A).
36. For the 1837 figure, see statement of the Bank of Montreal, 1 Dec. 1839 (RG4, series A1, vol. 392/I/52). For the 1840 figure, see state-

ment of the Bank of Montreal, 1 June 1840 (*Gazette*, 4 June 1840).

37. De Fonblanque, *Administration and organization of the British army*, 231.

38. For the £57,388 figure, see proceedings of a board of survey on the military chest, 29 Sept. 1832 (RG8/C343/18); for the £129,419 figure, see proceedings of a board of survey on the military chest, 31 Dec. 1831 (RG8/C345).

39. See, for example, warrant authorizing the commissary general to draw a bill of exchange for £200,000, 4 Dec. 1838 (RG8/C1278).

40. RG8/C343/100 (£122,605 amount); RG8/C343/249 (£80,722 amount); and proceedings of a board of survey on the military chest, 29 Sept. 1847 (RG8/C153) for the £11,233 amount.

41. Statement of the Bank of Montreal, 1 June 1840 (*Gazette*, 4 June 1840).

42. Routh to Stewart, 17 May 1831 (RG8/C79/128).

43. Statement of the Bank of Montreal, 1 June 1840 (*Gazette*, 4 June 1840).

44. Routh to Stewart, 17 May 1831 (RG8/C79/121–38).

45. Ibid.

46. Routh to Airey, 4 Dec. 1830 (RG8/C79/109–10).

47. Petition of a loyal mechanic to Lord Gosford, dated Montreal, 19 Dec. 1837 (RG4, series A1, vol. S392/80).

48. Specie payments did not resume until February 1838; see *Transcript*, 27 Feb. 1838.

49. RG4, series A1, vol. S392/80; see also Report of the committee of the whole, Executive Council, on the proposition of the Bank of Montreal for a copper coinage for Lower Canada, 28 Sept. 1837 (MG11/ Q239/I/111–12).

50. Routh to Stewart, 17 May 1831 (RG8/C79/121–38).

51. William Weir, *Sixty years in Canada*, 134; see pp. 135–83 for a discussion of currency from 1840 to 1870.

52. For the value of colonial money in 1844, see *Gazette*, 9 May 1844.

53. General orders, 15 June 1842 (RG8/C1194A/164); general order no. 1, 2 Dec. 1843 (RG8/C1194B/115).

54. Sir Charles Trevelyan to Commissary General Robinson, 6 Oct. 1854 (RG8/C157/172; see also 180–81).

CHAPTER THIRTEEN

1. WO17/1544/49.

2. Great Britain, *Hansard*, 3rd ser., 56 (1841), 1361–62.

3. General orders, 28 Oct. 1845 (RG8/C1194B/458); general orders, 10 Aug. 1847 (RG8/C1194C/295).

4. Compiled from figures in "Return of Officers . . . clerks and other Persons who have filled situations connected with, and subordinate to the Staff . . . from 1 Dec. 1840 to 31 Jan. 1841, shewing the pay or allowances authorized to be issued to them" (RG8/C1194S/2–9). This return does not show figures for the ordnance and commissariat staff which are estimated at about £2,000 a year.

5. General orders, 16 Feb. 1841 (McCord Museum, McCord papers, Queen's Light Dragoons box, see Orderly book).

6. Wily memoirs (MG29/F46/12).
7. See advertisement for tenders for army canteens in *Gazette*, 14 Sept. 1842.
8. Wily memoirs (MG29/F46/3).
9. Advertisement for tenders for army canteens in *Gazette*, 14 Sept. 1842.
10. Sir William Eyre to secretary of state for war, 9 Sept. 1858 (Eyre papers, MG24/F38).
11. Report by Lt.-Col. Charles Hay on the comfort and economy of the officers of the 19th Regiment stationed in Montreal (RG8/C860/87–89).
12. Maj. G. Talbot to Hon. Francis Hincks, 9 May 1850 (RG8/C1305/275).
13. Report by Hay on the comfort and economy of the officers of the 19th Regiment (RG8/C860/87–89).
14. Elgin to Grey, 2 Aug. 1850, cited in Charles P. Stacey, *Canada and the British army*, 24.
15. See Annual report of imports at the port of Montreal, in *Gazette*, 28 Jan. 1853.
16. RG8/C860/87–89.
17. Talbot to Hincks, 9 May 1850 (RG8/C1305/275).
18. Elgin to Grey, 2 Aug. 1850, cited in Stacey, *Canada and the British army*, 24.
19. See Annual report of imports at the port of Montreal, *Gazette*, 28 Jan. 1853.
20. Merrill Denison, *The barley and the stream*, 240.
21. Molson Archives, Cashbook, 1848–52, vol. 135, entries dated 5 July 1848 to Dec. 1849.
22. Ibid., see entries dated 10 July and 9 Aug. 1848.
23. Ibid., entry dated 10 Apr. 1849.
24. Ibid.; the figure of £253 is compiled from entries listed between July 1848 and July 1849; for rent of its house, see Molson Archives, Cashbook, 1845–49, vol. 125, entry dated 1 Dec. 1846.
25. Sir Richard Jackson to secretary at war, 21 Mar. 1842 (RG8/C1279/93).
26. General orders regarding keeping the winter dress of regiments' uniform, 3 Feb. 1845 (RG8/C1194B/315).
27. Ibid.; see also general order, no. 1, 6 Oct. 1840 (RG8/C1194/256).
28. Lt.-Gen. William Rowan to secretary at war, 6 Feb. 1855 (RG8/C1282/355).
29. Jackson to secretary at war, 22 Apr. 1842 (RG8/C1279).
30. See army notices in *Gazette*, 24 July 1840.
31. *Gazette*, 8 Oct. 1842.
32. Comparative statement for one year's issue of wood and fuel for troops in Quebec and Montreal barracks, 19 Nov. 1845 (RG8/C598/262).
33. RG8/C598/196 and 208.
34. *Gazette*, 14 Sept. 1842.
35. Sir Richard Jackson to lords of the Treasury, 21 Jan. 1843 (RG8/C1279/324).

36. Lt.-Col. Holdsworth to Eyre, 1 Sept. 1857 (Eyre papers, MG24/F38).
37. RG8/C36/294.
38. RG8/C36/268.
39. Memo to commissary general, 30 May 1842 (RG8/C1298).
40. Sir John Colborne to Lord Fitzroy Somerset, 18 Mar. 1838 (RG8/C1272/104–5).
41. Col. Charles Grey's journal, entry dated 18 Aug. 1838 (William G. Ormsby, *Crisis in the Canadas, 1838–9*, 107).
42. RG8/C1194C/63.
43. Capt. Walter Jones to Sir Benjamin D'Urban, 8 May 1849 (McCord Museum, McCord papers, Queen's Light Dragoons box, Orderly book, 8).
44. Bethune to Major Campbell, 24 May 1843 (RG8/C76).
45. Bethune to Assistant Commissary General J. E. Daniels, 25 Apr. 1843 (RG8/C76).
46. Bethune to Campbell, 24 May 1843 (RG8/C76).
47. For a brief history of the Montreal Water Works, see Sarah Lovell, *Reminiscences of seventy years*, 39.
48. McGill to Jackson, 19 Nov. 1839 (RG8/C606/243–47, 254).
49. Sir Randolph Routh to Capt. Brook Taylor, 8 Apr. 1842 (RG8/C606/254); Commissary General William Filder to Captain Wynyard, 3 Aug. 1843 (RG8/C606/256–57).
50. *Transcript*, 17 June 1843; J. C. Lamothe, *Histoire de la corporation de la cité de Montréal*, 45.
51. Sir John Colborne to the lords of the Treasury, 26 Sept. 1837 (RG8/C1278/21); Routh to Filder, 29 July 1844 (RG8/C606/267–68).
52. Sir Charles Trevelyan to Lord Cathcart, 2 Sept. 1845 (RG8/C76).
53. Lewis T. Drummond to Maj. H. S. Rowan, military secretary, 3 Mar. 1854 (RG8/C318/403–4).
54. PAC, Map division, AT350, Military property, Montreal, 1868, see references to leases and deeds, plans 1 to 5.
55. Ibid.
56. For a discussion, see Lord Cathcart to respective officers of the Board of Ordnance, 22 Oct. 1845 (RG8/C1194B/455).
57. Capt. Brook Taylor to Gore, 15 Mar. 1844 (RG8/C1300/77).
58. Sir William Rowan to secretary at war, 12 Mar. 1855 (RG8/C1282/366–67).
59. For the cost of a regimental mess, see Sir John Colborne to secretary at war, 10 July 1837 (RG8/C1277/206); for the cost of officers' quarters, see ordnance storekeeper's account, 15 July 1841 (RG8/C1297/13).
60. Report of the commanding officer, Royal Engineers, to Sir Benjamin D'Urban, 1 Sept. 1847 (WO1/560/196).
61. Rowan's memo on fitting up the Water Street Barracks, 21 Nov. 1849 (RG8/C860/122).
62. Statement of hired buildings in Montreal, circa 1849 (WO1/560/199).
63. Rowan to secretary at war, 5 Nov. 1852, and 16 Feb. 1855 (RG8/C1282/359).
64. Minute of Treasury Board, 29 Apr. 1845 (RG8/C606/257–61).

65. By 1870 when the imperial troops were withdrawn, Col. W. F. Coffin of the Department of the Secretary of State, Canada, put the value of the military property in Montreal at $52,405. He considered that the Quebec Gate Barracks and military hospital were fit only to be pulled down (Château Ramezay, Value of military property in Montreal relinquished to the government of Canada, 27 Dec. 1870, document no. 459).

66. Moses Judah Hays to Colonel Holloway, commanding officer, Royal Engineers, 26 Mar. 1845, Valuation of the Quebec Gate Barracks property (Château Ramezay, document no. 459).

67. Minute of Treasury Board, 29 Apr. 1845, encl. in letter of Sir Charles Trevelyan to Sir Richard Jackson, 2 May 1845 (RG8/C606).

68. Statement of receipts and expenditures of the ordnance storekeeper at Montreal between 1 Apr. and 21 Nov. 1845 (RG8/C343/278).

69. For a description of the size of each lot bought, see PAC, Map division, AT350, Military property, Montreal, 1868, plan 3, "Montreal exercising ground and burial ground."

70. Lord Cathcart to secretary of the Board of Ordnance, 22 Oct. 1845 (RG8/C1194B/455).

71. Cited in Denison, *The barley and the stream*, 230.

72. J. H. Ferns, *Military Montreal in the sixties*, 4.

CHAPTER FOURTEEN

1. A. N. Morin to Francis Hincks, 8 May 1841 (MG24/B68); Lt.-Col. Charles Grey to Earl Grey, 25 June 1838, in William G. Ormsby, *Crisis in the Canadas, 1838–9*, 51.

2. Elgin to Grey, 2 Dec. 1849 (*Elgin-Grey papers*, II, 553).

3. T. Bland Strange, *Gunner Jingo's jubilee*, 25.

4. *Transcript*, 25 Aug. 1838.

5. See proclamation in *Canada Gazette*, 3 Mar. 1858; general order no. 5, 10 Mar. 1858 (Eyre papers).

6. Wetherall to Eyre, 1 Apr. 1857 (Eyre papers).

7. Eyre to Sir Edmund Head, 26 Sept. 1857 (Eyre papers).

 Note on Sources

The major manuscript sources for the history of the British garrison in Montreal are the British military records (Record Group 8, C series), the Colborne papers, the Bellingham memoirs, and the Wily memoirs, all in the Public Archives, Ottawa, and the McCord military papers in the McCord Museum, Montreal. The most useful of the War Office papers, available on microfilm at the Public Archives, Ottawa, are the volumes on monthly troop returns (WO17) and the in-coming letters (WO1).

The British military records, the first major acquisition of the Public Archives, consist of close to 2,000 volumes of military documents, extending from the time of the arrival of Lord Dorchester in 1786 to the date of the withdrawal of imperial forces in 1871. For purposes of this study, the most useful of these were the letter books of the military secretary, containing the English and Canadian correspondence of the commanders of the forces for the years 1832 to 1855 (vols. 1271–1308); the volumes on civil government in Lower Canada, 1806–45 (76 and 76A); the correspondence on military aid at riots, 1800–1856 (vols. 316–18); and reports on political feeling, 1849–50 (vols. 616–18). Biographical material on military and former military personnel in Montreal was found in the volume on appointments and memorials, 1846–54 (26), as well as in volume 519, containing petitions for relief, 1839–45, and in volume 500, which deals with pensions.

Of particular interest in the Colborne papers are the reports of Lt.-Col. George Cathcart on rural police. The Wily memoirs provide a wealth of material on life in the lower ranks and on the relations of imperial troops with colonial units. The Bellingham memoirs supplement those of Wily, giving intimate glimpses into the relations between Montrealers and regulars during the difficult days of the rebellion period and of the political and social life of Montreal in the forties. Even when allowances are made for Bellingham's vagaries of memory and the propensity of an old man to romanticize the past, Bellingham's memoirs add much to an understanding of the role of the garrison in the life of the city.

The McCord papers contain John Samuel McCord's correspondence dealing with the raising of the Montreal volunteers in 1837 and 1838, particularly the Royal Montreal Cavalry and the Queen's Light Dragoons. They also contain much useful material on Masonic activities, genealogical material on Montreal families, and letters to and from Lord Cathcart and Col. George Cathcart on the dismissal of the Provincial Cavalry in 1850. The private papers of the Earl of Cathcart are invaluable because of the letters of Col. George Cathcart to his family in Britain in which he gives his candid opinions on colonial personalities, institutions, and politics.

The correspondence in Record Group 4 for the period from 1849 to 1855 contains letters to and from militia officers in Montreal and the Eastern Townships about their dismissal because of the annexation movement. These letters, with their marginal annotations by Provincial Secretary James Leslie, reveal the personal animosity that still prevailed between the reform and conservative wings of the British community in Montreal.

Manuscript sources of lesser importance were the Chapman papers, the Maitland diary, the Hale papers, the Chamberlin papers, and the Young papers. The Chapman papers contain Edmund O'Callaghan's lengthy letters to Thomas Falconer in England in which he describes La Fontaine's jealousy of Papineau. The Maitland diary, written by Capt. James Douglas, aide-decamp to his father-in-law, Lord Cathcart, provides a chronology of a young officer's social activities in Montreal, with an occasional comment on Montreal personalities and military personnel.

The Hale papers contain some 1,500 letters to and from Edward Hale of Sherbrooke, the eldest son of the Honourable John

Hale who came to Canada as aide-de-camp to the Duke of Kent. Edward Hale, as a member of a prominent British military family and as one who himself served in the army in India, bridged the military and social milieu of Montreal. His letters to his wife at Sherbrooke, written while Hale was in Montreal serving on the Special Council, provide vivid insights into the divisions within the council and intimate commentary on the military in Montreal. Rambling as they are, these letters, written with such charm and expressions of affection towards his wife and children, touch on topics and personalities with the candour that comes only in letters written under the impression that they would be seen by the eyes of the receiver alone.

The most useful letters in the Chamberlin collection were those written by Brown Chamberlin to his sister and other relatives at Frelighsburg in the 1840s when Chamberlin was in Montreal studying at McGill College. His letters reveal the reactions of a young student of conservative leanings to the troubled economic and political situation in Montreal and the continuing civil disorders. The Young papers are indispensable to an understanding of the development of the police forces in Quebec and Montreal and indicate the degree to which Montreal police authorities deferred to the advice of the Quebec superintendent of police, Thomas Ainslie Young.

Of the printed sources examined, by far the most important were contemporary Montreal newspapers. Here one finds the debates of the House of Assembly, reports of the various riots and subsequent coroners' inquests, and trials of those arrested in connection with the riots, as well as news of military activities, both abroad and in Montreal. Along with the British military records and the *Elgin-Grey papers*, the newspapers provide the major source for knowledge of internal disorders in Montreal in the 1840s.

Few native-born Montrealers have left memoirs of the period of the mid-nineteenth century. Of these few, the most valuable were the memoirs of Adele Clarke, the daughter of a Montreal fur baron, and Sarah Lovell, the daughter of an immigrant German jeweller and wife of Montreal's prominent publisher, John Lovell. These memoirs, interspersed as they are with accounts of social activities involving the officers of the garrison, show what an important and acceptable role British officers played in Montreal's social life.

Among military memoirs, Sir James Alexander's description of

265

the Gavazzi riot is perhaps the most balanced account of the affair. His description of the Rebellion Losses Bill agitation, when supplemented by that of Sir Richard Bonnycastle, gives a picture of these riots from the military point of view.

Such specialized studies as Professor John Cooper's work on the Anglican Diocese of Montreal and the Montreal Hunt added fragments of information on the military's role in Montreal. Jean Turmel's two-volume work on the history of the Montreal police force provided useful details of the internal structure of the Montreal police establishment in the nineteenth century.

Bibliography

ORIGINAL SOURCES: UNPUBLISHED

Ottawa

Public Archives
Bellingham memoirs (MG24/B25)
British military and naval records (RG8/C series)
Canadian military records (RG9)
Chamberlin papers (MG24/B19)
Chapman papers (MG24/B31)
Civil and provincial secretaries' correspondence (RG4)
Colborne papers (MG24/A40)
Denny papers (MG24/F33)
Durnford papers (MG24/F73)
Ellice diary (MG24/A2)
Ermatinger papers (MG24/G55)
Executive Council minutes (RG1)
Eyre papers (MG24/F38)
Freeling diary (MG24/F72)
Governor general's correspondence (RG7 and MG11/Q series)
Grant papers (MG24/A53)
Grey papers (MG24/A10)
Hincks papers (MG24/B68)
Maitland diary (MG24/I78)
Manson letter (MG24/B56)
Montizambert papers (MG24/B49)
Moyster papers (MG24/I87)

Nelson papers (MG24/B34)
Ogden autograph book (MG24/C19)
Papineau papers (MG24/B2)
Rowan papers (MG24/F55)
Townshend memoirs (MG24/F51)
Upper Canada Sundries (RG5/A1)
War Office papers (1/560–67 and 17/1536–59)
Wily memoirs (MG29/F46)
Young papers (MG24/B4)

Montreal

Anglican Archives
Charles Abrahall, "History of the Diocese of Montreal," 2 vols.
Dawson papers
Kelley papers

Château Ramezay Archives
William Coffin's evaluation of military property in Montreal relin-
   quished to the government of Canada, 27 Dec. 1870 (document 459)
Notice of Charles Dickens playing at the Theatre Royal with the Garri-
   son Amateurs, 28 May 1842 (document 2219)
O'Callaghan papers (document 2055)
Alfred Sandham, "Montreal illustrated," 18 vols.

Christ Church Cathedral Archives
Military index compiled by James Ramsay
Military registers of births, marriages, and deaths, 1766–1870

McCord Museum
Hale papers
McCord papers
Robert Lovelace, "The Montreal active volunteer force," 1864

McGill University Archives
Henry Mott papers
Patton papers

Molson Archives
Accounts current, 1844–51, vol. 125A
Cashbooks, 1845–49, vol. 125
Cashbook, 1848–52, vol. 135
Léon Trépanier collection. Mabel Good's notes, v

Montreal Military and Maritime Museum
1832 riot: Documents collected by Lt.-Col. A. F. Macintosh

Privately held
David family genealogy. Compiled by Harline David

Toronto

Public Archives Ontario
Mackenzie-Lindsey papers

Bibliography

Broomhall, Dunfermline, Scotland
Elgin papers, privately held by the Earl of Elgin

London, England
Cathcart papers, privately held by the Earl of Cathcart

ORIGINAL SOURCES: PUBLISHED

Parliamentary Papers and Proceedings

Great Britain
Bills, reports, estimates. xvii. Session 1. 1859.
Fourth report from the select committee appointed to enquire into the origin, nature, extent and tendency of the Orange Institutions in Great Britain and the colonies. H.C. [605] xvii. 1835.
Hansard's parliamentary debates. 3rd series. Vol. 56. 1841.

Lower Canada
Public accounts and statements of the income and expenditure for the year 1839 and an estimate of the civil expenditure of Lower Canada for the year ending October 10, 1840. Printed by order of the Special Council.
Journal of the Special Council. April to June 1840.

Canada
Appendix to the Journal. Legislative Assembly. 1841–55.
Returns to addresses of the Senate and House of Commons relative to the withdrawal of the troops from the Dominion; and on the defence of the country. Ottawa, 1871.

Government Publications

An act to amend and consolidate the provisions of the ordinance to incorporate the city and town of Montreal. Toronto, 1851.
Rules and regulations of the police force for the city and suburbs of Montreal. Printed by William Grey. Montreal, 1821.
Compilation of the by-laws and police regulations in force in the city of Montreal with an appendix containing extracts from provincial enactments. Printed by James Starke. Montreal, 1842.
WO. *Manual of military law.* Edited by Hugh Godley. London, 1914.

Letters, Journals, Diaries, Memoirs, Histories, and Travel Accounts

Ackland-Troyte, John Edward. *Through the ranks to a commission.* London, 1881.
Alexander, Sir James E. *L'Acadie, or seven years' explorations in British America.* 2 vols. London, 1849.
———. *Passages in the life of a soldier.* 2 vols. London, 1857.
Becket, Hugh W. *The Montreal Snow Shoe Club, its history and record with a synopsis of the racing events of other clubs throughout the Dominion from 1840 to the present time.* Montreal, 1882.
Bell, Sir George. *Soldier's glory: Being rough notes by an old soldier.* Edited by Brian Stuart. London, 1956.
Bellingham, Sydney. *Some personal recollections of the Rebellion of 1837 in Canada.* Dublin, 1902.
Bibaud, Michel. *Histoire du Canada et des Canadiens de 1832 à 1837*

269

sous la domination anglaise comprenant les administrations éminemment historiques de Lord Aylmer et de Lord Gosford. 3 vols. Montreal, 1878.

Bigsby, John Jeremiah. *Shoe and canoe; or pictures of travel in the Canadas.* 2 vols. London, 1850.

Blake, Catherine. "The riots of 1849 in Montreal." *Canadian Historical Review*, 15, no. 3 (Sept. 1934), 283–88.

Bonnycastle, Sir Richard. *The Canadas in 1841.* 2 vols. London, 1841.

———. *Canada as it was, is, and may be.* 2 vols. London, 1852.

Borthwick, John Douglas. *History and biographical gazetteer of Montreal to the year 1892.* Montreal, 1892.

———. *History of Montreal, including the streets of Montreal, their origin and history illustrated.* Montreal, 1897.

———. *History of the Montreal prison from 1784 to 1886, containing a complete record of the troubles of 1837–8, the burning of the parliament buildings in 1849, the St. Alban's raiders 1864 and the two Fenian raids of 1866 and 1870.* Montreal, 1886.

Bosworth, Newton. *Hochelaga depicta: The early history and present state of the city and island of Montreal.* Montreal, 1839.

Brown, James. *Views of Canada and the colonists, embracing the experience of a four-years' resident, 1839–1844.* Edinburgh, 1844.

Brumath, A. Leblond de. *Histoire populaire de Montréal depuis son origine jusqu'à nos jours.* Montreal, 1890.

Buckingham, James S. *Canada, Nova Scotia, New Brunswick and the other British provinces in North America with a plan of national colonization.* London, 1843.

Burnham, Hampden. *Canadians in the imperial naval and military service abroad.* Toronto, 1891.

Campbell, Robert. *A history of the Scotch Presbyterian Church, St. Gabriel Street.* Montreal, 1887.

Carrier, L. N. *Les événements de 1837–38, esquisse historique de l'insurrection du Bas-Canada.* Quebec, 1877.

Carter, Thomas. *Historical record of the 26th Regiment.* London, 1867.

Chalmers, Sir Robert. *A history of currency in the British colonies.* London, 1893.

Christie, Robert. *A history of the late province of Lower Canada.* 6 vols. Quebec, 1848–56.

Christmas, Henry. *The emigrant churchman in Canada by a pioneer in the wilderness.* 2 vols. London, 1849.

Clarke, Adele. *Old Montreal, John Clarke, his adventures, friends and family.* Montreal, 1906.

Clode, Charles M. *The military forces of the Crown, their administration and government.* 2 vols. London, 1869.

Côté, J. O. *Political appointments and elections in the province of Canada from 1841 to 1865.* Ottawa, 1866.

David, Laurent-Olivier. *Biographies et portraits.* Montreal, 1876.

———. *Les Patriotes de 1837–38.* Montreal, 1884.

———. *Mes contemporains.* Montreal, 1894.

Derbishire, Stewart. "Report to Lord Durham on Lower Canada, 1838."

Edited by Norah Storey. *Canadian Historical Review*, 18, no. 1 (Mar. 1937), 48–62.

Doughty, Sir Arthur, ed. *The Elgin-Grey papers, 1846–52*. 4 vols. Ottawa, 1937.

Duncan, Francis. *Our garrisons in the west, or sketches in British North America*. London, 1864.

Durnford, Mary. *Family recollections of Lieutenant General Elias Walker Durnford*. Montreal, 1863.

Fletcher, John. "Account of the 1852 fire." Clipping dated 24 Apr. 1889, scrapbook "Old Montreal," Montreal Military and Maritime Museum.

Fonblanque, Edward Barrington de. *Treatise on the administration and organization of the British army, with especial reference to finance and supply*. London, 1858.

Fraser, John. *Canadian pen and ink sketches*. Montreal, 1890.

Garneau, François-Xavier. *History of Canada from the time of its discovery till the union year 1840–41*. Translated by Andrew Bell. 3 vols. Montreal, 1862.

Gérin-Lajoie, A. *Dix ans au Canada de 1840 à 1850*. Quebec, 1888.

Girod, Amury. "Journal kept by the late Amury Girod, translated from the German and the Italian." *Public Archives Report* (1923), 370–80.

Graham, John H. *Outlines of the history of freemasonry in the province of Quebec*. Montreal, 1892.

Hawkins, Ernest. *Annals of the Diocese of Quebec*. London, 1849.

Hincks, Sir Francis. *Reminiscences of his public life*. Montreal, 1884.

Keppel, G. T. *Fifty years of my life*. London, 1876.

Kingsford, William. *The history of Canada*. Vol. x. Toronto, 1898.

Levinge, Sir Richard G. A. *Echoes from the backwoods, or sketches of transatlantic life*. London, 1846.

Lizars, Robina, and MacFarlane, Kathleen. *Humours of '37, grave, gay and grim: Rebellious times in the Canadas*. Toronto, 1897.

Lovell, Sarah. *Reminiscences of seventy years*. Montreal, 1908.

Lysons, Sir Daniel. *Early reminiscences*. London, 1896.

McGregor, John. *British America*. 2 vols. Edinburgh, 1833.

MacPherson, Charlotte H. *Old memories: Amusing and historical*. Montreal, 1890.

McRobie, William Orme. *Fighting the flames, or twenty-seven years in the Montreal fire brigade*. Montreal, 1881.

MacSuibhne, Peadar. *Paul Cullen and his contemporaries with their letters from 1820 to 1902*. 5 vols. Naas, Ireland, 1961–74.

Moodie, Susanna. *Roughing it in the bush, or forest life in Canada*. Toronto, 1913.

Moore, Sir John. *Diary*. Edited by Maj.-Gen. Sir J. F. Maurice. 2 vols. London, 1904.

O'Callaghan, Sir Desmond. *Guns, gunners and others: An autobiography*. London, 1925.

Ormsby, William G. *Crisis in the Canadas, 1838–9: The Grey journals and letters*. Toronto, 1964.

Papineau, Amédée. *Journal d'un Fils de la Liberté*. 2 vols. Quebec, Montreal, 1972, 1976.

Bibliography

Poutré, Félix. *Echappé de la potence, souvenirs d'un prisonnier d'état can-adien en 1838.* Montreal, 1862.

Prieur, François-Xavier. *Notes of a convict of 1838.* Translated by George Mackaness. Sydney, Australia, 1949.

Read, D. B. *The Canadian Rebellion of 1837.* Toronto, 1896.

Rhys, Horton. *A theatrical trip for a wager.* Vancouver, 1966.

Richardson, John. *Eight years in Canada.* Montreal, 1847.

Sanderson, Charles R. *The Arthur papers.* 2 vols. Toronto, 1957.

Sandham, Alfred. *Ville-Marie, or sketches of Montreal.* Montreal, 1870.

Seaver, William Rufus. "The Montreal riot of 1849." Edited by Josephine Foster. *Canadian Historical Review,* 32, no. 1 (Mar. 1951), 61–65.

Sellar, Robert. *History of the county of Huntingdon and of the seigniories of Châteauguay and Beauharnois from their earliest settlement to the year 1838.* Huntingdon, 1888.

Sleigh, B. W. A. *Pine forests and hacmatack clearings, or travel life and adventure in the British North American provinces.* London, 1853.

Somerville, Alexander. *Autobiography of a workingman.* London, 1951.

Strange, T. Bland. *Gunner Jingo's jubilee: An autobiography.* London, 1893.

Taylor, John Fennings. *Portraits of British Americans with biographical sketches.* 3 vols. Montreal, 1868.

Terrill, Frederick William. *A chronology of Montreal and of Canada, 1752 to 1893.* Montreal, 1893.

Turcotte, Louis Philippe. *Le Canada sous l'union, 1841–67.* Quebec, 1871.

Veith, Frederick H. *Recollections of the Crimean campaign . . . and also garrison life in the Canadian lower provinces.* Montreal, 1907.

Walrond, Theodore. *Letters and journals of James, eighth Earl of Elgin.* London, 1872.

Warre, Henry. *Sketches in North America and the Oregon territory.* London, 1848.

Weir, William. *Sixty years in Canada.* Montreal, 1903.

Wellington, Duke of. *Despatches, correspondence, and memoranda of Field Marshal Arthur Duke of Wellington.* 8 vols. London, 1867–80.

Whyte, W. H. *Scrapbooks on snowshoeing and other winter sports, as well as lacrosse.* Montreal, 1869.

Wolseley, Sir Garnet. *The story of a soldier's life.* 2 vols. Westminster, 1903.

Newspapers, Periodicals, Pamphlets, Directories, and Almanacs

The Albion, New York.

L'Ami du peuple, de l'ordre et des lois, Montreal.

Anon. *The Elgin period, the late Hon. Mrs. Robert Bruce, interesting rem-iniscences by Mufti.* Ottawa, 1890.

Anon. *The question answered, did the ministry intend to pay rebels? A letter to His Excellency the Right Honourable Earl of Elgin and Kincar-dine by a Canadian loyalist.* 4 June 1849.

Anon. *Ramble, a visitor to Montreal in 1816.*

Brown, Thomas Storrow. *Montreal fifty years ago.* Montreal, 1870.

Doidge, Thomas. *An alphabetical list of merchants, traders and house-holders residing in Montreal.* Montreal, 1819.

Ferns, J. Hamilton. *Military Montreal in the sixties, recalling the famil-iar figures of former days, interesting incidents, some famous batteries, factories replace barracks, the lash in use.* Montreal, 1920.

The Gazette, Montreal.

La Gazette du Québec, Quebec.

Gugy, B. C. A. *Some incidents related by credible witnesses in the life of a provincial.* Quebec, 1861.

The Herald, Montreal.

McGill, Robert. *The authority of law: A discourse delivered in St. Paul's Church, Montreal, on the Sabbath, 26 August, 1849, the city authorities having a few days before called for an enrolment of special constables to protect the peace of the city.*

Mackay, Robert W. S. *The stranger's guide to the island and city of Montreal.* Montreal, 1848.

La Minerve, Montreal.

Montreal almanac, 1840.

Montreal Courier, Montreal.

Montreal directory, 1842–55.

Orange Lily, Bytown.

The Pilot and Evening Journal of Commerce, Montreal.

Punch in Canada, Montreal.

Shakspeare Dramatic and Literary Club annual reports. Montreal, 1844–47.

Shakspeare Dramatic and Literary Club constitution and laws. Mon-treal, 1844.

Standing orders of the 23rd Regiment or Royal Welsh Fusiliers. Mon-treal, 1841.

Starke's Montreal pocket almanac and general register, 1843–55.

Telegraph, Prescott.

The Times, London.

Transcript, Montreal.

The United Service Journal and Naval and Military Magazine, London.

Weekly Witness, Montreal.

SECONDARY SOURCES

Books

Adams, Frank. *History of Christ Church Cathedral.* Montreal, 1941.

Aldington, Richard. *The duke, being an account of the life and achieve-ments of Arthur Wellesley, first Duke of Wellington.* New York, 1943.

Allaire, Jean-Baptiste. *Histoire de la paroisse de Saint-Denis-sur-Richelieu.* Saint-Hyacinthe, 1905.

———. *Dictionnaire biographique du clergé canadien-français.* 6 vols. Montreal, 1908–34.

Atherton, William H. *Montreal, 1535–1914.* 3 vols. Montreal, 1914.

Auclair, Elie J. *Histoire de Châteauguay.* Montreal, 1935.
Audet, Francis J. *Canadian historical events and dates, 1492–1915.* Ottawa, 1917.
Bell, Michael. *Painters in a new land.* Toronto, 1973.
Boss, W. *The Stormont, Dundas and Glengarry Highlanders, 1783–1951.* Ottawa, 1952.
Buchanan, A. W. Patrick. *The bench and bar of Lower Canada down to 1850.* Montreal, 1925.
Careless, J. M. S. *The union of the Canadas: The growth of Canadian institutions, 1841–1857.* Toronto, 1967.
Centenary of the Montreal Board of Trade. Montreal, 1922.
Chambers, Ernest J. *The Canadian militia: A history of the origin and development of the force.* Ottawa, 1907.
Chapais, Thomas. *Cours d'histoire du Canada depuis la conquête, 1760 à 1867.* 8 vols. Quebec, 1919.
Clark, S. D. *Movements of political protest in Canada, 1640–1840.* Toronto, 1959.
Clifford, Derek. *Collecting English watercolours.* London, 1970.
Collard, Edgar A. *Call back yesterdays.* Toronto, 1965.
Cooper, John I. *A history of the Montreal Hunt.* Montreal, 1953.
———. *The blessed communion: The origins and history of the Diocese of Montreal.* Montreal, 1960.
Cooper, Leonard. *British regular cavalry, 1644–1914.* London, 1965.
Corey, A. B. *The crisis of 1830–42 in Canadian-American relations.* New Haven, 1941.
Craig, Gerald. *Upper Canada: The formative years.* Toronto, 1963.
Cruikshank, E. A. *Inventory of the military documents in the Canadian Archives.* Ottawa, 1910.
Denison, Merrill. *The barley and the stream: The Molson story.* Toronto, 1955.
———. *History of the Bank of Montreal.* 2 vols. Montreal, 1967.
Devine, E. J. *Historic Caughnawaga.* Montreal, 1922.
Dictionary of Canadian biography, 1871–1880. Vols. IX, X. Toronto, 1972, 1976.
Dubois, Emile. *Le feu de la rivière du Chêne: Étude historique sur le mouvement insurrectionnel de 1837 au nord de Montréal.* Montreal, 1937.
Edwards, Murray D. *A stage in our past: English-language theatre in Eastern Canada from the 1790s to 1914.* Toronto, 1968.
Fauteux, Aegidius. *Patriotes de 1837–8.* Montreal, 1950.
Filteau, Gérard. *Histoire des Patriotes.* 3 vols. Montreal, 1937–42.
Firth, Edith. *Town of York, 1815–34.* Toronto, 1966.
Fortescue, J. W. *A history of the British army.* 13 vols. London, 1899–1930.
Gibbon, John Murray. *Our old Montreal.* Toronto, 1947.
Glover, Michael. *Wellington as a military commander.* London, 1968.
Glover, Richard. *Peninsular preparation: The reform of the British army, 1795–1809.* Cambridge, 1963.
Graham, Franklin. *Histrionic Montreal: Annals of the Montreal stage*

with biographical and critical notices of the plays and players of a century. Montreal, 1902.

Guedalla, Philip. *The Duke.* Montreal, 1937.

Guillet, Edwin C. *Early life in Upper Canada.* Toronto, 1933.

Hacker, Carlotta. *The indomitable lady doctors.* Toronto, 1974.

Halévy, Elie. *England in 1815.* London, 1961.

Hamelin, Jean, and Hamelin, Marcel. *Les moeurs électorales dans le Québec de 1791 à nos jours.* Montreal, 1962.

Hay, Ian. *The King's service: An informal history of the British infantry soldier.* London, 1938.

Hayward, Pat. *Surgeon Henry's trifles: Events of a military life.* London, 1970.

Hendrie, Lillian. *Early days in Montreal.* Montreal, 1932.

Hitsman, J. Mackay. *The incredible War of 1812: A military history.* Toronto, 1965.

———. *Safeguarding Canada, 1763–1871.* Toronto, 1968.

Jenkins, Kathleen. *Montreal: Island city of the St. Lawrence.* New York, 1966.

Jones, Robert L. *History of agriculture in Ontario, 1613–1880.* Toronto, 1946.

Kinchen, Oscar A. *The rise and fall of the Patriot Hunters.* New York, 1956.

Lamothe, J. C. *Histoire de la corporation de la cité de Montréal depuis son origine jusqu'à nos jours.* Montreal, 1903.

Luvaas, Jay. *The education of an army: British military thought, 1815–1940.* Chicago, 1964.

Manning, Helen Taft. *The revolt of French Canada, 1800–1835.* Toronto, 1962.

Massicotte, E.-Z. *Nos athlètes canadiens-français.* Montreal, 1908.

Mather, F. C. *Public order in the age of the Chartists.* New York, 1967.

Milborne, A. J. B. *Freemasonry in the province of Quebec, 1759–1959.* Knowlton, 1960.

Monet, Jacques. *The last cannon shot: A study of French Canadian nationalism, 1837–50.* Toronto, 1969.

Moore Smith, G. C. *The life of John Colborne, Field Marshal Lord Seaton.* London, 1903.

Morris, Richard B. *Encyclopedia of American history.* New York, 1961.

Nelson, Wolfred. *Wolfred Nelson et son temps.* Montreal, 1946.

Ouellet, Fernand. *Histoire économique et sociale du Québec, 1760–1850.* Montreal, 1966.

———. *Le Bas-Canada, 1791–1840.* Ottawa, 1976.

Pouliot, Léon. *La réaction catholique de Montréal, 1840–41.* Montreal, 1942.

———. *Monseigneur Bourget et son temps.* 2 vols. Montreal, 1955–56.

Rae, Isobel. *The strange story of Dr. James Barry.* London, 1958.

Raudzens, George. *The British Ordnance Department and Canada's canals, 1815–1855.* Waterloo, 1979.

Roberts, Leslie. *From mission colony to world city.* Toronto, 1969.

Sack, Benjamin G. *History of the Jews in Canada from the earliest begin-*

nings to the present day. 2 vols. Montreal, 1945.
Schull, Joseph. *Rebellion: Rising in French Canada, 1837.* Toronto, 1971.
Senior, Hereward. Orangeism in Ireland and Britain, 1795–1836. London, 1966.
Slattery, T. P. *Loyola and Montreal.* Montreal, 1962.
Smith, Paul. *Loyalists and redcoats: A study in British revolutionary policy.* Chapel Hill, N.C., 1964.
Stacey, Charles P. *Canada and the British army, 1846–1871: A study in the practice of responsible government.* Toronto, 1963.
Stanley, George F. *Canada's soldiers: The military history of an unmilitary people.* Toronto, 1960.
Stewart, Charles H. *The service of British regiments in Canada and North America.* Ottawa, 1964.
Thurston, Gavin. *The Clerkenwell riot.* London, 1967.
Tucker, G. N. *The Canadian commercial revolution, 1845–51.* Toronto, 1964.
Turmel, Jean. *Police de Montréal, historique du service: Premières structures et évolution de la police de Montréal, 1796–1971.* Écrit en collaboration avec le service de police de la ville de Montréal. 2 vols. Montreal, 1971–74.
Wade, Mason. *The French Canadians, 1760–1945.* Toronto, 1955.
Wallace, Stewart. *The Macmillan dictionary of Canadian biography.* Toronto, 1963.
Watteville, H. de. *The British soldier, his daily life from Tudor to modern times.* London, 1954.
Wheeler, Owen. *The war office: Past and present.* London, 1914.
Wood, W. C. H. *The storied province of Quebec.* 5 vols. Toronto, 1931–32.
Woodward, E. L. *The age of reform, 1815–1870.* Oxford, 1938.

Articles and Published Documents

Acheson, T. W. "The nature and structure of York commerce in the 1820's." In *Historical essays on Upper Canada*, edited by J. K. Johnson, pp. 171–93. Toronto, 1974.
Blanco, Richard. "Sir James McGrigor and the army medical corps." *History Today*, 21, no. 2 (Feb. 1971).
Burroughs, Peter. "Tackling army desertion in British North America." *Canadian Historical Review*, 61, no. 1 (Mar. 1980), 28–68.
Collard, Edgar A. "The town major." *Gazette*, 14 May 1966.
Cooper, John I. "George Etienne Cartier in the period of the forties." *Canadian Historical Association Report*, 1938.
———. "Social structure of Montreal in the 1850's." *Canadian Historical Association Report*, 1956.
Dechêne, Louise. "La Croissance de Montréal au 18ème siècle." *Revue d'histoire de l'Amérique française*, 27, no. 2 (Sept. 1973), 163–79.
Fuller, R. M. "The British army: 34th Regiment of Foot on the Detroit River frontier." *Western Ontario Historical Notes*, 13, no. 3 (Sept. 1955), 16–23.
Hamilton, C. F. "Defence, 1812–1912." In *Canada and its provinces*, edited by A. Shortt and A. G. Doughty, vol. VII, pp. 379–460. Toronto, 1914–17.

————. "The Canadian militia from 1816 to the Crimean War." *Canadian Defence Quarterly*, 5 (1928).

Hitsman, J. Mackay. "Please send us a garrison." *Ontario History*, 1, no. 4 (1958), 189–92.

Knaplund, Paul. "E. G. Wakefield on the colonial garrisons, 1851." *Canadian Historical Review*, 5, no. 3 (Sept. 1924), 228–36.

Landon, Fred. "British regiments in London." *Western Ontario Historical Notes*, 13, no. 3 (Sept. 1955), 1–15.

Lindsay, Sydenham B. "Early history of the Anglican Church in Montreal." *The Teachers' Magazine* (Montreal), June 1928.

Massicotte, E.-Z. "Les tribunaux de police à Montréal." *Le bulletin des recherches historiques*, 26, no. 5 (May 1920), 180–83.

————. "L'escrime et les maîtres d'armes à Montréal." *Le bulletin des recherches historiques*, 29, no. 9 (Sept. 1923), 260–63.

Morton, Desmond. "Aid to the civil power: The Canadian militia in support of civil order, 1867–1914." *Canadian Historical Review*, 51, no. 4 (Dec. 1970), 407–25.

Pearkes, G. R. "The burthen and the brunt: A short description of the services of the British regular army in Canada." *Canadian Defence Quarterly*, 17 (1935).

Philp, John. "The economic and social effects of the British garrisons in the development of western Upper Canada." *Ontario History*, 61, no. 1 (1949), 37–48.

Preston, Richard. "R. M. C. and Kingston: The effect of imperial and military influences on a Canadian community." *Ontario History*, 60, no. 3 (1958), 105–23.

————. "Military influence on the development of Canada." In *The Canadian military: A profile*, edited by Hector J. Massey, pp. 49–85. Toronto, 1972.

Raudzens, George. "A successful military settlement: Earl Grey's enrolled pensioners of 1846 in Canada." *Canadian Historical Review*, 52 (Dec. 1971), 398–403.

————. "The military impact on Canadian canals, 1815–1825." *Canadian Historical Review*, 56 (Sept. 1973), 273–86.

————. "The British Ordnance Department." *Journal of the Society for Army Historical Research*, 57, no. 230 (Summer 1979), 88–107.

Roy, Reginald. "The Canadian military tradition." In *The Canadian military: A profile*, edited by Hector J. Massey, pp. 6–48. Toronto, 1972.

Scott, S. Morely. "Civil and military authority in Canada, 1764–66." *Canadian Historical Review*, 9, no. 2 (June 1928), 117–36.

Senior, Elinor. "The British garrison in Montreal in the 1840s." *Journal of the Society for Army Historical Research* (London), 52, no. 210 (1974), 111–27.

————. "The Provincial Cavalry in Lower Canada, 1837–1850." *Canadian Historical Review*, 57, no. 1 (Mar. 1976), 1–24.

————. "The influence of the British garrison on the development of the Montreal police, 1832–1853." *Military Affairs* (Kansas), 42, no. 2 (Apr. 1979), 63–68.

Senior, Hereward. "Military Montreal." *Bulletin of the Organization of Military Museums of Canada*, 3 (Ottawa, 1974), 1–15.

Bibliography

Smith, Henry R. "Military aid to civil power." *Canadian Military Institution Selected Papers*, 10 (Toronto, 1873).
Spurr, John W. "The Kingston garrison, 1815–70." *Historic Kingston*, no. 20 (1972), 14–34.
Sylvain, Robert. "Le 9 juin 1853 à Montréal, encore l'affaire Gavazzi." *Revue d'histoire de l'Amérique française*, 14 (1960–61), 173–216.
Talman, James John. "British regiments in London." *Western Ontario Historical Notes*, 13, no. 3 (Sept. 1955), 1–23.
Tylden, G. "The Royal Canadian Rifle Regiment, 1840–1870." *Journal of the Society for Army Historical Research* (London), 34 (June 1956).
Yon, Armand. "Indésirable: L'apostat Gavazzi au Canada (1853)." *Le Canada français*, 26 (Dec. 1938), 329–47.

Theses and Unpublished Papers

Asbil, Walter G. "Under military chaplains, 1759–68." M.A. thesis, McGill University, 1967.
Bleasdale, R. "Class conflict on the canals of Upper Canada in the 1840s." Paper presented to the Learned Societies of Canada, University of Western Ontario, London, June 1978.
Conroy, Patricia. "History of the theatre in Montreal." M.A. thesis, McGill University, 1936.
Gallant, K. H. Barry. "The development of the Canadian army as a unilingual institution in a bilingual state." M.A. thesis, McGill University, 1968.
Hill, Robert A. "Robert Sellar and the *Huntingdon Gleaner*, the conscience of rural Protestant Quebec, 1863–1919." Ph.D. thesis, McGill University, 1970.
McDougall, Elizabeth Ann. "The Presbyterian Church in western Lower Canada, 1815–1842." Ph.D. thesis, McGill University, 1969.
"Montreal garrison, part II, 1813–69." Department of National Defence Library, Ottawa.
Steppler, Glenn. "Logistics of the War of 1812–14." M.A. thesis, McGill University, 1974.

ndex

Index

Index

Index

Index

Index

Index

law, 105; relies on local forces, 106
Elgin Guard, 94, 208
Elmwood, 175
Enlistment, 36
Ermatinger, Charles Oakes. *See* Police chiefs
Ermatinger, Lt.-Col. William, *31*, 42, 91, 96, 103, 109, 171, 175, 209; biographical sketch of, 33; injured, 94, 115–16; organizes Water Police, 110; requests aid of regulars, 111; in riots, 58, 62–63, 84, 92, 113, 118, 120
Eyre, Sir William, 158, 213

Fabre, Edouard-Raymond, 22, 87, 91, 102
Fenians, 205
Ferns, Hamilton, 205
Ferres, James Moir, 81, 87, *89*
Ferrier, Mayor James, 135–36, 162
Filder, Commissary General William, 162, 190
Fire Committee, 134
Fire companies, 135, 138, 142
Fire hazards: low water supply, 136; stoves, 135; wooden buildings, 139
Firemen: guarded by regulars, 138; role of, in Rebellion Losses Bill riots, 135–38
Fires: Cyrus Hotel, 105; La Fontaine's stables, 91; Parliament House, *86*, 87–88, 135, 138; troops at, 136–40
Fire Society, 134
Fire stations, 135
Fisher, Magistrate John, 15
Fletcher, Capt. John, 135, 138
Fleurimont, Josephe-Charlotte Noyëll de, 43
Flynn, Deputy Police Chief Eugene, 115
Forbes, C. J., 21
Freeling, Arthur, 181
French Canadian Missionary Society, 156
French Canadians: attitude of, to-

wards garrison, 65–66, 146; in British army, 46, 52; attitude of, towards paper money, 190; on Gavazzi inquest jury, 126–27; military attitude towards, 49–52, 212; military share in music with, 167; social relations of, with Anglophones, 42–43, 53
French coins, 187, 190

Garneau, François-Xavier, 23
Garrick Club, 171
Garrison: attitude towards, 4; composition of, 9; departure of, 10; main role of, 9, 12; mentality, 211; routine of, 151; size of, 7, 10, 76, 82–83, 133, 195, 200, 204–5, 210
Garrison Amateurs, 170, 211
Gavazzi, Father Alessandro, 109–10, 113, 120, 127
Gazette, 66–70, 73, 105–7, 159, 177, 179; on Gavazzi riot, 125–27; on mounted constabulary, 99; on Rebellion Losses Bill, 81; on troops used as police, 121
Gore, Sir Charles, 34, 76, 162–63, 203; prepares for renewed disturbances, 72, 74–75; receives reprimand, 137; at riots, 63, 84, 87–88, 92; and sports, 174
Gosford, Lord, 25
Gough, J. G., 147
Gowan, Ogle, 66
Grand Rural Festival of the Montreal Horticultural Society, 165
Grant, Capt. F. A., 94
Gregory, Maj. George, 14
Grey, Lt.-Col. Charles, 51, 155–56, 165
Grey, Earl, 72, 94–95, 100, 186
Griffin, Capt. Frank, 121
Groome, Peter, 106–7
Gugy, Lt.-Col. Bartholomew Conrad Augustus, *29*; becomes adjutant general, Canada East, 33, 48, 66; becomes superinten-

Sydenham), 30, 39–40, 162, 175, 209
Thumb, General Tom, 147
Torrance, F. W., 121
Tracey, Dr. Daniel, 11–12, 15, 21, 44, 110
Transcript: condemns inquest verdict, 127; condemns troop action, 125; criticizes 26th Regiment, 122, 131–32; deplores reduction in rural police, 32; praises deputy police chief, 115; praises 20th Regiment, 111; on the steeplechase, 175; urges increase in police, 121
Treasury, Lords of the, 187–90, 192, 194, 202
Trent incident, 205
Trinity Church, 153
Tully, John, 64, 99, 103
Turner, Maj. J. B., 171

Unlawful assembly, 57

Vallée, Guillaume, 20
Viger, Bonaventure, 79, 81
Viger, Jacques, 21, 43
Vindicator, 11, 21, 28, 44
Volunteers, 22, 52, 81–82, 102, 207

Waller, Jocelyn, 44
Walsh, James, 115, 126
Warde, Maj. Henry John, 180

Warre, Capt. Henry, 170
Weir, Lt. George, 158
Wellington, Duke of, 7, 71, 141
West Ward, 11, 60
Wetherall, Capt. Charles: on Beauharnois riot inquiry, 60; bilingual, 44; at 1844 election riot, 69; organizes mounted constabulary, 94–97, 208; role of, in Rebellion Losses Bill riots, 104–5, 209; rural magistrate, 32
Wetherall, Lt.-Col. George Augustus, 32, 35; attends Trinity Church, 154; contributes to Natural History Society, 172; deputy adjutant general, 62, 82; Montreal commandant, 25; opinion of, on raising colonial troops, 213
Whyte, Lt.-Col. John, 43, 174–75, 179–80
Wilgress, Lt.-Col. Edward, 156–57
Wilson, Mayor Charles, 110–23, 126, 128, 130
Wily, Thomas. *See* Police chiefs

Young, John, 69, 71
Young, Col. Plomer, 129
Young, Thomas Ainslie, 26

Zion Church, 109–13, *114*, 115–16, 120, 124–25

Due